THREE PLAYS

CHRISTOPHER MARLOWE

Christopher Marlowe

THREE PLAYS

TAMBURLAINE THE GREAT
DOCTOR FAUSTUS
EDWARD THE SECOND

Edited by John Hampden

THOMAS NELSON AND SONS LTD
LONDON EDINBURGH PARIS MELBOURNE
TORONTO AND NEW YORK

THOMAS NELSON AND SONS LTD
Parkside Works Edinburgh 9
3 Henrietta Street London WC2
312 Flinders Street Melbourne C1
5 Parker's Buildings Burg Street Cape Town

THOMAS NELSON AND SONS (CANADA) LTD
91–93 Wellington Street West Toronto 1

THOMAS NELSON AND SONS
19 East 47th Street New York 17

SOCIÉTÉ FRANÇAISE D'EDITIONS NELSON
25 rue Henri Barbusse Paris V^e

———

First issued in this series 1940

CONTENTS

INTRODUCTION vii

TAMBURLAINE THE GREAT, PART I. . . 25

TAMBURLAINE THE GREAT, PART II. . . 119

DOCTOR FAUSTUS 217

EDWARD THE SECOND 291

GLOSSARY 409

INTRODUCTION

CHRISTOPHER MARLOWE is one of that illustrious band of English poets, with John Keats at their head, who died too young. Born some ten weeks before Shakespeare, who was to learn more from him than from any other man, he was killed in a tavern brawl twenty-five years before the earth at Stratford closed over his great successor. He left behind him eight or nine plays of widely varying merit, some youthful translations from Ovid and Lucan, a lyric or two, an unfinished narrative poem, and a few half-obscure references to himself in contemporary books and state papers. His work has a permanent place in the history of English drama and the memory of all who care for English poetry ; what we know of his life is little more than a footnote to the turbulent history of Elizabethan London.

Before he came down from Cambridge his story was apparently uneventful enough. He was born in February 1564, at Canterbury, the son of a shoemaker, and grew up in a prosperous, pious home in that richly Gothic mediæval city. He was intended for holy orders, and in 1580 he passed from King's School, Canterbury, to Benet (now Corpus Christi) College, Cambridge, where he duly took his B.A. and M.A.

degrees. But he never entered the church. During those six years' submission to the narrow formalism, the barren metaphysics and theology, which Cambridge then required, he suffered some such disillusionment as that expressed in Faustus' opening soliloquy, and his ardent spirit sought other ways of life.

If he had set the stage of Elizabethan London for his own entrance he could hardly have made it more propitious for his genius. The year was 1587, the year in which Elizabeth agreed at last to the execution of Mary, Queen of Scots, and it became clear that the supreme trial of strength with Spain could not be much longer postponed. England was astir with the Renaissance spirit of adventure in thought and action. Spenser, Lyly, Peele, Greene, Kyd, and Shakespeare were at work, and between 1576 and 1587 six theatres, the first in England, had been built. Everything was ready for the man who was to make " the popular drama literary and the literary drama popular."

How Marlowe earned a living no one knows, for the evidence of his life in London is extremely scanty. Certainly he did not become a hack writer like the many playwrights and pamphleteers who divided their time precariously between garret and gaol. He appears to have had no wealthy patron. It is significant, however, that the first London record of him is an entry in the Privy Council Register, June 29, 1587, that " he had done Her Majestie good service & deserved to be rewarded for his faithfull dealinge," and the last record shows that he spent the day of

his death with three noted " complotters " of un-
savoury reputation. It is easy to believe that some
forms of secret service would appeal strongly to him.
He made good friends enough, however—Raleigh,
Chapman, and Sir Thomas Walsingham among them.
We get occasional glimpses of him—bold, aspiring,
over hasty, sometimes as brutal in speech and action
as Raleigh himself could be, with a biting wit and
a ready dagger, and given to wild talk which his
enemies probably reported as more blasphemous and
treasonable than it was.

When the plague of 1593 added to unrest in London,
and Thomas Kyd the playwright, with whom Marlowe
had shared a room, was charged with fostering that
unrest, Kyd laid as much blame as he could on Marlowe,
charging him, not unjustly, with atheism—which was
then almost as much a political as a religious offence.
Marlowe was summoned from Sir Thomas Walsingham's house at Scadbury to appear before the Privy
Council, but not kept under arrest. Possibly he found
lodgings at Deptford, and on May 30, 1593, he spent
the day with an Ingram Frizer and two other acquaint-
ances at the tavern kept by Eleanor Bull in Deptford
Strand. That evening Marlowe and Frizer quarrelled ;
Marlowe with Frizer's own dagger wounded him
slightly in the head, and Frizer forced back his hand
so that the blade entered Marlowe's eye, killing him
instantly   That at least was Frizer's deposition,
entered with a plea of self-defence by which he secured
a pardon. The story is questionable, but the whole

truth will never be known. On 1st June, the poet was buried in St. Nicholas Church, beside Deptford docks.

He had had only six years, but he had made his mark, for the spirit of the age worked with him. When he came upon the stage the professional theatre was drawing together the two great amateur traditions : the crude popular drama which derived from mediæval mystery plays and the stilted academic drama which imitated Seneca. Lyly's skilful affectations, Peele's lyric comedy, and Kyd's effective melodrama were already inaugurating a new era; and, like Shakespeare, Marlowe did not invent : he took the materials in common use and transfigured them by his genius. Unlike Shakespeare, however, he did not live to master fully the technique of his theatre. The triumph of *Tamburlaine*, as of *Doctor Faustus* and *The Jew of Malta*, is much rather that of poetic power than of dramatic skill. It was facilitated by Elizabethan conditions—the speed and continuity of action, the intimacy of an inn-yard or a small theatre with an apron stage, and the audience's ready response to poetry and rhetoric when " bombasted out " by such an actor as Alleyn.[1] Moreover, Tamburlaine speaks the very language of the Renaissance—the " high

---

[1] Edward Alleyn (1566–1626), one of the greatest and most successful of Elizabethan actors, " created " the parts of Tamburlaine, Faustus, and Barabas. Thomas Heywood described him as " Proteus for shapes and Roscius for a tongue, So could he speak, so vary." Fuller wrote, " He was the Roscius of our age, so acting to the life that he made any part (especially a majestic one) become him."

astounding terms " natural to an age which had become suddenly aware of strange new worlds to conquer. So Marlowe's deficiencies in stagecraft imposed no barrier between him and his audience. The elemental passion of his poetry swept his first play to immediate popularity, and with *Tamburlaine* drama was established as the representative art of the Elizabethan age.

By the same stroke Marlowe made blank verse the central metre of English poetry, and here, too, he did not invent but transform. Abjuring as deliberately as Milton the accustomed use of rhyme, he took that iambic pentameter which *Gorboduc* had brought lifeless on to the English stage twenty-five years before, and he filled it with vitality, beauty, and power. " His music had no echo of any man's before him," for in this, too, the style was the man, with all his perfections and imperfections on its head. Tamburlaine, Faustus, and Barabas speak with the accents of Marlowe himself, in the first English blank verse which bears unmistakably—and how magnificently—the imprint of its maker.

These first three plays have only one theme, an insatiate lust for power in various forms. Tamburlaine seeks the brittle glory of the conqueror :

> *Nature that fram'd us of foure Elements,*
> *Warring within our breasts for regiment,*
> *Doth teach us all to have aspyring minds.*
> *Our soules, whose faculties can comprehend*
> *The wondrous Architecture of the world,*

And measure every wandring plannets course,
Still climing after knowledge infinite
And alwaies mooving as the restles Spheares,
Wils us to weare our selves and never rest
Untill we reach the ripest fruit of all,
That perfect blisse and sole felicitie,
The sweet fruition of an earthly crowne.

To the modern mind the last line is bathos ; to the poet and his audience it was climax. For them divinity still hedged a king, and Marlowe invested his state with the full panoply of high romance :

" And ride in triumph through Persepolis " ?
Is it not brave to be a King, Techelles ?
Is it not passing brave to be a King
And ride in triumph through Persepolis ?

There is no limit to Tamburlaine's magniloquence and conceit :

And we will triumph over all the world.
I hold the Fates bound fast in yron chaines,
And with my hand turne Fortune's wheel about,
And sooner shall the Sun fall from his Spheare
Than Tamburlaine be slaine or overcome.

Yet this ranting, bloody-minded tyrant—who sweeps aside all opposition and dominates two continents, who harnesses kings to his chariot, massacres the virgins of Damascus, and murders his son—Tamburlaine, can speak with that other accent of the Renaissance which again we recognize as Marlowe's own :

If all the pens that ever poets held
Had fed the feeling of their maisters thoughts,
And every sweetnes that inspir'd their harts
Their minds and muses on admyred theames,—
If all the heavenly Quintessence they still
From their immortall flowers of Poesy,
Wherein as in a myrrour we perceive
The highest reaches of a humaine wit,—
If these had made one Poems period
And all combin'd in Beauties worthinesse,
Yet should ther hover in their restlesse heads
One thought, one grace, one woonder at the least
Which into words no vertue can digest.

There are few such interludes, however, and in such
an epic of violence there is no room, no time, for that
conflict and development of character, that subtle
interplay of good and evil, thought and desire, which
make the supreme masterpieces of drama. Tamburlaine is the play, his dominance its unity, and it is
redeemed from turgid monotony and absurdity only
by the fitful splendour of " Marlowe's mighty line."

Faustus is consumed with a lust for power not less
than Tamburlaine's, but he seeks it through knowledge, and there is a conflict within himself which
gives far more poignancy and subtlety to his tragic
story than to the Scythian's tale of conquests. " How
greatly it is all planned ! " said Goethe when he was
meditating a translation of *Doctor Faustus.* The
adjective was ill-chosen if it referred to structure, for
all Marlowe's work is inadequately articulated, and
this tragedy too is more dramatic poem than play.

The poet took the mediæval legend of a pact with the devil, to which the *Faustbuch* had given finally a local habitation and a name, interpreted it in terms of Renaissance thought, and invested it with immortal significance. Here more than ever Marlowe's raptures are all air and fire, and his characteristic avoidance of ugliness and gross material horrors is plainly evident. There is transcendent beauty in the famous passages which no repetition can dim :

> *Was this the face that lancht a thousand shippes ?*
> *And burnt the toplesse Towres of Ilium ?*
> *Sweete Helen, make me immortall with a kisse . . .*

There is hardly less beauty in those many incidental felicities of expression, the prodigalities of genius, in which the play abounds.

> *All things that moove betweene the quiet Poles . . .*

Not Shakespeare himself could have chosen and placed an adjective with more superb evocative power than that " quiet." And even Shakespeare has not put upon the stage a scene of more extreme beauty and terror than the death of Faustus. The reason may be that no play of Marlowe's has in it so much of his own life and thought as this, to which Mephistophilis supplies the key-note :

> *Thinkst thou that I who saw the face of God*
> *And tasted the eternal joyes of heaven*
> *Am not tormented with ten thousand hels . . . ?*

Mutilated as the text is, and full of crudities and trivialities, which we must not hastily ascribe to the revisers, its essential power survives for us, a deep diapason of spiritual ardour and anguish. In our day as in his own, *Doctor Faustus* is generally accepted, for all its obvious faults, as Marlowe's highest achievement.

The Jew of Malta, which probably followed a few months later, marks the beginning of a new period— a promise of dramatic power which found its first fulfilment in *Edward II.* but never reached maturity. The Jew Barabas, consumed by the lust for money, is akin to Tamburlaine and Faustus, but the first two acts of the play show a mastery of characterization, dialogue, and dramatic structure which neither Marlowe nor any other English dramatist had approached before. The last three acts, however, are much inferior. Barabas degenerates into a fiend of cruelty, a caricature without human interest; the writing is careless, and one horror is piled upon another more absurdly than in *Tamburlaine* without the earlier play's redeeming poetry.

A similar carelessness mars the two lesser plays, *The Tragedy of Dido* (in which Nashe may have had a hand), probably undergraduate work revised about 1592; and *The Massacre at Paris*, a topical drama dealing with the assassination of Henry III., which was probably written as late as 1592. The text is shockingly garbled.

Marlowe may well have written a good deal of the

three-part play of *Henry VI.* which appears in the Shakespeare canon, and quite probably contributed also to *Richard III.*, but only one " history " is undoubtedly his. This is *Edward II.*, which for some readers challenges the pre-eminence of *Faustus*, and which Charles Lamb praised in one of the most famous passages of English dramatic criticism : " The reluctant pangs of abdicating Royalty in Edward furnished hints which Shakespeare scarcely improved in his *Richard the Second* ; and the death-scene of Marlowe's King moves pity and terror beyond any scene, ancient or modern, with which I am acquainted."

In this tragedy there is nothing of the grandiose magnificence of *Tamburlaine* and little of those wild excesses which mark all the other plays in varying degree. By taking thought Marlowe has reduced his *dramatis personæ* to the stature of men and women, and schooled his mighty line, sacrificing something of its splendour, into dialogue which permits the interplay of thought and motive ; its movement is that of human life, not of an avalanche. Yet he has not fully achieved unity and order, always particularly difficult in the " history," and from sheer indolence, one is tempted to think, he has left the characterization defective. A little more care would have made far more convincing the Queen's transition from love to hatred of the King, and the development of the King himself from the ineffectual dilettante of the opening scenes to the almost majestic figure of the end.

Yet *Edward II.*, hardly less than *Tamburlaine*, shows Marlowe as the mighty pioneer, for in this he gave the Elizabethan chronicle play its final shape. When Shakespeare shortly afterwards answered the challenge with *Richard II.* he showed indeed greater subtlety and dramatic skill, but he could make no radical improvement in the form. It is impossible to believe that Marlowe could ever have equalled Shakespeare in range and power, humour and insight, for he was too ill-balanced in himself, but *Edward II.* suggests how much he might have achieved if he too had had another quarter of a century.

Marlowe's translations from Lucan and Ovid are early work, immature in both poetry and scholarship, though all contain lines which foreshadow *Tamburlaine*. Of the lyrics which he must surely have written only one is known certainly as his—*The Passionate Shepherd to his Love*; and *Hero and Leander*—perhaps the loveliest of all English narrative poems—he left unfinished at his death. George Chapman, daring too much, completed it. The first known edition appeared in 1598. Its popularity was enormous— there were apparently at least eleven editions in the first thirty years—and it was fully justified. Of the six sestiads in which the classical story is retold with romantic beauty only two are Marlowe's, but they are the fine flower of his genius. Though even here there is the lack of constructive skill which was his besetting fault, the fragment has a sinewy strength, a pellucid sensuous beauty, a " most strangely intellectual fire," which have rarely been surpassed. With *Doctor Faustus* and *Edward II.* it establishes Marlowe as the first great poet to write in modern English.

Shakespeare paid tribute to him by quoting aptly from *Hero and Leander* :

> *Dead Shepheard, now I find thy saw of might :*
> *" Who ever lov'd that lov'd not at first sight ? "*

It was a lesser poet, however, Michael Drayton, who wrote the most felicitous of his epitaphs :

> *Neat Marlow, bathed in the Thespian springs,*
> *Had in him those brave translunary things*
> *That the first Poets had ; his raptures were*
> *All ayre and fire, which made his verses cleere,*
> *For that fine madnes still he did retaine*
> *Which rightly should possesse a Poet's braine.*

J. H.

TAMBURLAINE THE GREAT
PART I

The First Part of 'Tamburlaine the Great' was probably completed and performed during 1587. The author took his material from a number of books dealing with the famous Tartar conqueror, Timūr Khan (1336–1405), mainly from the Latin 'Magni Tamerlanis Scythiarum Imperatoris Vita' (1553), by Petrus Perondinus, and 'The Foreste, or Collection of Histories' (1571), by Thomas Fortescue, a translation of Pedro Mexia's 'Silva de Varia Lection' (1542).

The Second Part was written (to follow up the success of the first) and first performed about 1587–88, and was largely of the author's invention, though he took incidents from Ariosto's 'Orlando Furioso' (1516–32) and Belleforest's 'Cosmographie Universelle' (1575).

Marlowe's name does not appear on the title-page of any early edition, and there is no absolute proof of his authorship, but it is accepted on the strength of tradition, some rather obscure contemporary references, and the strong internal evidence of style and thought.

The first edition, containing both parts and presenting a good text, was published in octavo in 1590. This is the editio princeps from which all subsequent editions have been derived, and it has been followed very closely by the present editor, who has used Wagner's reprint in 'Marlowes Werke: historisch-kritische Ausgabe von Hermann Breymann und Albrecht Wagner: Heilbronn, 1885.' Spelling, punctuation, and use of capitals have been modernized, and minor emendations have ben made without notice, but nothing has been omitted, and all editorial additions have been enclosed in 'square' brackets.

J. H.

Tamburlaine

the Great.

Who, from a Scythian Shephearde,
by his rare and woonderfull Conquests,
became a most puissant and migh-
tye Monarque.

And (for his tyranny, and terrour in
Warre) was tearmed,

The Scourge of God.

Deuided into two Tragicall Dis-
courses, as they were sundrie times
shewed vpon Stages in the Cittie
of London.

By the right honorable the Lord
Admyrall, his seruantes.

Now first, and newlie published.

LONDON.
Printed by Richard Ihones: at the signe
of the Rose and Crowne neere Hol-
borne Bridge. 1590.

To the Gentlemen Readers and Others that Take
Pleasure in Reading Histories :

Gentlemen and courteous readers whosoever, I have here
published in print for your sakes the two tragical discourses
of the Scythian shepherd Tamburlaine, that became so great
a conqueror and so mighty a monarch. My hope is that
they will be now no less acceptable unto you to read after
your serious affairs and studies than they have been (lately)
delightful for many of you to see when the same were
showed in London upon stages. I have (purposely) omitted
and left out some fond and frivolous gestures, digressing
(and in my poor opinion) far unmeet for the matter, which
I thought might seem more tedious unto the wise than any
way else to be regarded, though (haply) they have been of
some vain, conceited fondlings greatly gaped at, what times
they were showed upon the stage in their graced deformities.
Nevertheless now to be mixtured in print with such matter
of worth, it would prove a great disgrace to so honourable
and stately a history. Great folly were it in me to commend
unto your wisdoms either the eloquence of the author that
writ them or the worthiness of the matter itself ; I therefore
leave unto your learned censures both the one and the other
and myself the poor printer of them unto your most
courteous and favourable protection, which if you vouchsafe
to accept, you shall evermore bind me to employ what
travail and service I can to the advancing and pleasuring of
your excellent degree.

Yours, most humble at commandment,

R. J., Printer.

[DRAMATIS PERSONÆ

MYCETES, *King of Persia.*
COSROE, *his brother.*
MEANDER,
THERIDAMAS,
ORTYGIUS, }*Persian lords.*
CENEUS,
MENAPHON,
TAMBURLAINE, *a Scythian shepherd.*
TECHELLES,
USUMCASANE, } *his followers.*
BAJAZETH, *Emperor of the Turks.*
KING OF FEZ.
KING OF MOROCCO.
KING OF ARGIER.
KING OF ARABIA.
SOLDAN OF EGYPT.
GOVERNOR OF DAMASCUS.
AGYDAS,
MAGNETES, } *Median lords.*
CAPOLIN, *an Egyptian.*
PHILEMUS, BASSOES, LORDS, CITIZENS, MOORS, SOLDIERS, *and*
    ATTENDANTS.

ZENOCRATE, *daughter to the Soldan of Egypt.*
ANIPPE, *her maid.*
ZABINA, *wife to* BAJAZETH.
EBEA, *her maid.*
VIRGINS OF DAMASCUS.]

The two Tragical Discourses of mighty Tamburlaine, the Scythian Shepherd, etc.

THE PROLOGUE

FROM jigging veins of riming mother wits,
And such conceits as clownage keeps in pay,
We'll lead you to the stately tent of war,
Where you shall hear the Scythian Tamburlaine
Threatening the world with high astounding terms
And scourging kingdoms with his conquering sword.
View but his picture in this tragic glass,
And then applaud his fortunes as you please.

ACT I

SCENE I

MYCETES, COSROE, MEANDER, THERIDAMAS,
ORTYGIUS, CENEUS, [MENAPHON,] *with others.*

Mycetes. Brother Cosroe, I find myself agriev'd ;
   Yet insufficient to express the same,

Act I, Scene I, in the original appears as Actus I, Scæna I, and headings
are repeated in full throughout—*e.g.* Actus I.   Scæna II.

For it requires a great and thundering speech :
Good brother, tell the cause unto my lords ;
I know you have a better wit than I.

Cosroe. Unhappy Persia, that in former age
Hast been the seat of mighty conquerors,
That, in their prowess and their policies,
Have triumphed over Afric, and the bounds
Of Europe where the sun dares scarce appear
For freezing meteors and congealed cold,
Now to be ruled and governed by a man
At whose birthday Cynthia with Saturn joined,
And Jove, the Sun, and Mercury denied
To shed their influence in his fickle brain !
Now Turks and Tartars shake their swords at thee,
Meaning to mangle all thy provinces.

Mycetes. Brother, I see your meaning well enough,
And thorough your planets I perceive you think
I am not wise enough to be a king :
But I refer me to my noblemen,
That know my wit, and can be witnesses.
I might command you to be slain for this.
Meander, might I not ?

Meander. Not for so small a fault, my sovereign lord.

Mycetes. I mean it not, but yet I know I might.
Yet live ; yea, live ; Mycetes wills it so.
Meander, thou, my faithful counsellor,
Declare the cause of my conceived grief,
Which is (God knows) about that Tamburlaine,
That, like a fox in midst of harvest-time,
Doth prey upon my flocks of passengers,

And, as I hear, doth mean to pull my plumes ;
Therefore 'tis good and meet for to be wise.
Meander. Oft have I heard your majesty complain
  Of Tamburlaine, that sturdy Scythian thief,
  That robs your merchants of Persepolis
  Trading by land unto the Western Isles,
  And in your confines with his lawless train
  Daily commits incivil outrages,
  Hoping (misled by dreaming prophecies)
  To reign in Asia, and with barbarous arms
  To make himself the monarch of the East :
  But, ere he march in Asia, or display
  His vagrant ensign in the Persian fields,
  Your grace hath taken order by Theridamas,
  Charged with a thousand horse, to apprehend
  And bring him captive to your highness' throne.
Mycetes. Full true thou speakst, and like thyself, my
      lord,
  Whom I may term a Damon for thy love :
  Therefore 'tis best, if so it like you all,
  To send my thousand horse incontinent
  To apprehend that paltry Scythian.
  How like you this, my honourable lords ?
  Is it not a kingly resolution ?
Cosroe. It cannot choose, because it comes from you.
Mycetes. Then hear thy charge, valiant Theridamas,
  The chiefest captain of Mycetes' host,
  The hope of Persia, and the very legs
  Whereon our state doth lean as on a staff,
  That holds us up and foils our neighbour foes.

Thou shalt be leader of this thousand horse,
Whose foaming gall with rage and high disdain
Have sworn the death of wicked Tamburlaine.
Go frowning forth, but come thou smiling home,
As did Sir Paris with the Grecian dame.
Return with speed, time passeth swift away,
Our life is frail, and we may die to-day.

Theridamas. Before the moon renew her borrowed light,
Doubt not, my lord and gracious sovereign,
But Tamburlaine and that Tartarian rout
Shall either perish by our warlike hands,
Or plead for mercy at your highness' feet.

Mycetes. Go, stout Theridamas, thy words are swords,
And with thy looks thou conquerest all thy foes :
I long to see thee back return from thence,
That I may view these milk-white steeds of mine
All loaden with the heads of killed men,
And from their knees even to their hoofs below
Besmeared with blood that makes a dainty show.

Theridamas. Then now, my lord, I humbly take my
leave.   [*Exit.*]

Mycetes. Therid[amas,] farewell ten thousand times.
Ah, Menaphon, why stayest thou thus behind,
When other men press forward for renown ?
Go, Menaphon, go into Scythia,
And foot by foot follow Theridamas.

Cosroe. Nay, pray you, let him stay ; a greater [task]
Fits Menaphon than warring with a thief :
Create him pro-rex of [all] Africa,
That he may win the Babylonians' hearts,

Which will revolt from Persian government,
Unless they have a wiser king than you.

Mycetes. Unless they have a wiser king than you?
These are his words, Meander, set them down.

Cosroe. And add this to them, that all Asia
Lament to see the folly of their king.

Mycetes. Well, here I swear by this my royal seat—

Cosroe. You may do well to kiss it, then.

Mycetes.—Embossed with silk as best beseems my state,
To be reveng'd for these contemptuous words!
O where is duty and allegiance now?
Fled to the Caspian or the Ocean main?
What, shall I call thee brother? no, a foe,
Monster of nature, shame unto thy stock,
That darst presume thy sovereign for to mock!
Meander, come, I am abus'd, Meander.   *Exit.*

Manent COSROE *and* MENAPHON.

Menaphon. How now, my lord, what, mated and
    amaz'd
To hear the king thus threaten like himself?

Cosroe. Ah Menaphon, I pass not for his threats.
The plot is laid by Persian noblemen
And captains of the Median garrisons
To crown me emperor of Asia.
But this it is that doth excruciate
The very substance of my vexed soul!
To see our neighbours that were wont to quake
And tremble at the Persian monarch's name,

Now sits and laughs our regiment to scorn ;
And that which might resolve me into tears,
Men from the farthest equinoctial line
Have swarm'd in troops into the Eastern India,
Lading their ships with gold and precious stones,
And made their spoils from all our provinces.

Menaphon. This should entreat your highness to rejoice,
Since Fortune gives you opportunity
To gain the title of a conqueror
By curing of this maimed Empery.
Afric and Europe bordering on your land,
And continent to your dominions,
How easily may you, with a mighty host,
Pass into Græcia, as did Cyrus once,
And cause them to withdraw their forces home,
Lest you subdue the pride of Christendom !

　　　　　　　　　　　　[*Trumpet sounds within.*]

Cosroe. But Menaph[on,] what means this trumpet's
　　sound ?

Menaphon. Behold, my lord, Ortygius and the rest
Bringing the crown to make you emperor !

Enter ORTYGIUS *and* CENEUS, *bearing a crown, with others.*

Ortygius. Magnificent and mighty prince Cosroe,
We, in the name of other Persian states
And commons of this mighty monarchy,
Present thee with th' imperial diadem.

Ceneus. The warlike soldiers and the gentlemen,
That heretofore have filled Persepolis

With Afric captains taken in the field,
Whose ransom made them march in coats of gold,
With costly jewels hanging at their ears,
And shining stones upon their lofty crests,
Now living idle in the walled towns,
Wanting both pay and martial discipline,
Begin in troops to threaten civil war,
And openly exclaim against the king.
Therefore, to stay all sudden mutinies,
We will invest your highness emperor ;
Whereat the soldiers will conceive more joy
Than did the Macedonians at the spoil
Of great Darius and his wealthy host.

Cosroe. Well, since I see the state of Persia droop
And languish in my brother's government,
I willingly receive th' imperial crown,
And vow to wear it for my country's good,
In spite of them shall malice my estate.

Ortygius. And, in assurance of desir'd success,
We here do crown thee monarch of the East,
Emperor of Asia and of Persia,
Great lord of Media and Armenia,
Duke of Africa and Albania,
Mesopotamia and of Parthia,
East India and the late discovered isles,
Chief lord of all the wide vast Euxine Sea,
And of the ever-raging Caspian Lake.
Long live Cosroe, mighty emperor !

Cosroe. And Jove may never let me longer live
Than I may seek to gratify your love,

And cause the soldiers that thus honour me
To triumph over many provinces !
By whose desires of discipline in arms
I doubt not shortly but to reign sole king,
And with the army of Theridamas,
Whither we presently will fly (my lords),
To rest secure against my brother's force.

Ortygius. We knew, my lord, before we brought the
    crown,
Intending your investion so near
The residence of your despised brother,
The lords would not be too exasperate
To injure or suppress your worthy title.
Or if they would, there are in readiness
Ten thousand horse to carry you from hence,
In spite of all suspected enemies.

Cosroe. I know it well, my lord, and thank you all.

Ortygius. Sound up the trumpets, then. God save the
    king !   [*Flourish of trumpets.*] *Exeunt.*

SCENE II

TAMBURLAINE *leading* ZENOCRATE : TECHELLES,
USUMCASANE, [AGYDAS, MAGNETES,] *other* Lords
and Soldiers *loaden with treasure.* [TAMBURLAINE *is
wearing a shepherd's dress over his armour.*]

Tamburlaine. Come lady, let not this appal your
    thoughts ;

32

The jewels and the treasure we have ta'en
Shall be reserv'd, and you in better state
Than if you were arriv'd in Syria,
Even in the circle of your father's arms,
The mighty Soldan of Egyptia.

Zenocrate. Ah shepherd, pity my distressed plight!
(If, as thou seem'st, thou art so mean a man)
And seek not to enrich thy followers
By lawless rapine from a silly maid,
Who, travelling with these Median lords
To Memphis, from my uncle's country of Media,
Where all my youth I have been governed,
Have passed the army of the mighty Turk,
Bearing his privy signet and his hand
To safe conduct us thorough Africa.

Magnetes. And since we have arrived in Scythia,
Besides rich presents from the puissant Cham,
We have his highness' letters to command
Aid and assistance, if we stand in need.

Tamburlaine. But now you see these letters and com-
mands
Are countermanded by a greater man,
And through my provinces you must expect
Letters of conduct from my mightiness,
If you intend to keep your treasure safe,
But since I love to live at liberty,
As easily may you get the Soldan's crown,
As any prizes out of my precinct.
For they are friends that help to wean my state,
Till men and kingdoms help to strengthen it,

33   2

And must maintain my life exempt from servitude.
But tell me madam, is your grace betroth'd?
Zenocrate. I am (my lord)—for so you do import.
Tamburlaine. I am a lord, for so my deeds shall prove,
  And yet a shepherd by my parentage.
  But lady, this fair face and heavenly hue
  Must grace his bed that conquers Asia,
  And means to be a terror to the world,
  Measuring the limits of his empery
  By east and west, as Phœbus doth his course.
  Lie here, ye weeds that I disdain to wear!

                    [Removing his shepherd's dress.]

  This complete armour and this curtle-axe
  Are adjuncts more beseeming Tamburlaine.
  And madam, whatsoever you esteem
  Of this success, and loss unvalued,
  Both may invest you empress of the East.
  And these, that seem but silly country swains,
  May have the leading of so great an host
  As with their weight shall make the mountains
    quake,
  Even as when windy exhalations,
  Fighting for passage, tilt within the earth.
Techelles. As princely lions when they rouse themselves,
  Stretching their paws, and threatening herds of
    beasts,
  So in his armour looketh Tamburlaine.
  Methinks I see kings kneeling at his feet,
  And he with frowning brows and fiery looks
  Spurning their crowns from off their captive heads.

Usumcasane. And making thee and me, Techelles,
    kings,
  That even to death will follow Tamburlaine.
Tamburlaine. Nobly resolv'd, sweet friends and fol-
    lowers !
  These lords (perhaps) do scorn our estimates,
  And think we prattle with distempered spirits.
  But since they measure our deserts so mean,
  That in conceit bear empires on our spears,
  Affecting thoughts coequal with the clouds,
  They shall be kept our forced followers
  Till with their eyes they view us emperors.
Zenocrate. The gods, defenders of the innocent,
  Will never prosper your intended drifts,
  That thus oppress poor friendless passengers.
  Therefore at least admit us liberty,
  Even as thou hop'st to be eternised
  By living Asia's mighty emperor.
Agydas. I hope our lady's treasure and our own
  May serve for ransom to our liberties :
  Return our mules and empty camels back,
  That we may travel into Syria,
  Where her betrothed lord, Alcidamus,
  Expects th' arrival of her highness' person.
Magnetes. And wheresoever we repose ourselves,
  We will report but well of Tamburlaine.
Tamburlaine. Disdains Zenocrate to live with me ?
  Or you, my lords, to be my followers ?
  Think you I weigh this treasure more than you ?
  Not all the gold in India's wealthy arms

Shall buy the meanest soldier in my train.
Zenocrate, lovelier than the love of Jove,
Brighter than is the silver Rhodope,
Fairer than whitest snow on Scythian hills,
Thy person is more worth to Tamburlaine
Than the possession of the Persian crown,
Which gracious stars have promis'd at my birth.
A hundred Tartars shall attend on thee,
Mounted on steeds swifter than Pegasus.
Thy garments shall be made of Median silk,
Enchas'd with precious jewels of mine own,
More rich and valurous than Zenocrate's.
With milk-white harts upon an ivory sled
Thou shalt be drawn amidst the frozen pools,
And scale the icy mountains' lofty tops,
Which with thy beauty will be soon resolv'd.
My martial prizes, with five hundred men,
Won on the fifty-headed Volga's waves,
Shall all we offer to Zenocrate,
And then myself to fair Zenocrate.

Techelles. What now ? in love ?

Tamburlaine. Techelles, women must be flattered,
But this is she with whom I am in love.

Enter a Soldier.

Soldier. News, news !

Tamburlaine. How now, what's the matter ?

Soldier. A thousand Persian horsemen are at hand,
Sent from the king to overcome us all.

Tamburlaine. How now, my lords of Egypt and
 Zenocrate ?

Now must your jewels be restor'd again,

And I that triumphed so be overcome.

How say you, lordings ? Is not this your hope ?

Agydas. We hope yourself will willingly restore them.

Tamburlaine. Such hope, such fortune, have the
 thousand horse.

Soft ye, my lords, and sweet Zenocrate.

You must be forced from me ere you go.

A thousand horsemen ! We five hundred foot !

An odds too great for us to stand against.

But are they rich ? And is their armour good ?

Soldier. Their plumed helms are wrought with beaten
 gold,

Their swords enamelled, and about their necks

Hangs massy chains of gold down to the waist ;

In every part exceeding brave and rich.

Tamburlaine. Then shall we fight courageously with
 them ?

Or look you I should play the orator ?

Techelles. No ; cowards and faint-hearted runaways

Look for orations when the foe is near.

Our swords shall play the orators for us.

Usumcasane. Come, let us meet them at the mountain
 foot,

And with a sudden and an hot alarum

Drive all their horses headlong down the hill.

Techelles. Come, let us march.

Tamburlaine. Stay, Techelles ; ask a parley first.

The Soldiers *enter.*

Open the mails, yet guard the treasure sure,
Lay out our golden wedges to the view,
That their reflections may amaze the Persians.
And look we friendly on them when they come :
But if they offer word or violence,
We'll fight, five hundred men at arms to one,
Before we part with our possession.
And 'gainst the general we will lift our swords,
And either lanch his greedy thirsting throat,
Or take him prisoner, and his chain shall serve
For manacles till he be ransom'd home.

Techelles. I hear them come ; shall we encounter them ?
Tamburlaine. Keep all your standings, and not stir a
    foot,
    Myself will bide the danger of the brunt.

Enter THERIDAMAS, *with others.*

Theridamas. Where is this Scythian Tamburlaine ?
Tamburlaine. Whom seekst thou, Persian ? I am
    Tamburlaine.
Theridamas. Tamburlaine ! A Scythian shepherd so
    embellished
    With nature's pride and richest furniture !
    His looks do menace heaven and dare the gods,
    His fiery eyes are fixed upon the earth,
    As if he now devis'd some stratagem,
    Or meant to pierce Avernas' darksome vaults
    To pull the triple-headed dog from hell.

Tamburlaine. Noble and mild this Persian seems to be,
 If outward habit judge the inward man.
Techelles. His deep affections make him passionate.
Tamburlaine. With what a majesty he rears his looks !—
 In thee, thou valiant man of Persia,
 I see the folly of thy emperor ;
 Art thou but captain of a thousand horse,
 That by characters graven in thy brows,
 And by thy martial face and stout aspect,
 Deserv'st to have the leading of an host ?
 Forsake thy king and do but join with me,
 And we will triumph over all the world.
 I hold the Fates bound fast in iron chains,
 And with my hand turn Fortune's wheel about,
 And sooner shall the sun fall from his sphere
 Than Tamburlaine be slain or overcome.
 Draw forth thy sword, thou mighty man at arms,
 Intending but to raze my charmed skin,
 And Jove himself will stretch his hand from heaven
 To ward the blow, and shield me safe from harm.
 See how he rains down heaps of gold in showers,
 As if he meant to give my soldiers pay,
 And as a sure and grounded argument
 That I shall be the monarch of the East,
 He sends this Soldan's daughter rich and brave,
 To be my queen and portly emperess.
 If thou wilt stay with me, renowmed man,
 And lead thy thousand horse with my conduct,
 Besides thy share of this Egyptian prize,
 Those thousand horse shall sweat with martial spoil

Of conquered kingdoms and of cities sacked.
Both we will walk upon the lofty clifts,
And Christian merchants, that with Russian stems
Plough up huge furrows in the Caspian Sea,
Shall vail to us as lords of all the lake.
Both we will reign as consuls of the earth,
And mighty kings shall be our senators ;
Jove sometimes masked in a shepherd's weed,
And by those steps that he hath scal'd the heavens,
May we become immortal like the gods.
Join with me now in this my mean estate,
(I call it mean, because, being yet obscure,
The nations far remov'd admire me not,)
And when my name and honour shall be spread,
As far as Boreas claps his brazen wings,
Or fair Bootes sends his cheerful light,
Then shalt thou be competitor with me,
And sit with Tamburlaine in all his majesty.
Theridamas. Not Hermes, prolocutor to the gods,
Could use persuasions more pathetical.
Tamburlaine. Nor are Apollo's oracles more true
Than thou shalt find my vaunts substantial.
Techelles. We are his friends, and if the Persian king
Should offer present dukedoms to our state,
We think it loss to make exchange for that
We are assured of by our friend's success.
Usumcasane. And kingdoms at the least we all expect,
Besides the honour in assured conquests,
Where kings shall crouch unto our conquering
swords,

And hosts of soldiers stand amaz'd at us,
When with their fearful tongues they shall confess,
These are the men that all the world admires.

Theridamas. What strong enchantments tice my yield-
　　ing soul ?
Ah, these resolved noble Scythians !
But shall I prove a traitor to my king ?

Tamburlaine. No, but the trusty friend of Tamburlaine.

Theridamas. Won with thy words, and conquered with
　　thy looks,
I yield myself, my men, and horse to thee :
To be partaker of thy good or ill,
As long as life maintains Theridamas.

Tamburlaine. Theridamas, my friend, take here my
　　hand.
Which is as much as if I swore by heaven,
And call'd the gods to witness of my vow,
Thus shall my heart be still combined with thine,
Until our bodies turn to elements,
And both our souls aspire celestial thrones.
Techelles, and Casane, welcome him.

Techelles. Welcome renowmed Persian to us all.

[*Usum*]*casane.* Long may Theridamas remain with us.

Tamburlaine. These are my friends in whom I more
　　rejoice,
Than doth the King of Persia in his crown :
And by the love of Pylades and Orestes,
Whose statues we adore in Scythia,
Thyself and them shall never part from me,
Before I crown you kings in Asia.

　　Make much of them, gentle Theridamas,
　　And they will never leave thee till the death.

Theridamas. Nor thee, nor them, thrice-noble Tambur-
　　　　laine,
　　Shall want my heart to be with gladness pierc'd,
　　To do you honour and security.

Tamburlaine. A thousand thanks worthy Theridamas,
　　And now fair madam, and my noble lords,
　　If you will willingly remain with me,
　　You shall have honours as your merits be :
　　Or else you shall be forc'd with slavery.

Agydas. We yield unto thee, happy Tamburlaine.

Tamburlaine. For you then madam, I am out of doubt.

Zenocrate. I must be pleased perforce, wretched Zeno-
　　　　crate !　　　　　　　　　　　　　　　*Exeunt.*

ACT II

SCENE I

COSROE, MENAPHON, ORTYGIUS, CENEUS, *with other* Soldiers.

Cosroe. Thus far are we towards Theridamas,
 And valiant Tamburlaine, the man of fame,
 The man that in the forehead of his fortune
 Bears figures of renown and miracle.
 But tell me, that hast seen him, Menaphon,
 What stature wields he, and what personage ?
Menaphon. Of stature tall, and straightly fashioned,
 Like his desire, lift upwards and divine,
 So large of limbs, his joints so strongly knit,
 Such breadth of shoulders as might mainly bear
 Old Atlas' burthen ; 'twixt his manly pitch,
 A pearl more worth than all the world is placed,
 Wherein by curious sovereignty of art
 Are fixed his piercing instruments of sight,
 Whose fiery circles bear encompassed
 A heaven of heavenly bodies in their spheres,
 That guides his steps and actions to the throne
 Where honour sits invested royally.

Pale of complexion, wrought in him with passion,
Thirsting with sovereignty, with love of arms,
His lofty brows in folds do figure death,
And in their smoothness amity and life.
About them hangs a knot of amber hair,
Wrapped in curls, as fierce Achilles' was,
On which the breath of heaven delights to play,
Making it dance with wanton majesty :
His arms and fingers long and sinewy,
Betokening valour and excess of strength :
In every part proportioned like the man
Should make the world subdued to Tamburlaine.

Cosroe. Well hast thou pourtrayed in thy terms of life
The face and personage of a wondrous man :
Nature doth strive with Fortune and his stars
To make him famous in accomplished worth :
And well his merits shew him to be made
His fortune's master and the king of men,
That could persuade, at such a sudden pinch,
With reasons of his valour and his life,
A thousand sworn and overmatching foes.
Then, when our powers in points of swords are
    join'd,
And closed in compass of the killing bullet,
Though strait the passage and the port be made
That leads to palace of my brother's life,
Proud is his fortune if we pierce it not.
And when the princely Persian diadem
Shall overweigh his weary witless head,
And fall like mellowed fruit, with shakes of death,

In fair Persia noble Tamburlaine
Shall be my regent, and remain as king.

Ortygius. In happy hour we have set the crown
Upon your kingly head, that seeks our honour
In joining with the man ordain'd by heaven
To further every action to the best.

Ceneus. He that with shepherds and a little spoil,
Durst, in disdain of wrong and tyranny,
Defend his freedom 'gainst a monarchy,
What will he do supported by a king?
Leading a troop of gentlemen and lords,
And stuffed with treasure for his highest thoughts?

Cosroe. And such shall wait on worthy Tamburlaine.
Our army will be forty thousand strong,
When Tamburlaine and brave Theridamas
Have met us by the river Araris:
And all conjoin'd to meet the witless king,
That now is marching near to Parthia,
And with unwilling soldiers faintly arm'd,
To seek revenge on me and Tamburlaine.
To whom, sweet Menaphon, direct me straight.

Menaphon. I will, my lord.   *Exeunt*

SCENE II

MYCETES, MEANDER, *with other* Lords *and* Soldiers.

Mycetes. Come my Meander, let us to this gear.
I tell you true, my heart is swoln with wrath

On this same thievish villain Tamburlaine,
And of that false Cosroe, my traitorous brother.
Would it not grieve a king to be so abused,
And have a thousand horsemen ta'en away?
And, which is worse, to have his diadem
Sought for by such scald knaves as love him not?
I think it would: well then, by heavens I swear,
Aurora shall not peep out of her doors,
But I will have Cosroe by the head,
And kill proud Tamburlaine with point of sword.
Tell you the rest, Meander, I have said.
Meander. Then, having passed Armenian deserts now,
And pitched our tents under the Georgian hills,
Whose tops are covered with Tartarian thieves
That lie in ambush, waiting for a prey,
What should we do but bid them battle straight,
And rid the world of those detested troops?
Lest, if we let them linger here a while,
They gather strength by power of fresh supplies.
This country swarms with vile outrageous men,
That live by rapine and by lawless spoil,
Fit soldiers for the wicked Tamburlaine.
And he that could with gifts and promises
Inveigle him that led a thousand horse,
And make him false his faith unto his king,
Will quickly win such as are like himself.
Therefore cheer up your minds; prepare to fight.
He that can take or slaughter Tamburlaine,
Shall rule the province of Albania.
Who brings that traitor's head, Theridamas,

Shall have a government in Media,
Beside the spoil of him and all his train.
But if Cosroe (as our spials say,
And as we know) remains with Tamburlaine,
His highness' pleasure is that he should live,
And be reclaim'd with princely lenity.

[*Enter a Spy.*]

Spy. An hundred horsemen of my company,
    Scouting abroad upon these champion plains,
    Have view'd the army of the Scythians,
    Which make reports it far exceeds the king's.
Meander. Suppose they be in number infinite,
    Yet being void of martial discipline,
    All running headlong after greedy spoils,
    And more regarding gain than victory,
    Like to the cruel brothers of the earth,
    Sprung of the teeth of dragons venomous,
    Their careless swords shall lanch their fellows'
        throats
    And make us triumph in their overthrow.
Mycetes. Was there such brethren, sweet Meander, say,
    That sprung of teeth of dragons venomous?
Meander. So poets say, my lord.
Mycetes. And 'tis a pretty toy to be a poet.
    Well, well, Meander, thou art deeply read;
    And having thee, I have a jewel sure.
    Go on my lord, and give your charge, I say;
    Thy wit will make us conquerors to-day.

Meander. Then noble soldiers, to entrap these thieves,
  That live confounded in disordered troops,
  If wealth or riches may prevail with them,
  We have our camels laden all with gold,
  Which you that be but common soldiers
  Shall fling in every corner of the field ;
  And while the base-born Tartars take it up,
  You, fighting more for honour than for gold,
  Shall massacre those greedy minded slaves.
  And when their scattered army is subdu'd,
  And you march on their slaughtered carcasses,
  Share equally the gold that bought their lives,
  And live like gentlemen in Persia.
  Strike up the drum, and march courageously ;
  Fortune herself doth sit upon our crests.
Mycetes. He tells you true, my masters, so he does.
  Drums, why sound ye not when Meander speaks ?
                               Exeunt.

SCENE III

Cosroe, Tamburlaine, Theridamas, Techelles,
Usumcasane, Ortygius, *with others.*

Cosroe. Now, worthy Tamburlaine, have I reposed
  In thy approved fortunes all my hope.
  What thinkst thou, man, shall come of our attempts ?
  For, even as from assured oracle,
  I take thy doom for satisfaction.

Tamburlaine. And so mistake you not a whit, my
　　lord.
　For fates and oracles [of] heaven have sworn
　To royalise the deeds of Tamburlaine,
　And make them blest that share in his attempts.
　And doubt you not but, if you favour me
　And let my fortunes and my valour sway
　To some direction in your martial deeds,
　The world will strive with hosts of men at arms
　To swarm unto the ensign I support.
　The hosts of Xerxes, which by fame is said
　To drink the mighty Parthian Araris,
　Was but a handful to that we will have ;
　Our quivering lances shaking in the air
　And bullets like Jove's dreadful thunderbolts
　Enrolled in flames and fiery smouldering mists
　Shall threat the gods more than Cyclopian wars ;
　And with our sun-bright armour, as we march,
　We'll chase the stars from heaven and dim their
　　eyes
　That stand and muse at our admired arms.
Theridamas. You see, my lord, what working words he
　　hath.
　But, when you see his actions top his speech,
　Your speech will stay, or so extol his worth
　As I shall be commended and excused
　For turning my poor charge to his direction.
　And these his two renowmed friends, my lord,
　Would make one thrust and strive to be retain'd
　In such a great degree of amity.

Techelles. With duty and with amity we yield
  Our utmost service to the fair Cosroe.
Cosroe. Which I esteem as portion of my crown.
  Usumcasane and Techelles both,
  When she that rules in Rhamnis' golden gates
  And makes a passage for all prosperous arms,
  Shall make me solely emperor of Asia,
  Then shall your meeds and valours be advanced
  To rooms of honour and nobility.
Tamburlaine. Then haste, Cosroe, to be king alone,
  That I with these my friends and all my men
  May triumph in our long expected fate.
  The king your brother is now hard at hand ;
  Meet with the fool, and rid your royal shoulders
  Of such a burden as outweighs the sands
  And all the craggy rocks of Caspea.

[*Enter a* Messenger.]

Messenger. My lord, we have discovered the enemy
  Ready to charge you with a mighty army.
Cosroe. Come, Tamburlaine, now whet thy winged
      sword
  And lift thy lofty arm into the clouds,
  That it may reach the king of Persia's crown
  And set it safe on my victorious head.
Tamburlaine. See where it is, the keenest curtle-axe
  That e'er made passage thorough Persian arms !
  These are the wings shall make it fly as swift
  As doth the lightning or the breath of heaven,

   And kill as sure as it swiftly flies.
Cosroe. Thy words assure me of kind success.
   Go, valiant soldier, go before and charge
   The fainting army of that foolish king.
Tamburlaine. Usumcasane and Techelles, come.
   We are enough to scare the enemy,
   And more than needs to make an emperor.
                                    [*Exeunt.*]

[SCENE IV]

To the battle and MYCETES *comes out alone with his
crown in his hand, offering to hide it.*

Mycetes. Accurst be he that first invented war !
   They knew not, ah, they knew not, simple men,
   How those were hit by pelting cannon shot
   Stand staggering like a quivering aspen leaf
   Fearing the force of Boreas' boisterous blasts.
   In what a lamentable case were I,
   If nature had not given me wisdom's lore !
   For kings are clouts that every man shoots at,
   Our crown the pin that thousands seek to cleave ;
   Therefore in policy I think it good
   To hide it close ; a goodly stratagem,
   And far from any man that is a fool.
   So shall not I be known ; or if I be,
   They cannot take away my crown from me.
   Here will I hide it in this simple hole.

Enter TAMBURLAINE.

Tamburlaine. What fearful coward straggling from the
    camp,
  When kings themselves are present in the field ?
Mycetes. Thou liest.
Tamburlaine. Base villain, darst thou give the lie ?
Mycetes. Away ! I am the king. Go, touch me not.
  Thou breakst the law of arms unless thou kneel
  And cry me " Mercy, noble king ! "
Tamburlaine. Are you the witty king of Persia ?
Mycetes. Ay, marry, am I ; have you any suit to me ?
Tamburlaine. I would entreat you to speak but three
    wise words.
Mycetes. So I can when I see my time.
Tamburlaine. Is this your crown ?
Mycetes. Ay. Didst thou ever see a fairer ?
Tamburlaine. You will not sell it, will ye ?
Mycetes. Such another word, and I will have thee
    executed. Come, give it me.
Tamburlaine. No ; I took it prisoner.
Mycetes. You lie ; I gave it you.
Tamburlaine. Then 'tis mine.
Mycetes. No ; I mean I let you keep it.
Tamburlaine. Well, I mean you shall have it again.
  Here, take it for a while ; I lend it thee,
  Till I may see thee hemm'd with armed men.
  Then shalt thou see me pull it from thy head ;
  Thou art no match for mighty Tamburlaine.

                              [Exit.]

Mycetes. O gods, is this Tamburlaine the thief ?
  I marvel much he stole it not away.
                    Sound trumpets to the battle and he runs in.

[SCENE V]

COSROE, TAMBURLAINE, THERIDAMAS, MENAPHON,
    MEANDER, ORTYGIUS, TECHELLES, USUMCASANE,
    with others.

Tamburlaine. Hold thee, Cosroe ; wear two imperial
        crowns.
  Think thee invested now as royally,
  Even by the mighty hand of Tamburlaine,
  As if as many kings as could encompass thee
  With greatest pomp had crown'd thee emperor.
Cosroe. So do I, thrice renowmed man at arms ;
  And none shall keep the crown but Tamburlaine.
  Thee do I make my regent of Persia,
  And general lieutenant of my armies.
  Meander, you that were our brother's guide,
  And chiefest counsellor in all his acts,
  Since he is yielded to the stroke of war,
  On your submission we with thanks excuse,
  And give you equal place in our affairs.
Meander. Most happy emperor, in humblest terms
  I vow my service to your majesty,
  With utmost virtue of my faith and duty.

Cosroe. Thanks, good Meander. Then, Cosroe, reign,
  And govern Persia in her former pomp.
  Now send embassage to thy neighbour kings,
  And let them know the Persian king is chang'd
  From one that knew not what a king should do
  To one that can command what 'longs thereto.
  And now we will to fair Persepolis
  With twenty thousand expert soldiers.
  The lords and captains of my brother's camp
  With little slaughter take Meander's course,
  And gladly yield them to my gracious rule.
  Ortygius and Menaphon, my trusty friends,
  Now will I gratify your former good,
  And grace your calling with a greater sway.

Ortygius. And as we ever aimed at your behoof,
  And sought your state all honour it deserv'd,
  So will we with our powers and our lives
  Endeavour to preserve and prosper it.

Cosroe. I will not thank thee, sweet Ortygius ;
  Better replies shall prove my purposes.
  And now, Lord Tamburlaine, my brother's camp
  I leave to thee and to Theridamas,
  To follow me to fair Persepolis.
  Then will we march to all those Indian mines
  My witless brother to the Christians lost,
  And ransom them with fame and usury.
  And till thou overtake me, Tamburlaine,
  (Staying to order all the scattered troops,)
  Farewell, lord regent and his happy friends.
  I long to sit upon my brother's throne.

Menaphon. Your majesty shall shortly have your wish,
  And ride in triumph through Persepolis.   *Exeunt.*
  [*Manent* TAMBURLAINE, THERIDAMAS, TECHELLES,
    AND USUMCASANE.

Tamburlaine. And ride in triumph through Persepolis !
  Is it not brave to be a king, Techelles ?
  Usumcasane and Theridamas,
  Is it not passing brave to be a king,
  And ride in triumph through Persepolis ?

Techelles. O, my lord, 'tis sweet and full of pomp !

Usumcasane. To be a king, is half to be a god.

Theridamas. A god is not so glorious as a king :
  I think the pleasure they enjoy in heaven,
  Cannot compare with kingly joys in earth ;
  To wear a crown enchas'd with pearl and gold,
  Whose virtues carry with it life and death ;
  To ask and have, command and be obeyed ;
  When looks breed love, with looks to gain the prize,
  Such power attractive shines in princes' eyes.

Tamburlaine. Why, say, Theridamas, wilt thou be a
    king ?

Theridamas. Nay, though I praise it, I can live without
    it.

Tamburlaine. What says my other friends, will you be
    kings ?

Techelles. I, if I could, with all my heart, my lord.

Tamburlaine. Why, that's well said, Techelles ;   so
    would I.
  And so would you, my masters, would you not ?

Usumcasane. What then my lord ?

Tamburlaine. Why then, Casane, shall we wish for
     ought
   The world affords in greatest novelty,
   And rest attemptless, faint and destitute ?
   Methinks we should not. I am strongly mov'd,
   That if I should desire the Persian crown,
   I could attain it with a wondrous ease ;
   And would not all our soldiers soon consent,
   If we should aim at such a dignity ?
Theridamas. I know they would with our persuasions.
Tamburlaine. Why then, Theridamas, I'll first assay
   To get the Persian kingdom to myself ;
   Then thou for Parthia ; they for Scythia and
     Media ;
   And if I prosper, all shall be assure
   As if the Turk, the Pope, Afric and Greece
   Came creeping to us with their crowns a-piece.
Techelles. Then shall we send to this triumphing king,
   And bid him battle for his novel crown ?
Usumcasane. Nay, quickly, then, before his room be hot.
Tamburlaine. 'Twill prove a pretty jest, in faith, my
     friends.
Theridamas. A jest to charge on twenty thousand men ?
   I judge the purchase more important far.
Tamburlaine. Judge by thyself, Theridamas, not me ;
   For presently Techelles here shall haste
   To bid him battle ere he pass too far,
   And lose more labour than the gain will quite.
   Then shalt thou see the Scythian Tamburlaine
   Make but a jest to win the Persian crown.

Techelles, take a thousand horse with thee
And bid him turn him back to war with us,
That only made him king to make us sport.
We will not steal upon him cowardly,
But give him warning and more warriors.
Haste thee, Techelles ; we will follow thee.

                       [*Exit Techelles.*]

What saith Theridamas ?
Theridamas. Go on, for me.   *Exeunt.*

SCENE VI

Cosroe, Meander, Ortygius, Menaphon,
with other Soldiers.

Cosroe. What means this devilish shepherd, to aspire
With such a giantly presumption,
To cast up hills against the face of heaven,
And dare the force of angry Jupiter ?
But as he thrust them underneath the hills,
And pressed out fire from their burning jaws,
So will I send this monstrous slave to hell,
Where flames shall ever feed upon his soul.
Meander. Some powers divine, or else infernal, mixed
Their angry seeds at his conception ;
For he was never sprung of human race,
Since with the spirit of his fearful pride,
He dares so doubtlessly resolve of rule,

   And by profession be ambitious.

Ortygius. What god or fiend or spirit of the earth
   Or monster turned to a manly shape,
   Or of what mould or mettle he be made,
   What star or state soever govern him,
   Let us put on our meet encountering minds,
   And in detesting such a devilish thief,
   In love of honour and defence of right,
   Be arm'd against the hate of such a foe,
   Whether from earth or hell or heaven he grow.

Cosroe. Nobly resolv'd, my good Ortygius.
   And since we all have sucked one wholesome air,
   And with the same proportion of elements
   Resolve, I hope we are resembled,
   Vowing our loves to equal death and life.
   Let's cheer our soldiers to encounter him,
   That grievous image of ingratitude,
   That fiery thirster after sovereignty,
   And burn him in the fury of that flame
   That none can quench but blood and empery.
   Resolve, my lords and loving soldiers, now
   To save your king and country from decay.
   Then strike up, drum ; and all the stars that make
   The loathsome circle of my dated life,
   Direct my weapon to his barbarous heart,
   That thus opposeth him against the gods,
   And scorns the powers that govern Persia !

                         [Exeunt.]

[SCENE VII]

Enter to the battle, and after the battle enter Cosroe
    wounded, Theridamas, Tamburlaine, Techelles,
    Usumcasane, *with others.*

Cosroe. Barbarous and bloody Tamburlaine,
    Thus to deprive me of my crown and life !
    Treacherous and false Theridamas,
    Even at the morning of my happy state,
    Scarce being seated in my royal throne,
    To work my downfall and untimely end !
    An uncouth pain torments my grieved soul
    And death arrests the organ of my voice,
    Who, entering at the breach thy sword hath made,
    Sacks every vein and artier of my heart.
    Bloody and insatiate Tamburlaine !
Tamburlaine. The thirst of reign and sweetness of a
       crown,
    That caused the eldest son of heavenly Ops
    To thrust his doting father from his chair,
    And place himself in the imperial heaven,
    Mov'd me to manage arms against thy state.
    What better precedent than mighty Jove ?
    Nature, that fram'd us of four elements
    Warring within our breasts for regiment,
    Doth teach us all to have aspiring minds :
    Our souls, whose faculties can comprehend

The wondrous architecture of the world,
And measure every wandering planet's course,
Still climbing after knowledge infinite,
And always moving as the restless spheres,
Wills us to wear ourselves and never rest,
Until we reach the ripest fruit of all,
That perfect bliss and sole felicity,
The sweet fruition of an earthly crown.

Theridamas. And that made me to join with Tambur-
laine ;
For he is gross and like the massy earth
That moves not upwards, nor by princely deeds
Doth mean to soar above the highest sort.

Techelles. And that made us, the friends of Tamburlaine,
To lift our swords against the Persian king.

Usumcasane. For as, when Jove did thrust old Saturn
down,
Neptune and Dis gain'd each of them a crown,
So do we hope to reign in Asia,
If Tamburlaine be plac'd in Persia.

Cosroe. The strangest men that ever nature made !
I know not how to take their tyrannies.
My bloodless body waxeth chill and cold ;
And with my blood my life slides through my
wound ;
My soul begins to take her flight to hell,
And summons all my senses to depart ;
The heat and moisture which did feed each other,
For want of nourishment to feed them both

Is dry and cold ; and now doth ghastly death
With greedy talents gripe my bleeding heart,
And like a harpy tires on my life.
Theridamas and Tamburlaine, I die :
And fearful vengeance light upon you both !

> [*Tamburlaine*] *takes the crown, and puts it on.*

Tamburlaine. Not all the curses which the furies
    breathe
Shall make me leave so rich a prize as this.
Theridamas, Techelles, and the rest,
Who think you now is King of Persia ?

All. Tamburlaine !   Tamburlaine !

Tamburlaine. Though Mars himself, the angry god of
    arms,
And all the earthly potentates conspire
To dispossess me of this diadem,
Yet will I wear it in despite of them,
As great commander of this eastern world,
If you but say that Tamburlaine shall reign.

All. Long live Tamburlaine, and reign in Asia !

Tamburlaine. So ; now it is more surer on my head
Than if the gods had held a parliament,
And all pronounc'd me King of Persia.   [*Exeunt.*]

Finis Actus 2

ACT III

SCENE I

BAJAZETH, *the* KINGS OF FEZ, MOROCCO, *and*
ARGIER, *with others, in great pomp.*

Bajazeth. Great kings of Barbary, and my portly
　bassoes,
We hear the Tartars and the eastern thieves,
Under the conduct of one Tamburlaine,
Presume a bickering with your emperor,
And thinks to rouse us from our dreadful siege
Of the famous Grecian Constantinople.
You know our army is invincible ;
As many circumcised Turks we have,
And warlike bands of Christians renied,
As hath the ocean or the Terrene sea
Small drops of water when the moon begins
To join in one her semicircled horns :
Yet would we not be brav'd with foreign power,
Nor raise our siege before the Grecians yield,
Or breathless lie before the city-walls.
Fez. Renowmed emperor and mighty general,
What if you sent the bassoes of your guard

To charge him to remain in Asia,
Or else to threaten death and deadly arms
As from the mouth of mighty Bajazeth?

Bajazeth. Hie thee, my basso, fast to Persia.
Tell him thy lord, the Turkish emperor,
Dread lord of Afric, Europe and Asia,
Great king and conqueror of Græcia,
The ocean, Terrene, and the coal-black sea,
The high and highest monarch of the world,
Wills and commands (for say not I entreat),
Not once to set his foot in Africa,
Or spread his colours in Græcia,
Lest he incur the fury of my wrath.
Tell him I am content to take a truce,
Because I hear he bears a valiant mind;
But if, presuming on his silly power,
He be so mad to manage arms with me,
Then stay thou with him, say I bid thee so.
And if, before the sun have measur'd heaven
With triple circuit, thou regreet us not,
We mean to take his morning's next arise
For messenger he will not be reclaim'd,
And mean to fetch thee in despite of him.

Basso. Most great and puissant monarch of the earth,
Your basso will accomplish your behest,
And shew your pleasure to the Persian,
As fits the legate of the stately Turk.   [*Exit Basso.*

Argier. They say he is the king of Persia;
But, if he dare attempt to stir your siege,
'Twere requisite he should be ten times more,

For all flesh quakes at your magnificence.

Bajazeth. True, Argier, and tremble at my looks.

Morocco. The spring is hindered by your smothering
    host ;

For neither rain can fall upon the earth,

Nor sun reflex his virtuous beams thereon,

The ground is mantled with such multitudes.

Bajazeth. All this is true as holy Mahomet ;

And all the trees are blasted with our breaths.

Fez. What thinks your greatness best to be achiev'd

In pursuit of the city's overthrow ?

Bajazeth. I will the captive pioners of Argier

Cut off the water that by leaden pipes

Runs to the city from the mountain Carnon ;

Two thousand horse shall forage up and down,

That no relief or succour come by land,

And all the sea my galleys countermand.

Then shall our footmen lie within the trench,

And with their cannons, mouth'd like Orcus' gulf,

Batter the walls, and we will enter in ;

And thus the Grecians shall be conquered.   *Exeunt.*

SCENE II

AGYDAS, ZENOCRATE, ANIPPE, *with others.*

[*Agydas.*] Madam Zenocrate, may I presume

To know the cause of these unquiet fits

That work such trouble to your wonted rest ?

'Tis more than pity such a heavenly face
Should by heart's sorrow wax so wan and pale,
When your offensive rape by Tamburlaine
(Which of your whole displeasures should be most)
Hath seem'd to be digested long ago.

Zenocrate. Although it be digested long ago,
As his exceeding favours have deserv'd,
And might content the Queen of Heaven, as well
As it hath chang'd my first conceiv'd disdain ;
Yet since a farther passion feeds my thoughts
With ceaseless and disconsolate conceits,
Which dyes my looks so lifeless as they are,
And might, if my extremes had full events,
Make me the ghastly counterfeit of death.

Agydas. Eternal heaven sooner be dissolv'd,
And all that pierceth Phœbe's silver eye,
Before such hap fall to Zenocrate !

Zenocrate. Ah, life and soul still hover in his breast,
And leave my body senseless as the earth,
Or else unite you to his life and soul,
That I may live and die with Tamburlaine !

Enter TAMBURLAINE, *with* TECHELLES, *and others.*

Agydas. With Tamburlaine !   Ah, fair Zenocrate,
Let not a man so vile and barbarous,
That holds you from your father in despite,
And keeps you from the honours of a queen,
Being supposed his worthless concubine,
Be honoured with your love but for necessity !

So now the mighty Soldan hears of you,
Your highness needs not doubt but in short time
He will, with Tamburlaine's destruction,
Redeem you from this deadly servitude.

Zenocrate. [Agydas,] leave to wound me with these
    words,
And speak of Tamburlaine as he deserves.
The entertainment we have had of him
Is far from villany or servitude,
And might in noble minds be counted princely.

Agydas. How can you fancy one that looks so fierce,
Only disposed to martial stratagems?
Who, when he shall embrace you in his arms,
Will tell how many thousand men he slew;
And, when you look for amorous discourse,
Will rattle forth his facts of war and blood,
Too harsh a subject for your dainty ears.

Zenocrate. As looks the sun through Nilus' flowing
    stream,
Or when the Morning holds him in her arms,
So looks my lordly love, fair Tamburlaine;
His talk much sweeter than the Muses' song
They sung for honour 'gainst Pierides,
Or when Minerva did with Neptune strive;
And higher would I rear my estimate
Than Juno, sister to the highest god,
If I were matched with mighty Tamburlaine.

Agydas. Yet be not so inconstant in your love,
But let the young Arabian live in hope,
After your rescue to enjoy his choice.

You see, though first the king of Persia,
Being a shepherd, seem'd to love you much,
Now, in his majesty, he leaves those looks,
Those words of favour, and those comfortings,
And gives no more than common courtesies.

Zenocrate. Thence rise the tears that so distain my
      cheeks,
Fearing his love through my unworthiness.

*Tamburlaine goes to her, and takes her away lovingly
by the hand, looking wrathfully on Agydas, and says
nothing.* [*Exeunt all except Agydas.*]

Agydas. Betrayed by fortune and suspicious love,
Threatened with frowning wrath and jealousy,
Surpris'd with fear of hideous revenge,
I stand aghast ; but most astonied
To see his choler shut in secret thoughts,
And wrapt in silence of his angry soul.
Upon his brows was pourtrayed ugly death,
And in his eyes the fury of his heart,
That shine as comets, menacing revenge,
And casts a pale complexion on his cheeks.
As when the seaman sees the Hyades
Gather an army of Cimmerian clouds,
(Auster and Aquilon with winged steeds,
All sweating, tilt about the watery heavens,
With shivering spears enforcing thunderclaps,
And from their shields strike flames of lightning)
All fearful folds his sails and sounds the main,

Lifting his prayers to the heavens for aid
Against the terror of the winds and waves ;
So fares Agydas for the late felt frowns,
That sent a tempest to my daunted thoughts,
And makes my soul divine her overthrow.

Enter TECHELLES *with a naked dagger,* [*and*
USUMCASANE.]

Techelles. See you, Agydas, how the king salutes you
   He bids you prophesy what it imports.
Agydas. I prophesied before and now I prove
   The killing frowns of jealousy and love.
   He needed not with words confirm my fear,
   For words are vain where working tools present
   The naked action of my threatened end.
   It says, Agydas, thou shalt surely die.
   And of extremities elect the least ;
   More honour and less pain it may procure
   To die by this resolved hand of thine,
   Than stay the torments he and heaven have sworn.
   Then haste, Agydas, and prevent the plagues
   Which thy prolonged fates may draw on thee ;
   Go wander free from fear of tyrant's rage,
   Removed from the torments and the hell
   Wherewith he may excruciate thy soul ;
   And let Agydas by Agydas die,
   And with this stab slumber eternally.
                                        [*Stabs himself.*]
Techelles. Usumcasane, see how right the man
   Hath hit the meaning of my lord the king !

Usumcasane. Faith, and, Techelles, it was manly done ;
  And, since he was so wise and honourable,
  Let us afford him now the bearing hence,
  And crave his triple worthy burial.
Techelles. Agreed, Casane ; we will honour him.
                [*Exeunt, bearing out the body.*]

SCENE III

TAMBURLAINE, TECHELLES, USUMCASANE, THERI-
DAMAS, BASSO, ZENOCRATE, *with others.*

Tamburlaine. Basso, by this thy lord and master knows
  I mean to meet him in Bithynia :
  See how he comes ! tush, Turks are full of brags
  And menace more than they can well perform.
  He meet me in the field and fetch thee hence !
  Alas, poor Turk ! his fortune is too weak
  T' encounter with the strength of Tamburlaine.
  View well my camp, and speak indifferently ;
  Do not my captains and my soldiers look
  As if they meant to conquer Africa ?
Basso. Your men are valiant, but their number few,
  And cannot terrify his mighty host ;
  My lord, the great commander of the world,
  Besides fifteen contributory kings,
  Hath now in arms ten thousand janizaries,
  Mounted on lusty Mauritanian steeds,

Brought to the war by men of Tripoly ;
Two hundred thousand footmen that have serv'd
In two set battles fought in Græcia ;
And for the expedition of this war,
If he think good, can from his garrisons
Withdraw as many more to follow him.

Techelles. The more he brings, the greater is the spoil ;
For, when they perish by our warlike hands,
We mean to seat our footmen on their steeds,
And rifle all those stately janizars.

Tamburlaine. But will those kings accompany your
     lord ?

Basso. Such as his highness please ; but some must
     stay
To rule the provinces he late subdued.

Tamburlaine. Then fight courageously ; their crowns
     are yours,
This hand shall set them on your conquering heads
That made me emperor of Asia.

Usumcasane. Let him bring millions infinite of men,
Unpeopling Western Africa and Greece,
Yet we assure us of the victory.

Theridamas. Even he, that in a trice vanquished two
     kings
More mighty than the Turkish emperor,
Shall rouse him out of Europe, and pursue
His scattered army till they yield or die.

Tamburlaine. Well said, Theridamas ! speak in that
     mood ;
For Will and Shall best fitteth Tamburlaine,

Whose smiling stars gives him assured hope
Of martial triumph ere he meet his foes.
I that am term'd the Scourge and Wrath of God,
The only fear and terror of the world,
Will first subdue the Turk, and then enlarge
Those Christian captives which you keep as slaves,
Burdening their bodies with your heavy chains,
And feeding them with thin and slender fare,
That naked row about the Terrene sea,
And, when they chance to breathe and rest a space,
Are punished with bastones so grievously
That they lie panting on the galley's side,
And strive for life at every stroke they give.
These are the cruel pirates of Argier,
That damned train, the scum of Africa,
Inhabited with straggling runagates,
That make quick havoc of the Christian blood.
But, as I live, that town shall curse the time
That Tamburlaine set foot in Africa.

Enter BAJAZETH *with his Bassoes and contributory*
Kings, [ZABINA *and* EBEA.]

Bajazeth. Bassoes and janizaries of my guard,
   Attend upon the person of your lord,
   The greatest potentate of Africa.
Tamburlaine. Techelles and the rest, prepare your
      swords ;
   I mean t' encounter with that Bajazeth.
Bajazeth. Kings of Fesse, Moroccus, and Argier,

He calls me Bajazeth, whom you call lord !
Note the presumption of this Scythian slave !
I tell thee, villain, those that lead my horse
Have to their names titles of dignity ;
And dar'st thou bluntly call me Bajazeth ?

Tamburlaine. And know thou, **Turk**, that those which lead my horse
Shall lead thee captive thorough Africa ;
And dar'st thou bluntly call me Tamburlaine ?

Bajazeth. By Mahomet my kinsman's sepulchre,
And by the holy Alcaron I swear,
He shall be made a chaste and lustless eunuch,
And in my sarell tend my concubines ;
And all his captains, that thus stoutly stand,
Shall draw the chariot of my emperess,
Whom I have brought to see their overthrow.

Tamburlaine. By this my sword that conquer'd Persia,
Thy fall shall make me famous through the world !
I will not tell thee how I'll handle thee,
But every common soldier of my camp
Shall smile to see thy miserable state.

Fez. What means the mighty Turkish emperor,
To talk with one so base as Tamburlaine ?

Morocco. Ye Moors and valiant men of Barbary,
How can ye suffer these indignities ?

Argier. Leave words, and let them feel your lances' points,
Which glided through the bowels of the Greeks.

Bajazeth. Well said, my stout contributory kings !
Your threefold army and my hugy host

  Shall swallow up these base born Persians.

Techelles. Puissant, renowmed, and mighty Tamburlaine,

  Why stay we thus prolonging all their lives?

Theridamas. I long to see those crowns won by our swords,

  That we may reign as kings of Africa.

Usumcasane. What coward would not fight for such a prize?

Tamburlaine. Fight all courageously, and be you kings:

  I speak it, and my words are oracles.

Bajazeth. Zabina, mother of three braver boys

  Than Hercules, that in his infancy

  Did pash the jaws of serpents venomous,

  Whose hands are made to gripe a warlike lance,

  Their shoulders broad for complete armour fit,

  Their limbs more large and of a bigger size

  Than all the brats y-sprung from Typhon's loins;

  Who, when they come unto their father's age,

  Will batter turrets with their manly fists—

  Sit here upon this royal chair of state,

  And on thy head wear my imperial crown,

  Until I bring this sturdy Tamburlaine

  And all his captains bound in captive chains.

Zabina. Such good success happen to Bajazeth!

Tamburlaine. Zenocrate, the loveliest maid alive,

  Fairer than rocks of pearl and precious stone,

  The only paragon of Tamburlaine;

  Whose eyes are brighter than the lamps of heaven,

  And speech more pleasant than sweet harmony;

That with thy looks canst clear the darkened sky,
And calm the rage of thundering Jupiter ;
Sit down by her, adorned with my crown,
As if thou wert the empress of the world.
Stir not, Zenocrate, until thou see
Me march victoriously with all my men,
Triumphing over him and these his kings,
Which I will bring as vassals to thy feet.
Till then, take thou my crown, vaunt of my worth,
And manage words with her, as we will arms.

Zenocrate. And may my love, the king of Persia,
Return with victory and free from wound !

Bajazeth. Now shalt thou feel the force of Turkish
arms,
Which lately made all Europe quake for fear.
I have of Turks, Arabians, Moors and Jews,
Enough to cover all Bithynia.
Let thousands die : their slaughtered carcasses
Shall serve for walls and bulwarks to the rest ;
And as the heads of Hydra, so my power,
Subdued, shall stand as mighty as before.
If they should yield their necks unto the sword,
Thy soldiers' arms could not endure to strike
So many blows as I have heads for thee.
Thou knowest not, foolish-hardy Tamburlaine,
What 'tis to meet me in the open field,
That leave no ground for thee to march upon.

Tamburlaine. Our conquering swords shall marshal us
the way
We use to march upon the slaughtered foe,

74

Trampling their bowels with our horses' hoofs,
Brave horses bred on the white Tartarian hills.
My camp is like to Julius Cæsar's host,
That never fought but had the victory ;
Nor in Pharsalia was there such hot war
As these my followers willingly would have.
Legions of spirits fleeting in the air
Direct our bullets and our weapons' points
And make our strokes to wound the senseless lure ;
And when she sees our bloody colours spread,
Then Victory begins to take her flight,
Resting herself upon my milk-white tent.
But come, my lords, to weapons let us fall ;
The field is ours, the Turk, his wife and all.

> *Exit with his followers.*

Bajazeth. Come, kings and bassoes, let us glut our
    swords
That thirst to drink the feeble Persians' blood.

> *Exit with his followers.*

Zabina. Base concubine, must thou be plac'd by me
    That am the empress of the mighty Turk ?

Zenocrate. Disdainful Turkess, and unreverend boss,
    Call'st thou me concubine, that am betroth'd
    Unto the great and mighty Tamburlaine ?

Zabina. To Tamburlaine, the great Tartarian thief !

Zenocrate. Thou wilt repent these lavish words of thine
    When thy great basso master and thyself
    Must plead for mercy at his kingly feet,
    And sue to me to be your advocates.

Zabina. And sue to thee ! I tell thee, shameless girl,

    Thou shalt be laundress to my waiting maid.

    How lik'st thou her, Ebea ? will she serve ?

Ebea.   Madam, she thinks perhaps she is too fine ;

    But I shall turn her into other weeds,

    And make her dainty fingers fall to work.

Zenocrate.   Hearst thou, Anippe, how thy drudge doth talk,

    And how my slave, her mistress, menaceth ?

    Both for their sauciness shall be employed

    To dress the common soldiers' meat and drink ;

    For we will scorn they should come near ourselves.

Anippe.   Yet sometimes let your highness send for them

    To do the work my chambermaid disdains.

>   *They sound to the battle within and stay.*

Zenocrate.   Ye gods and powers that govern Persia,

    And made my lordly love her worthy king,

    Now strengthen him against the Turkish Bajazeth,

    And let his foes, like flocks of fearful roes

    Pursued by hunters, fly his angry looks,

    That I may see him issue conqueror !

Zabina.   Now, Mahomet, solicit God himself,

    And make him rain down murdering shot from heaven,

    To dash the Scythians' brains, and strike them dead,

    That dare to manage arms with him

    That offered jewels to thy sacred shrine

    When first he warr'd against the Christians !

>   *To the battle again.*

Zenocrate.   By this the Turks lie weltring in their blood,

And Tamburlaine is lord of Africa.

Zabina. Thou art deceiv'd. I heard the trumpets
    sound

As when my emperor overthrew the Greeks,

And led them captive into Africa.

Straight will I use thee as thy pride deserves ;

Prepare thyself to live and die my slave.

Zenocrate. If Mahomet should come from heaven and
    swear

My royal lord is slain or conquered,

Yet should he not persuade me otherwise

But that he lives and will be conqueror.

BAJAZETH *flies and he pursues him. The battle* [is]
    short and they enter. BAJAZETH *is overcome.*

Tamburlaine. Now, king of bassoes, who is conqueror ?

Bajazeth. Thou, by the fortune of this damned foil.

Tamburlaine. Where are your stout contributory kings ?

Enter TECHELLES, THERIDAMAS, *and* USUMCASANE.

Techelles. We have their crowns ; their bodies strow
    the field.

Tamburlaine. Each man a crown ! why, kingly fought,
    i'faith.

Deliver them into my treasury.

Zenocrate. Now let me offer to my gracious lord

His royal crown again so highly won.

Tamburlaine. Nay, take the Turkish crown from her,
    Zenocrate,

And crown me emperor of Africa.

Zabina. No, Tamburlaine ; though now thou gat the
  best,
  Thou shalt not yet be lord of Africa.
Theridamas. Give her the crown, Turkess, you were best.
                    He takes it from her, and gives it Zenocrate.
Zabina. Injurious villains, thieves, runagates,
  How dare you thus abuse my majesty ?
Theridamas. Here, madam, you are empress ; she is
  none.
Tamburlaine. Not now, Theridamas ; her time is past :
  The pillars that have bolstered up those terms
  Are faln in clusters at my conquering feet.
Zabina. Though he be prisoner, he may be ransom'd.
Tamburlaine. Not all the world shall ransom Bajazeth.
Bajazeth. Ah, fair Zabina, we have lost the field ;
  And never had the Turkish emperor
  So great a foil by any foreign foe.
  Now will the Christian miscreants be glad,
  Ringing with joy their superstitious bells,
  And making bonfires for my overthrow :
  But, ere I die, those foul idolaters
  Shall make me bonfires with their filthy bones ;
  For, though the glory of this day be lost,
  Afric and Greece have garrisons enough
  To make me sovereign of the earth again.
Tamburlaine. Those walled garrisons will I subdue,
  And write myself great lord of Africa.
  So from the East unto the furthest West
  Shall Tamburlaine extend his puissant arm.
  The galleys and those pilling brigandines,

78

That yearly sail to the Venetian gulf,
And hover in the straits for Christians' wreck,
Shall lie at anchor in the Isle Asant,
Until the Persian fleet and men-of-war,
Sailing along the oriental sea,
Have fetched about the Indian continent,
Even from Persepolis to Mexico,
And thence unto the Straits of Jubalter,
Where they shall meet and join their force in one,
Keeping in awe the Bay of Portingale,
And all the ocean by the British shore ;
And by this means I'll win the world at last.

Bajazeth. Yet set a ransom on me, Tamburlaine.

Tamburlaine. What, thinkst thou Tamburlaine esteems
    thy gold ?
I'll make the kings of India, ere I die,
Offer their mines, to sue for peace, to me,
And dig for treasure to appease my wrath.
Come, bind them both, and one lead in the Turk ;
The Turkess let my love's maid lead away.

       They bind them.

Bajazeth. Ah, villains, dare ye touch my sacred arms ?
O Mahomet ! O sleepy Mahomet !

Zabina. O cursed Mahomet, that makest us thus
The slaves to Scythians rude and barbarous !

Tamburlaine. Come, bring them in ; and for this
    happy conquest
Triumph and solemnise a martial feast. *Exeunt.*

Finis Actus Tertii

ACT IV

SCENE I

SOLDAN OF EGYPT *with three or four* Lords,
CAPOLIN, [*and a* Messenger.]

Soldan. Awake, ye men of Memphis ! hear the clang
　　Of Scythian trumpets ; hear the basilisks,
　　That roaring shake Damascus' turrets down.
　　The rogue of Volga holds Zenocrate,
　　The Soldan's daughter, for his concubine,
　　And with a troop of thieves and vagabonds,
　　Hath spread his colours to our high disgrace,
　　While you faint-hearted, base Egyptians,
　　Lie slumbering on the flowery banks of Nile,
　　As crocodiles that unaffrighted rest
　　While thundering cannons rattle on their skins.
Messenger. Nay, mighty Soldan, did your greatness see
　　The frowning looks of fiery Tamburlaine,
　　That with his terror and imperious eyes
　　Commands the hearts of his associates,
　　It might amaze your royal majesty.
Soldan. Villain, I tell thee, were that Tamburlaine
　　As monstrous as Gorgon prince of hell,

 The Soldan would **not** start a foot from him.
 But speak, what **power** hath he ?

Messenger. Mighty lord,
 Three hundred thousand men in armour clad,
 Upon their prancing steeds, disdainfully
 With wanton paces trampling on the ground ;
 Five hundred thousand footmen threatening shot,
 Shaking their swords, their spears and iron bills,
 Environing their standard round, that stood
 As bristle-pointed as a thorny wood **;**
 Their warlike engines and munition
 Exceed the forces of their martial men.

Soldan. Nay, could their numbers countervail the stars,
 Or ever drizzling drops of April showers,
 Or withered leaves that autumn shaketh down,
 Yet would the Soldan by his conquering power
 So scatter and consume them in his rage,
 That not a man should live to rue their fall.

Capolin. So might your highness, had you time to sort
 Your fighting men, and raise your royal host.
 But Tamburlaine by expedition
 Advantage takes of your unreadiness.

Soldan. Let him take all th' advantages he can.
 Were all the world conspir'd to fight for him,
 Nay, were he devil, as he is no man,
 Yet in revenge of fair Zenocrate,
 Whom he detaineth in despite of us,
 This arm should send him down to Erebus,
 To shroud his shame in darkness of the night.

Messenger. Pleaseth your mightiness to understand,

His resolution far exceedeth all.
The first day when he pitcheth down his tents,
White is their hue, and on his silver crest,
A snowy feather spangled white he bears,
To signify the mildness of his mind,
That, satiate with spoil, refuseth blood :
But when Aurora mounts the second time,
As red as scarlet is his furniture ;
Then must his kindled wrath be quenched with
        blood,
Not sparing any that can manage arms :
But if these threats move not submission,
Black are his colours, black pavilion ;
His spear, his shield, his horse, his armour, plumes,
And jetty feathers menace death and hell ;
Without respect of sex, degree, or age,
He razeth all his foes with fire and sword.
Soldan. Merciless villain, peasant, ignorant
  Of lawful arms or martial discipline,
  Pillage and murder are his usual trades,
  The slave usurps the glorious name of war !
  See Capolin the fair Arabian king,
  That hath been disappointed by this slave
  Of my fair daughter and his princely love,
  May have fresh warning to go war with us,
  And be reveng'd for her disparagement.   [*Exeunt.*]

SCENE II

TAMBURLAINE, TECHELLES, THERIDAMAS, USUM-
    CASANE, ZENOCRATE, ANIPPE, *two* Moors *drawing*
    BAJAZETH *in his cage, and his wife following him.*

Tamburlaine. Bring out my footstool.
                              They take him out of the cage.
Bajazeth. Ye holy priests of heavenly Mahomet,
    That, sacrificing, slice and cut your flesh,
    Staining his altars with your purple blood,
    Make heaven to frown and every fixed star
    To suck up poison from the moorish fens,
    And pour it in this glorious tyrant's throat !
Tamburlaine. The chiefest God, first mover of that
        sphere
    Enchas'd with thousands ever shining lamps,
    Will sooner burn the glorious frame of heaven
    Than it should so conspire my overthrow.
    But, villain, thou that wishest this to me,
    Fall prostrate on the low disdainful earth,
    And be the footstool of great Tamburlaine,
    That I may rise into my royal throne.
Bajazeth. First shalt thou rip my bowels with thy
        sword
    And sacrifice my heart to death and hell,
    Before I yield to such a slavery.
Tamburlaine. Base villain, vassal, slave to Tamburlaine,
    Unworthy to embrace or touch the ground

    That bears the honour of my royal weight,
    Stoop, villain, stoop ! Stoop, for so he bids
    That may command thee piecemeal to be torn,
    Or scattered like the lofty cedar trees
    Struck with the voice of thundering Jupiter.
Bajazeth. Then as I look down to the damned fiends,
    Fiends, look on me ! and thou, dread god of hell,
    With ebon sceptre strike this hateful earth,
    And make it swallow both of us at once !

                 He gets up upon him to his chair.
Tamburlaine. Now clear the triple region of the air,
    And let the majesty of heaven behold
    Their scourge and terror tread on emperors.
    Smile, stars that reign'd at my nativity,
    And dim the brightness of their neighbour lamps ;
    Disdain to borrow light of Cynthia,
    For I, the chiefest lamp of all the earth,
    First rising in the east with mild aspect,
    But fixed now in the meridian line,
    Will send up fire to your turning spheres,
    And cause the sun to borrow light of you.
    My sword struck fire from his coat of steel,
    Even in Bithynia, when I took this Turk ;
    As when a fiery exhalation,
    Wrapt in the bowels of a freezing cloud,
    Fighting for passage, makes the welkin crack,
    And casts a flash of lightning to the earth.
    But ere I march to wealthy Persia,
    Or leave Damascus and th' Egyptian fields,
    As was the fame of Clymene's brainsick son

That almost brent the axletree of heaven,
So shall our swords, our lances and our shot
Fill all the air with fiery meteors ;
Then, when the sky shall wax as red as blood,
It shall be said I made it red myself,
To make me think of naught but blood and war.

Zabina. Unworthy king, that by thy cruelty
Unlawfully usurpest the Persian seat,
Dar'st thou, that never saw an emperor
Before thou met my husband in the field,
Being thy captive, thus abuse his state,
Keeping his kingly body in a cage,
That roofs of gold and sun-bright palaces
Should have prepar'd to entertain his grace ?
And treading him beneath thy loathsome feet,
Whose feet the kings of Africa have kissed ?

Techelles. You must devise some torment worse, my
        lord,
To make these captives rein their lavish tongues.

Tamburlaine. Zenocrate, look better to your slave.

Zenocrate. She is my handmaid's slave, and she shall
        look
That these abuses flow not from her tongue.
Chide her, Anippe.

Anippe. Let these be warnings for you then, my slave,
How you abuse the person of the king ;
Or else I swear to have you whipt stark nak'd.

Bajazeth. Great Tamburlaine, great in my overthrow,
Ambitious pride shall make thee fall as low,
For treading on the back of Bajazeth,

That should be horsed on four mighty kings.

Tamburlaine. Thy names and titles and thy dignities
   Are fled from Bajazeth and remain with me,
   That will maintain it against a world of kings.—
   Put him in again.   [*They put him into the cage.*]

Bajazeth. Is this a place for mighty Bajazeth?
   Confusion light on him that helps thee thus.

Tamburlaine. There, whiles he lives, shall Bajazeth be
      kept ;
   And where I go be thus in triumph drawn ;
   And thou his wife shalt feed him with the scraps
   My servitors shall bring thee from my board ;
   For he that gives him other food than this,
   Shall sit by him and starve to death himself :
   This is my mind and I will have it so.
   Not all the kings and emperors of the earth,
   If they would lay their crowns before my feet,
   Shall ransom him, or take him from his cage ;
   The ages that shall talk of Tamburlaine,
   Even from this day to Plato's wondrous year,
   Shall talk how I have handled Bajazeth ;
   These Moors, that drew him from Bithynia
   To fair Damascus, where we now remain,
   Shall lead him with us wheresoe'er we go.
   Techelles, and my loving followers,
   Now may we see Damascus' lofty towers,
   Like to the shadows of Pyramides
   That with their beauties graced the Memphian fields
   The golden stature of their feathered bird,
   That spreads her wings upon the city walls,

Shall not defend it from our battering shot.
The townsmen mask in silk and cloth of gold,
And every house is as a treasury ;
The men, the treasure and the town is ours.

Theridamas. Your tents of white now pitch'd before
        the gates,
And gentle flags of amity displayed,
I doubt not but the governor will yield,
Offering Damascus to your majesty.

Tamburlaine. So shall he have his life, and all the rest.
But if he stay until the bloody flag
Be once advanc'd on my vermilion tent,
He dies, and those that kept us out so long ;
And when they see me march in black array,
With mournful streamers hanging down their heads,
Were in that city all the world contain'd,
Not one should scape, but perish by our swords.

Zenocrate. Yet would you have some pity for my sake,
Because it is my country's and my father's.

Tamburlaine. Not for the world, Zenocrate, if I have
        sworn.
Come, bring in the Turk.   *Exeunt.*

SCENE III

SOLDAN, ARABIA, CAPOLIN, *with streaming colours,*
and Soldiers.

Soldan. Methinks we march as Meleager did,
    Environed with brave Argolian knights,

To chase the savage Calydonian boar,
Or Cephalus, with lusty Theban youths,
Against the wolf that angry Themis sent
To waste and spoil the sweet Aonian fields.
A monster of five hundred thousand heads,
Compact of rapine, piracy and spoil,
The scum of men, the hate and scourge of God,
Raves in Egyptia, and annoyeth us.
My lord, it is the bloody Tamburlaine,
A sturdy felon and a base bred thief,
By murder raised to the Persian crown,
That dares control us in our territories.
To tame the pride of this presumptuous beast,
Join your Arabians with the Soldan's power;
Let us unite our royal bands in one,
And hasten to remove Damascus' siege.
It is a blemish to the majesty
And high estate of mighty emperors,
That such a base usurping vagabond
Should brave a king, or wear a princely crown.

Arabia. Renowmed Soldan, have ye lately heard
   The overthrow of mighty Bajazeth
   About the confines of Bithynia?
   The slavery wherewith he persecutes
   The noble Turk and his great emperess?

Soldan. I have, and sorrow for his bad success;
   But, noble lord of great Arabia,
   Be so persuaded that the Soldan is
   No more dismayed with tidings of his fall,
   Than in the haven when the pilot stands,

And views a stranger's ship rent in the winds,
And shivered against a craggy rock.
Yet in compassion of his wretched state,
A sacred vow to heaven and him I make,
Confirming it with Ibis' holy name,
That Tamburlaine shall rue the day, the hour,
Wherein he wrought such ignominious wrong
Unto the hallowed person of a prince,
Or kept the fair Zenocrate so long,
As concubine, I fear, to feed his lust.

Arabia. Let grief and fury hasten on revenge ;
Let Tamburlaine for his offences feel
Such plagues as heaven and we can pour on him.
I long to break my spear upon his crest,
And prove the weight of his victorious arm ;
For fame, I fear, hath been too prodigal
In sounding through the world his partial praise.

Soldan. Capolin, hast thou surveyed our powers ?

Capolin. Great emperors of Egypt and Arabia,
The number of your hosts united is,
A hundred and fifty thousand horse,
Two hundred thousand foot, brave men-at-arms,
Courageous and full of hardiness,
As frolic as the hunters in the chase
Of savage beasts amid the desert woods.

Arabia. My mind presageth fortunate success ;
And, Tamburlaine, my spirit doth foresee
The utter ruin of thy men and thee.

Soldan. Then rear your standards ; let your sounding
drums

Direct our soldiers to Damascus' walls.
Now, Tamburlaine, the mighty Soldan comes,
And leads with him the great Arabian king,
To dim thy baseness and obscurity,
Famous for nothing but for theft and spoil ;
To raze and scatter thy inglorious crew
Of Scythians and slavish Persians.   *Exeunt.*

SCENE IV

The banquet, and to it cometh TAMBURLAINE *all in scarlet,*
    THERIDAMAS, TECHELLES, USUMCASANE, *the Turk*
    with others.

Tamburlaine. Now hang our bloody colours by
     Damascus,
Reflexing hues of blood upon their heads,
While they walk quivering on their city walls,
Half dead for fear before they feel my wrath.
Then let us freely banquet and carouse
Full bowls of wine unto the god of war,
That means to fill your helmets full of gold,
And make Damascus spoils as rich to you
As was to Jason Colchos' golden fleece.
And now, Bajazeth, hast thou any stomach ?
Bajazeth. Ay, such a stomach, cruel Tamburlaine, as I
     could willingly feed upon thy blood-raw heart.
Tamburlaine. Nay, thine own is easier to come by ;

pluck out that and 'twill serve thee and thy wife.
Well, Zenocrate, Techelles, and the rest, fall to
your victuals.

Bajazeth. Fall to, and never may your meat digest !
Ye Furies, that can mask invisible,
Dive to the bottom of Avernas pool,
And in your hands bring hellish poison up,
And squeeze it in the cup of Tamburlaine !
Or, winged snakes of Lerna, cast your stings,
And leave your venoms in this tyrant's dish.

Zabina. And may this banquet prove as ominous
As Progne's to th' adulterous Thracian king
That fed upon the substance of his child !

Zenocrate. My lord, how can you suffer these
Outrageous curses by these slaves of yours ?

Tamburlaine. To let them see, divine Zenocrate,
I glory in the curses of my foes,
Having the power from the imperial heaven
To turn them all upon their proper heads.

Techelles. I pray you, give them leave, madam ; this
speech is a goodly refreshing to them.

Theridamas. But if his highness would let them be fed,
it would do them more good.

Tamburlaine. Sirrah, why fall you not to ? are you so
daintily brought up, you cannot eat your own
flesh ?

Bajazeth. First, legions of devils shall tear thee in
pieces.

Usumcasane. Villain, knowest thou to whom thou
speakest ?

Tamburlaine. O, let him alone. Here; eat, sir; take
it from my sword's point, or I'll thrust it to thy
heart.   *He takes it, and stamps upon it.*

Theridamas. He stamps it under his feet, my lord.

Tamburlaine. Take it up, villain, and eat it; or I will
make thee slice the brawns of thy arms into
carbonadoes and eat them.

Usumcasane. Nay, 'twere better he killed his wife, and
then she shall be sure not to be starv'd, and he
be provided for a month's victual beforehand.

Tamburlaine. Here is my dagger; despatch her while
she is fat, for if she live but a while longer, she
will fall into a consumption with fretting, and
then she will not be worth the eating.

Theridamas. Dost thou think that Mahomet will suffer
this?

Techelles. 'Tis like he will, when he cannot let it.

Tamburlaine. Go to; fall to your meat. What, not a
bit? Belike he hath not been watered to-day;
give him some drink.

> *They give him water to drink, and he flings it on the
> ground.*

Fast, and welcome, sir, while hunger make you eat.
How now, Zenocrate, doth not the Turk and his
wife make a goodly show at a banquet?

Zenocrate. Yes, my lord.

Theridamas. Methinks 'tis a great deal better than a
consort of music.

Tamburlaine. Yet music would do well to cheer up
Zenocrate. Pray thee tell, why art thou so sad? if

  thou wilt have a song, the Turk shall strain his
  voice. But why is it?

Zenocrate. My lord, to see my father's town besieg'd,
 The country wasted, where myself was born,
 How can it but afflict my very soul?
 If any love remain in you, my lord,
 Or if my love unto your majesty
 May merit favour at your highness' hands,
 Then raise your siege from fair Damascus walls,
 And with my father take a friendly truce.

Tamburlaine. Zenocrate, were Egypt Jove's own land,
 Yet would I with my sword make Jove to stoop.
 I will confute those blind geographers
 That make a triple region in the world,
 Excluding regions which I mean to trace,
 And with this pen reduce them to a map,
 Calling the provinces, cities and towns
 After my name and thine, Zenocrate.
 Here at Damascus will I make the point
 That shall begin the perpendicular;
 And wouldst thou have me buy thy father's love
 With such a loss? tell me, Zenocrate.

Zenocrate. Honour still wait on happy Tamburlaine.
 Yet give me leave to plead for him, my lord.

Tamburlaine. Content thyself; his person shall be safe,
 And all the friends of fair Zenocrate,
 If with their lives they will be pleas'd to yield,
 Or may be forc'd to make me emperor;
 For Egypt and Arabia must be mine.
 [*To Bajazeth.*] Feed, you slave; thou mayest think

thyself happy to be fed from my trencher.

Bajazeth. My empty stomach, full of idle heat,
Draws bloody humours from my feeble parts,
Preserving life by hasting cruel death.
My veins are pale, my sinews hard and dry,
My joints benumb'd ; unless I eat, I die.

Zabina. Eat, Bajazeth. Let us live in spite of them,
looking some happy power will pity and enlarge
us.

Tamburlaine. Here Turk, wilt thou have a clean
trencher ?

Bajazeth. Ay, tyrant, and more meat.

Tamburlaine. Soft sir, you must be dieted ; too much
eating will make you surfeit.

Theridamas. So it would, my lord, specially having so
small a walk and so little exercise.

Enter a second course of crowns.

Tamburlaine. Theridamas, Techelles and Casane, here
are the cates you desire to finger, are they not ?

Theridamas. Ay, my lord ; but none save kings must
feed with these.

Techelles. 'Tis enough for us to see them, and for
Tamburlaine only to enjoy them.

Tamburlaine. Well ; here is now to the Soldan of
Egypt, the King of Arabia, and the Governor of
Damascus.
Now, take these three crowns,
And pledge me, my contributory kings.

I crown you here, Theridamas, king of Argier ;
Techelles, king of Fesse ; and Usumcasane,
King of Moroccus.   How say you to this, Turk ?
These are not your contributory kings.

Bajazeth. Nor shall they long be thine, I warrant them.

Tamburlaine. Kings of Argier, Moroccus, and of Fesse,
You that have marched with happy Tamburlaine
As far as from the frozen place of heaven
Unto the watery morning's ruddy bower,
And thence by land unto the torrid zone,
Deserve these titles I endow you with,
By valour and by magnanimity.
Your births shall be no blemish to your fame ;
For virtue is the fount whence honour springs,
And they are worthy she investeth kings.

Theridamas. And, since your highness hath so well
          vouchsafed,
If we deserve them not with higher meeds
Than erst our states and actions have retain'd,
Take them away again and make us slaves.

Tamburlaine. Well said, Theridamas.   When holy
          Fates
Shall 'stablish me in strong Egyptia,
We mean to travel to th' antarctic pole,
Conquering the people underneath our feet,
And be renowm'd as never emperors were.
Zenocrate, I will not crown thee yet,
Until with greater honours I be grac'd.

Finis Actus quarti.

ACT V

SCENE I

The GOVERNOR OF DAMASCO *with three or four* Citizens, *and four* Virgins *with branches of laurel in their hands.*

Governor. Still doth this man, or rather god of war,
  Batter our walls and beat our turrets down ;
  And to resist with longer stubbornness,
  Or hope of rescue from the Soldan's power,
  Were but to bring our wilful overthrow,
  And make us desperate of our threatened lives.
  We see his tents have now been altered
  With terrors to the last and cruel'st hue ;
  His coal-black colours, everywhere advanced,
  Threaten our city with a general spoil ;
  And if we should with common rites of arms
  Offer our safeties to his clemency,
  I fear the custom proper to his sword,
  Which he observes as parcel of his fame,
  Intending so to terrify the world,
  By any innovation or remorse
  Will never be dispensed with till our deaths.
  Therefore, for these our harmless virgins' sakes,

Whose honours and whose lives rely on him,
Let us have hope that their unspotted prayers,
Their blubbered cheeks and hearty humble moans
Will melt his fury into some remorse,
And use us like a loving conqueror.

[1.] *Virgin.* If humble suits or imprecations
(Uttered with tears of wretchedness and blood
Shed from the heads and hearts of all our sex,
Some made your wives, and some your children,)
Might have entreated your obdurate breasts
To entertain some care of our securities
Whiles only danger beat upon our walls,
These more than dangerous warrants of our death
Had never been erected as they be,
Nor you depend on such weak helps as we.

Governor. Well, lovely virgins, think our country's
    care,
Our love of honour, loath to be enthrall'd
To foreign powers and rough imperious yokes,
Would not with too much cowardice or fear,
Before all hope of rescue were denied,
Submit yourselves and us to servitude.
Therefore, in that your safeties and our own,
Your honours, liberties, and lives were weigh'd
In equal care and balance with our own,
Endure as we the malice of our stars,
The wrath of Tamburlaine and power of wars ;
Or be the means the overweighing heavens
Have kept to qualify these hot extremes,
And bring us pardon in your cheerful looks.

2. *Virgin.* Then here, before the majesty of heaven
   And holy patrons of Egyptia.
   With knees and hearts submissive we entreat
   Grace to our words and pity to our looks,
   That this device may prove propitious,
   And through the eyes and ears of Tamburlaine
   Convey events of mercy to his heart.
   Grant that these signs of victory we yield
   May bind the temples of his conquering head,
   To hide the folded furrows of his brows,
   And shadow his displeased countenance
   With happy looks of ruth and lenity.
   Leave us, my lord, and loving countrymen :
   What simple virgins may persuade, we will.
Governor. Farewell, sweet virgins, on whose safe return
   Depends our city, liberty, and lives.

                    Exeunt [all except the Virgins.]

SCENE II

TAMBURLAINE, TECHELLES, THERIDAMAS, USUM-
   CASANE, *with others.* TAMBURLAINE *all in black
   and very melancholy.*

Tamburlaine. What, are the turtles frayed out of their
   nests ?
   Alas, poor fools, must you be first shall feel
   The sworn destruction of Damascus ?

They know my custom ; could they not as well
Have sent ye out when first my milk-white flags,
Through which sweet Mercy threw her gentle beams,
Reflexed them on your disdainful eyes,
As now when fury and incensed hate
Flings slaughtering terror from my coal-black tents,
And tells for truth submissions comes too late ?

1. *Virgin.* Most happy king and emperor of the
          earth,
Image of honour and nobility,
For whom the powers divine have made the world,
And on whose throne the holy graces sit ;
In whose sweet person is compris'd the sum
Of nature's skill and heavenly majesty ;
Pity our plights ! O, pity poor Damascus !
Pity old age, within whose silver hairs
Honour and reverence evermore have reign'd,
Pity the marriage bed, where many a lord
In prime and glory of his loving joy
Embraceth now with tears of ruth and blood
The jealous body of his fearful wife,
Whose cheeks and hearts, so punished with conceit,
To think thy puissant never-stayed arm
Will part their bodies and prevent their souls
From heavens of comfort yet their age might bear,
Now wax all pale and withered to the death,
As well for grief our ruthless governor
Have thus refused the mercy of thy hand,
(Whose sceptre angels kiss and furies dread,)
As for their liberties, their loves, or lives.

O, then, for these and such as we ourselves,
For us, for infants, and for all our bloods,
That never nourished thought against thy rule,
Pity, O pity, sacred emperor,
The prostrate service of this wretched town ;
And take in sign thereof this gilded wreath,
Whereto each man of rule hath given his hand,
And wished, as worthy subjects, happy means
To be investers of thy royal brows
Even with the true Egyptian diadem.

Tamburlaine. Virgins, in vain ye labour to prevent
That which mine honour swears shall be perform'd
Behold my sword ; what see you at the point ?

Virgins. Nothing but fear and fatal steel, my lord.

Tamburlaine. Your fearful minds are thick and misty
    then,
For there sits Death ; there sits imperious Death,
Keeping his circuit by the slicing edge.
But I am pleased you shall not see him there ;
He now is seated on my horsemen's spears,
And on their points his fleshless body feeds.
Techelles, straight go charge a few of them
To charge these dames, and shew my servant Death,
Sitting in scarlet on their armed spears.

Omnes. O, pity us !

Tamburlaine. Away with them, I say, and shew them
    Death.   *They take them away*
I will not spare these proud Egyptians,
Nor change my martial observations
For all the wealth of Gihon's golden waves,

Or for the love of Venus, would she leave
The angry god of arms and lie with me.
They have refused the offer of their lives,
And know my customs are as peremptory
As wrathful planets, death, or destiny.

Enter TECHELLES

What, have your horsemen shown the virgins
      Death ?
Techelles. They have, my lord, and on Damascus' walls
   Have hoisted up their slaughtered carcasses.
Tamburlaine. A sight as baneful to their souls, I think,
   As are Thessalian drugs or mithridate.
   But go, my lords, put the rest to the sword.
                                    [*Exeunt.*

Ah, fair Zenocrate, divine Zenocrate,
Fair is too foul an epithet for thee,
That in thy passion for thy country's love,
And fear to see thy kingly father's harm,
With hair dishevelled wip'st thy watery cheeks ;
And like to Flora in her morning's pride,
Shaking her silver tresses in the air,
Rain'st on the earth resolved pearl in showers,
And sprinklest sapphires on thy shining face,
Where Beauty, mother to the Muses, sits,
And comments volumes with her ivory pen,
Taking instructions from thy flowing eyes,
Eyes, when that Ebena steps to heaven,
In silence of thy solemn evening's walk,

Making the mantle of the richest night,
The moon, the planets, and the meteors, light.
There angels in their crystal armours fight
A doubtful battle with my tempted thoughts
For Egypt's freedom and the Soldan's life,
His life that so consumes Zenocrate ;
Whose sorrows lay more siege unto my soul
Than all my army to Damascus' walls ;
And neither Persia's sovereign nor the Turk
Troubled my senses with conceit of foil
So much by much as doth Zenocrate.
What is beauty, saith my sufferings, then ?
If all the pens that ever poets held
Had fed the feeling of their masters' thoughts,
And every sweetness that inspir'd their hearts,
Their minds and muses on admired themes—
If all the heavenly quintessence they still
From their immortal flowers of poesy,
Wherein as in a mirror we perceive
The highest reaches of a human wit—
If these had made one poem's period,
And all combin'd in beauty's worthiness,
Yet should there hover in their restless heads
One thought, one grace, one wonder, at the least,
Which into words no virtue can digest.
But how unseemly is it for my sex,
My discipline of arms and chivalry,
My nature, and the terror of my name,
To harbour thoughts effeminate and faint !
Save only that in beauty's just applause,

With whose instinct the soul of man is touched,
And every warrior that is rapt with love
Of fame, of valour, and of victory,
Must needs have beauty beat on his conceits,
I thus conceiving, and subduing both,
That which hath stopt the tempest of the gods,
Even from the fiery spangled veil of heaven,
To feel the lovely warmth of shepherds' flames,
And march in cottages of strowed weeds,
Shall give the world to note, for all my birth,
That virtue solely is the sum of glory,
And fashions men with true nobility.
Who's within there ?

Enter two or three.

Hath Bajazeth been fed to-day ?
Attendant. Ay, my lord.
Tamburlaine. Bring him forth ; and let us know if the
    town be ransacked.

Enter TECHELLES, THERIDAMAS, USUMCASANE,
    and others.

Techelles. The town is ours, my lord, and fresh supply
    Of conquest and of spoil is offered us.
Tamburlaine. That's well, Techelles.   What's the
    news ?
Techelles. The Soldan and the Arabian king together
    March on us with such eager violence
    As if there were no way but one with us.

Tamburlaine. No more there is not, I warrant thee,
    Techelles.

They bring in the Turk.

Theridamas. We know the victory is ours, my lord,
    But let us save the reverend Soldan's life
    For fair Zenocrate that so laments his state.
Tamburlaine. That will we chiefly see unto, Theri-
    damas,
    For sweet Zenocrate, whose worthiness
    Deserves a conquest over every heart.
    And now, my footstool, if I lose the field,
    You hope of liberty and restitution.
    Here let him stay, my masters, from the tents,
    Till we have made us ready for the field.
    Pray for us, Bajazeth ; we are going.   *Exeunt.*
Bajazeth. Go, never to return with victory !
    Millions of men encompass thee about,
    And gore thy body with as many wounds !
    Sharp, forked arrows light upon thy horse !
    Furies from the black Cocytus' lake,
    Break up the earth, and with their firebrands
    Enforce thee run upon the baneful pikes !
    Vollies of shot pierce through thy charmed skin,
    And every bullet dipt in poisoned drugs !
    Or roaring cannons sever all thy joints,
    Making thee mount as high as eagles soar !
Zabina. Let all the swords and lances in the field
    Stick in his breast as in their proper rooms !
    At every pore let blood come dropping forth,

    That lingering pains may massacre his heart,
    And madness send his damned soul to hell !
Bajazeth. Ah, fair Zabina, we may curse his power,
    The heavens may frown, the earth for anger quake ;
    But such a star hath influence in his sword
    As rules the skies and countermands the gods
    More than Cimmerian Styx or Destiny :
    And then shall we in this detested guise,
    With shame, with hunger and with horror ay
    Griping our bowels with retorqued thoughts,
    And have no hope to end our ecstasies.
Zabina. Then is there left no Mahomet, no God,
    No fiend, no fortune, nor no hope of end
    To our infamous, monstrous slaveries.
    Gape, earth, and let the fiends infernal view
    A hell as hopeless and as full of fear
    As are the blasted banks of Erebus,
    Where shaking ghosts with ever howling groans
    Hover about the ugly ferryman,
    To get a passage to Elysian.
    Why should we live ? O wretches, beggars, slaves !
    Why live we, Bajazeth, and build up nests
    So high within the region of the air,
    By living long in this oppression,
    That all the world will see and laugh to scorn
    The former triumphs of our mightiness
    In this obscure infernal servitude ?
Bajazeth. O life, more loathsome to my vexed thoughts
    Than noisome parbreak of the Stygian snakes,
    Which fills the nooks of hell with standing air,

Infecting all the ghosts with cureless griefs !
O dreary engines of my loathed sight,
That sees my crown, my honour and my name
Thrust under yoke and thraldom of a thief,
Why feed ye still on day's accursed beams,
And sink not quite into my tortur'd soul ?
You see my wife, my queen, and emperess,
Brought up and propped by the hand of Fame,
Queen of fifteen contributory queens,
Now thrown to rooms of black abjection,
Smear'd with blots of basest drudgery,
And villeiness to shame, disdain, and misery.
Accursed Bajazeth, whose words of ruth,
That would with pity cheer Zabina's heart,
And make our souls resolve in ceaseless tears,
Sharp hunger bites upon the gripes the root
From whence the issues of my thoughts do break.
O poor Zabina ! O my queen, my queen !
Fetch me some water for my burning breast,
To cool and comfort me with longer date,
That, in the shortened sequel of my life,
I may pour forth my soul into thine arms
With words of love, whose moaning intercourse
Hath hitherto been stayed with wrath and hate
Of our expressless banned inflictions.

Zabina. Sweet Bajazeth, I will prolong thy life
As long as any blood or spark of breath
Can quench or cool the torments of my grief.

She goes out.

Bajazeth. Now, Bajazeth, abridge thy baneful days,

And beat thy brains out of thy conquer'd head,
Since other means are all forbidden me,
That may be ministers of my decay.
O highest lamp of ever-living Jove,
Accursed day, infected with my griefs,
Hide now thy stained face in endless night,
And shut the windows of the lightsome heavens.
Let ugly darkness with her rusty coach,
Engirt with tempests wrapt in pitchy clouds,
Smother the earth with never-fading mists,
And let her horses from their nostrils breathe
Rebellious winds and dreadful thunder claps,
That in this terror Tamburlaine may live,
And my pin'd soul, resolv'd in liquid air,
May still excruciate his tormented thoughts.
Then let the stony dart of senseless cold
Pierce through the centre of my withered heart,
And make a passage for my loathed life.

                    He brains himself against the cage.

                    Enter ZABINA.

Zabina. What do mine eyes behold ? my husband
          dead !
     His skull all riven in twain ! his brains dash'd out,
     The brains of Bajazeth, my lord and sovereign !
     O Bajazeth, my husband and my lord !
     O Bajazeth ! O Turk ! O emperor !
                                        [*She runs mad.*]
     Give him his liquor ? not I. Bring milk and fire,

and my blood I bring him again. Tear me in
pieces, give me the sword with a ball of wild-fire
upon it. Down with him, down with him. Go
to my child ; away, away, away ! ah, save that
infant ! save him, save him ! I, even I, speak to
her. The sun was down, streamers white, red,
black. Here, here, here ! Fling the meat in his
face Tamburlaine, Tamburlaine ! Let the
soldiers be buried. Hell, death, Tamburlaine,
hell ! Make ready my coach, my chair, my
jewels. I come, I come, I come !

> *She runs against the cage, and brains herself.*

[*Enter*] ZENOCRATE *with* ANIPPE.

[*Zenocrate.*] Wretched Zenocrate, that livest to see
Damascus' walls dy'd with Egyptian blood,
Thy father's subjects and thy countrymen ;
Thy streets strowed with disseevered joints of men,
And wounded bodies gasping yet for life ;
But most accursed, to see the sun-bright troop
Of heavenly virgins and unspotted maids,
Whose looks might make the angry god of arms
To break his sword and mildly treat of love,
On horsemen's lances to be hoisted up,
And guiltlessly endure a cruel death.
For every fell and stout Tartarian steed,
That stamped on others with their thundring hoofs,
When all their riders charg'd their quivering spears,
Began to check the ground and rein themselves,

Gazing upon the beauty of their looks.
Ah, Tamburlaine, wert thou the cause of this,
That term'st Zenocrate thy dearest love ?
Whose lives were dearer to Zenocrate
Than her own life, or aught save thine own love.
But see another bloody spectacle.
Ah, wretched eyes, the enemies of my heart,
How are ye glutted with these grievous objects,
And tell my soul more tales of bleeding ruth !
See, see, Anippe, if they breathe or no.

Anippe. No breath, nor sense, nor motion, in them
    both.
Ah, madam, this their slavery hath enforc'd,
And ruthless cruelty of Tamburlaine.

Zenocrate. Earth, cast up fountains from thy entrails,
And wet thy cheeks for their untimely deaths ;
Shake with their weight in sign of fear and grief.
Blush heaven, that gave them honour at their birth,
And let them die a death so barbarous.
Those that are proud of fickle empery
And place their chiefest good in earthly pomp,
Behold the Turk and his great emperess !
Ah, Tamburlaine, my love, sweet Tamburlaine,
That fightst for sceptres and for slippery crowns,
Behold the Turk and his great emperess !
Thou that, in conduct of thy happy stars,
Sleep'st every night with conquest on thy brows,
And yet wouldst shun the wavering turns of war,
In fear and feeling of the like distress,
Behold the Turk and his great emperess !

Ah, mighty Jove and holy Mahomet,
Pardon my love ! O, pardon his contempt
Of earthly fortune and respect of pity ;
And let not conquest, ruthlessly pursued,
Be equally against his life incensed
In this great Turk and hapless emperess !
And pardon me that was not mov'd with ruth
To see them live so long in misery.
Ah, what may chance to thee, Zenocrate ?

Anippe. Madam, content yourself, and be resolv'd,
Your love hath Fortune so at his command,
That she shall stay and turn her wheel no more,
As long as life maintains his mighty arm
That fights for honour to adorn you head.

Enter a Messenger [PHILEMUS].

Zenocrate. What other heavy news now brings Phile-
    mus ?

Philemus. Madam, your father and th' Arabian king,
The first affecter of your excellence,
Comes now as Turnus 'gainst Æneas did,
Armed with lance into the Ægyptian fields,
Ready for battle 'gainst my lord the king.

Zenocrate. Now shame and duty, love and fear presents
A thousand sorrows to my martyred soul.
Whom should I wish the fatal victory,
When my poor pleasures are divided thus,
And racked by duty from my cursed heart ?
My father and my first betrothed love

Must fight against my life and present love ;
Wherein the change I use condemns my faith,
And makes my deeds infamous through the world.
But as the gods, to end the Trojan's toil,
Prevented Turnus of Lavinia,
And fatally enriched Æneas' love,
So, for a final issue to my griefs,
To pacify my country and my love,
Must Tamburlaine by their resistless powers,
With virtue of a gentle victory,
Conclude a league of honour to my hope ;
Then, as the powers divine have pre-ordained,
With happy safety of my father's life
Send like defence of fair Arabia.

*They sound to the battle.   And Tamburlaine enjoys the
victory ; after, Arabia enters wounded.*

Arabia. What cursed power guides the murdering
          hands
  Of this infamous tyrant's soldiers,
  That no escape may save their enemies,
  Nor fortune keep themselves from victory ?
  Lie down, Arabia, wounded to the death,
  And let Zenocrate's fair eyes behold,
  That, as for her thou bearst these wretched arms,
  Even so for her thou diest in these arms,
  Leaving thy blood for witness of thy love.
Zenocrate. Too dear a witness for such love, my lord.
  Behold Zenocrate, the cursed object

Whose fortunes never mastered her griefs ;
Behold her wounded in conceit for thee,
As much as thy fair body is for me !
Arabia. Then shall I die with full contented heart,
  Having beheld divine Zenocrate,
  Whose sight with joy would take away my life,
  As now it bringeth sweetness to my wound,
  If I had not been wounded as I am—
  Ah, that the deadly pangs I suffer now
  Would lend an hour's licence to my tongue,
  To make discourse of some sweet accidents
  Have chanc'd thy merits in this worthless bondage,
  And that I might be privy to the state
  Of thy deserv'd contentment and thy love !
  But making now a virtue of thy sight,
  To drive all sorrow from my fainting soul,
  Since death denies me further cause of joy,
  Depriv'd of care, my heart with comfort dies,
  Since thy desired hand shall close mine eyes.

Enter TAMBURLAINE *leading the* SOLDAN, TECH-
ELLES, THERIDAMAS, USUMCASANE, *with others.*

Tamburlaine. Come, happy father of Zenocrate,
  A title higher than thy Soldan's name.
  Though my right hand have thus enthralled thee,
  Thy princely daughter here shall set thee free,
  She that hath calmed the fury of my sword,
  Which had ere this been bathed in streams of blood
  As vast and deep as Euphrates or Nile.

Zenocrate. O sight thrice welcome to my joyful soul,
  To see the king my father issue safe
  From dangerous battle of my conquering love !
Soldan. Well met, my only dear Zenocrate,
  Though with the loss of Egypt and my crown.
Tamburlaine. 'Twas I, my lord, that got the victory,
  And therefore grieve not at your overthrow,
  Since I shall render all into your hands,
  And add more strength to your dominions
  Then ever yet confirm'd th' Egyptian crown.
  The god of war resigns his room to me,
  Meaning to make me general of the world ;
  Jove, viewing me in arms, looks pale and wan,
  Fearing my power should pull him from his throne ;
  Where'er I come the fatal sisters sweat,
  And grisly death, by running to and fro
  To do their ceaseless homage to my sword ;
  And here in Afric, where it seldom rains,
  Since I arriv'd with my triumphant host,
  Have swelling clouds, drawn from wide gasping
      wounds,
  Been oft resolv'd in bloody purple showers,
  A meteor that might terrify the earth,
  And make it quake at every drop it drinks ;
  Millions of souls sit on the banks of Styx,
  Waiting the back return of Charon's boat ;
  Hell and Elysium swarm with ghosts of men
  That I have sent from sundry foughten fields
  To spread my fame through hell and up to heaven ;
  And see, my lord, a sight of strange import,

Emperors and kings lie breathless at my feet ;
The Turk and his great empress, as it seems,
Left to themselves while we were at the fight,
Have desperately despatched their slavish lives ;
With them Arabia too hath left his life :
All sights of power to grace my victory.
And such are objects fit for Tamburlaine,
Wherein, as in a mirror, may be seen
His honour, that consists in shedding blood
When men presume to manage arms with him.

Soldan. Mighty hath God and Mahomet made thy
hand,
Renowmed Tamburlaine, to whom all kings
Of force must yield their crowns and emperies ;
And I am pleased with this my overthrow,
If, as beseems a person of thy state,
Thou hast with honour used Zenocrate.

Tamburlaine. Her state and person wants no pomp,
you see ;
And for all blot of foul inchastity,
I record heaven, her heavenly self is clear :
Then let me find no further time to grace
Her princely temples with the Persian crown ;
But here these kings that on my fortunes wait,
And have been crown'd for proved worthiness
Even by this hand that shall establish them,
Shall now, adjoining all their hands with mine,
Invest her here my Queen of Persia.
What saith the noble Soldan and Zenocrate ?

Soldan. I yield with thanks and protestations

Of endless honour to thee for her love.

Tamburlaine. Then doubt I not but fair Zenocrate
  Will soon consent to satisfy us both.

Zenocrate. Else should I much forget myself, my lord.

Theridamas. Then let us set the crown upon her head,
  That long hath lingered for so high a seat.

Techelles. My hand is ready to perform the deed,
  For now her marriage time shall work us rest.

Usumcasane. And here's the crown, my lord ; help set
    it on.

Tamburlaine. Then sit thou down, divine Zenocrate ;
  And here we crown thee Queen of Persia,
  And all the kingdoms and dominions
  That late the power of Tamburlaine subdued.
  As Juno, when the giants were suppressed
  That darted mountains at her brother Jove,
  So looks my love, shadowing in her brows
  Triumphs and trophies for my victories ;
  Or as Latona's daughter, bent to arms,
  Adding more courage to my conquering mind.
  To gratify thee, sweet Zenocrate,
  Egyptians, Moors, and men of Asia,
  From Barbary unto the Western Indie,
  Shall pay a yearly tribute to thy sire ;
  And from the bounds of Afric to the banks
  Of Ganges shall his mighty arm extend.
  And now, my lords and loving followers,
  That purchas'd kingdoms by your martial deeds,
  Cast off your armour, put on scarlet robes,
  Mount up your royal places of estate,

Environed with troops of noble men,
And there make laws to rule your provinces :
Hang up your weapons on Alcides' post ;
For Tamburlaine takes truce with all the world.
Thy first betrothed love, Arabia,
Shall we with honour, as beseems, entomb,
With this great Turk and his fair emperess.
Then, after all these solemn exequies,
We will our rites of marriage solemnise.

Finis Actus quinti & ultimi huius primae partis.

TAMBURLAINE THE GREAT
PART II

[DRAMATIS PERSONÆ

TAMBURLAINE, *King of Persia.*
CALYPHAS, ⎫
AMYRAS, ⎬ *his sons.*
CELEBINUS, ⎭
THERIDAMAS, *King of Argier.*
TECHELLES, *King of Fez.*
USUMCASANE, *King of Morocco.*
ORCANES, *King of Natolia.*
KING OF TREBIZON.
KING OF SORIA.
KING OF JERUSALEM.
KING OF AMASIA.
GAZELLUS, *Viceroy of Byron.*
URIBASSA.
SIGISMUND, *King of Hungary.*
FREDERICK, ⎫
BALDWIN, ⎭ *lords of Buda and Bohemia.*
CALLAPINE, *son to* BAJAZETH, *and prisoner to* TAMBURLAINE.
ALMEDA, *his keeper.*
GOVERNOR OF BABYLON.
CAPTAIN OF BALSERA.
HIS SON.
ANOTHER CAPTAIN.
MAXIMUS, PERDICAS, PHYSICIANS, LORDS, CITIZENS, MESSENGERS,
    SOLDIERS, *and* ATTENDANTS.

ZENOCRATE, *wife to* TAMBURLAINE.
OLYMPIA, *wife to the* CAPTAIN OF BALSERA.
TURKISH CONCUBINES.]

The second part of
The bloody Conquests
of mighty Tamburlaine.

With his impassionate fury, for the death of
his Lady and love, fair Zenocrate: his form of
exhortation and discipline to his three sons,
and the manner of his own death.

THE PROLOGUE

THE general welcomes Tamburlaine receiv'd,
When he arrived last upon our stage,
Hath made our poet pen his second part,
Where death cuts off the progress of his pomp,
And murderous Fates throws all his triumphs down.
But what became of fair Zenocrate,
And with how many cities' sacrifice
He celebrated her sad funeral,
Himself in presence shall unfold at large.

ACT I

SCENE I

ORCANES *king of Natolia,* GAZELLUS *viceroy of Byron,* URIBASSA, *and their train, with drums and trumpets.*

Orcanes. Egregious viceroys of these eastern parts,
   Plac'd by the issue of great Bajazeth,
   And sacred lord, the mighty Callapine,
   Who lives in Egypt prisoner to that slave
   Which kept his father in an iron cage,
   Now have we marched from fair Natolia
   Two hundred leagues, and on Danubius' banks
   Our warlike host in complete armour rest,
   Where Sigismund, the king of Hungary,
   Should meet our person to conclude a truce.
   What? shall we parle with the Christian,
   Or cross the stream, and meet him in the field?
Byron. King of Natolia, let us treat of peace;
   We are all glutted with the Christians' blood,
   And have a greater foe to fight against,
   Proud Tamburlaine, that now in Asia,
   Near Guyron's head, doth set his conquering feet,
   And means to fire Turkey as he goes:
   'Gainst him, my lord, must you address your power.

Uribassa. Besides, King Sigismund hath brought from
        Christendom
  More than his camp of stout Hungarians,
  Slavonians, Almains, Rutters, Muffs and Danes,
  That with the halberd, lance and murdering axe,
  Will hazard that we might with surety hold.
Orcanes. Though from the shortest northern parallel,
  Vast Gruntland, compassed with the frozen sea,
  Inhabited with tall and sturdy men,
  Giants as big as hugy Polypheme,
  Millions of soldiers cut the arctic line,
  Bringing the strength of Europe to these arms,
  Our Turkey blades shall glide through all their
        throats,
  And make this champion mead a bloody fen ;
  Danubius' stream, that runs to Trebizon,
  Shall carry, wrapt within his scarlet waves,
  As martial presents to our friends at home,
  The slaughtered bodies of these Christians ;
  The Terrene main, wherein Danubius falls,
  Shall by this battle be the bloody sea ;
  The wandering sailors of proud Italy
  Shall meet those Christians fleeting with the tide,
  Beating in heaps against their argosies,
  And make fair Europe, mounted on her bull,
  Trapped with the wealth and riches of the world,
  Alight and wear a woful mourning weed.
Byron. Yet, stout Orcanes, Prorex of the world,
  Since Tamburlaine hath mustered all his men,
  Marching from Cairon northward with his camp

To Alexandria and the frontier towns,
Meaning to make a conquest of our land,
'Tis requisite to parle for a peace
With Sigismund, the king of Hungary,
And save our forces for the hot assaults
Proud Tamburlaine intends Natolia.

Orcanes. Viceroy of Byron, wisely hast thou said.
My realm, the centre of our empery,
Once lost, all Turkey would be overthrown ;
And for that cause the Christians shall have peace.
Slavonians, Almains, Rutters, Muffs and Danes
Fear not Orcanes, but great Tamburlaine ;
Nor he, but Fortune that hath made him great.
We have revolted Grecians, Albanese,
Cicilians, Jews, Arabians, Turks and Moors,
Natolians, Sorians, black Egyptians,
Illyrians, Thracians and Bithynians,
Enough to swallow forceless Sigismund,
Yet scarce enough t' encounter Tamburlaine.
He brings a world of people to the field,
From Scythia to the oriental plage
Of India, where raging Lantchidol
Beats on the regions with his boisterous blows,
That never seaman yet discovered,
All Asia is in arms with Tamburlaine ;
Even from the midst of fiery Cancer's tropic
To Amazonia under Capricorn,
And thence, as far as Archipelago,
All Afric is in arms with Tamburlaine ;
Therefore, viceroys, the Christians must have peace.

SCENE II

[*Enter to them*] SIGISMUND, FREDERICK, BALDWIN,
      and their train, with drums and trumpets.

Sigismund. Orcanes, as our legates promised thee,
   We, with our peers, have crossed Danubius' stream,
   To treat of friendly peace or deadly war.
   Take which thou wilt ; for, as the Romans used,
   I here present thee with a naked sword ;
   Wilt thou have war, then shake this blade at me ;
   If peace, restore it to my hands again,
   And I will sheathe it, to confirm the same.
Orcanes. Stay, Sigismund ; forgetst thou I am he
   That with the cannon shook Vienna walls,
   And made it dance upon the continent,
   As when the massy substance of the earth
   Quivers about the axle-tree of heaven ?
   Forgetst thou that I sent a shower of darts,
   Mingled with powdered shot and feathered steel,
   So thick upon the blink-ey'd burghers' heads,
   That thou thyself, then County Palatine,
   The King of Boheme, and the Austric Duke,
   Sent heralds out, which basely on their knees,
   In all your names, desired a truce of me ?
   Forgetst thou that, to have me raise my siege,
   Waggons of gold were set before my tent,
   Stampt with the princely fowl that in her wings

123

Carries the fearful thunderbolts of Jove ?
How canst thou think of this, and offer war ?

Sigismund. Vienna was besieg'd, and I was there,
Then County Palatine, but now a king,
And what we did was in extremity.
But now, Orcanes, view my royal host,
That hides these plains, and seems as vast and wide
As doth the desert of Arabia
To those that stand on Badgeth's lofty tower,
Or as the ocean to the traveller
That rests upon the snowy Appenines ;
And tell me whether I should stoop so low,
Or treat of peace with the Natolian king.

Byron. Kings of Natolia and of Hungary,
We came from Turkey to confirm a league,
And not to dare each other to the field.
A friendly parle might become ye both.

Frederick. And we from Europe, to the same intent ;
Which if your general refuse or scorn,
Our tents are pitched, our men stand in array,
Ready to charge you ere you stir your feet.

Orcanes. So prest are we : but yet, if Sigismund
Speak as a friend, and stand not upon terms,
Here is his sword ; let peace be ratified
On these conditions specified before,
Drawn with advice of our ambassadors.

Sigismund. Then here I sheathe it and give thee my
            hand,
Never to draw it out, or manage arms
Against thyself or thy confederates ;

But whilst I live will be at truce with thee.

Orcanes. But, Sigismund, confirm it with an oath,
And swear in sight of heaven and by thy Christ.

Sigismund. By him that made the world and sav'd my
        soul,
The son of God and issue of a maid,
Sweet Jesus Christ, I solemnly protest
And vow to keep this peace inviolable.

Orcanes. By sacred Mahomet, the friend of God,
Whose holy Alcaron remains with us,
Whose glorious body, when he left the world,
Closed in a coffin mounted up the air,
And hung on stately Mecca's temple roof,
I swear to keep this truce inviolable !
Of whose conditions and our solemn oaths,
Sign'd with our hands, each shall retain a scroll,
As memorable witness of our league.
Now, Sigismund, if any Christian king
Encroach upon the confines of thy realm,
Send word, Orcanes of Natolia
Confirm'd this league beyond Danubius' stream,
And they will, trembling, sound a quick retreat ;
So am I fear'd among all nations.

Sigismund. If any heathen potentate or king
Invade Natolia, Sigismund will send
A hundred thousand horse train'd to the war,
And back'd by stout lanceres of Germany,
The strength and sinews of the imperial seat.

Orcanes. I thank thee, Sigismund ; but when I war,
All Asia Minor, Africa, and Greece

Follow my standard and my thundering drums.
Come, let us go and banquet in our tents :
I will despatch chief of my army hence
To fair Natolia and to Trebizon,
To stay my coming 'gainst proud Tamburlaine :
Friend Sigismund, and peers of Hungary,
Come, banquet and carouse with us a while,
And then depart we to our territories.   *Exeunt.*

SCENE III

CALLAPINE *with* ALMEDA *his keeper.*

Callapine. Sweet Almeda, pity the ruthful plight
  Of Callapine, the son of Bajazeth,
  Born to be monarch of the western world,
  Yet here detain'd by cruel Tamburlaine.
Almeda. My lord, I pity it, and with my heart
  Wish your release ; but he whose wrath is death,
  My sovereign lord, renowmed Tamburlaine,
  Forbids you further liberty than this.
Callapine. Ah, were I now but half so eloquent
  To paint in words what I'll perform in deeds,
  I know thou wouldst depart from hence with me !
Almeda. Not for all Afric ; therefore move me not.
Callapine. Yet hear me speak, my gentle Almeda.
Almeda. No speech to that end, by your favour, sir.
Callapine. By Cario runs—

Almeda. No talk of running, I tell you, sir.

Callapine. A little further, gentle Almeda.

Almeda. Well sir, what of this ?

Callapine. By Cario runs to Alexandria bay
  Darotes' streams, wherein at anchor lies
  A Turkish galley of my royal fleet,
  Waiting my coming to the river side,
  Hoping by some means I shall be released ;
  Which, when I come aboard, will hoist up sail,
  And soon put forth into the Terrene sea,
  Where, 'twixt the isles of Cyprus and of Crete,
  We quickly may in Turkish seas arrive.
  Then shalt thou see a hundred kings and more,
  Upon their knees, all bid me welcome home.
  Amongst so many crowns of burnished gold,
  Choose which thou wilt, all are at thy command :
  A thousand galleys, mann'd with Christian slaves,
  I freely give thee, which shall cut the Straits,
  And bring armadoes, from the coasts of Spain,
  Fraughted with gold of rich America :
  The Grecian virgins shall attend on thee,
  Skilful in music and in amorous lays,
  As fair as was Pygmalion's ivory girl
  Or lovely Io metamorphosed :
  With naked negroes shall thy coach be drawn,
  And, as thou rid'st in triumph through the streets,
  The pavement underneath thy chariot wheels
  With Turkey carpets shall be covered,
  And cloth of arras hung about the walls,
  Fit objects for thy princely eye to pierce ;

A hundred bassoes, cloth'd in crimson silk,
Shall ride before thee on Barbarian steeds ;
And, when thou goest, a golden canopy
Enchas'd with precious stones, which shine as bright
As that fair veil that covers all the world,
When Phœbus, leaping from his hemisphere,
Descendeth downward to th' Antipodes—
And more than this, for all I cannot tell.

Almeda. How far hence lies the galley, say you ?

Callapine. Sweet Almeda, scarce half a league from
    hence.

Almeda. But need we not be spied going aboard ?

Callapine. Betwixt the hollow hanging of a hill,
And crooked bending of a craggy rock,
The sails wrapt up, the mast and tacklings down,
She lies so close that none can find her out.

Almeda. I like that well : but, tell me, my lord, if I
    should let you go, would you be as good as your
    word ? shall I be made a king for my labour ?

Callapine. As I am Callapine the emperor,
And by the hand of Mahomet I swear,
Thou shalt be crown'd a king and be my mate !

Almeda. Then here I swear, as I am Almeda,
Your keeper under Tamburlaine the Great,
(For that's the style and title I have yet,)
Although he sent a thousand armed men
To intercept this haughty enterprise,
Yet would I venture to conduct your grace,
And die before I brought you back again !

Callapine. Thanks, gentle Almeda ; then let us haste,

Lest time be past, and lingering let us both.

Almeda. When you will, my lord; I am ready.

Callapine. Even straight: and farewell, cursed Tamburlaine!

Now go I to revenge my father's death.   *Exeunt.*

SCENE IV

TAMBURLAINE, *with* ZENOCRATE, *and his three sons,* CALYPHAS, AMYRAS, *and* CELEBINUS, *with drums and trumpets.*

Tamburlaine. Now, bright Zenocrate, the world's fair eye,

Whose beams illuminate the lamps of heaven,

Whose cheerful looks do clear the cloudy air,

And clothe it in a crystal livery,

Now rest thee here on fair Larissa plains,

Where Egypt and the Turkish empire parts,

Between thy sons, that shall be emperors,

And every one commander of a world.

Zenocrate. Sweet Tamburlaine, when wilt thou leave these arms,

And save thy sacred person free from scathe,

And dangerous chances of the wrathful war?

Tamburlaine. When heaven shall cease to move on both the poles,

And when the ground, whereon my soldiers march,

Shall rise aloft and touch the horned moon ;
And not before, my sweet Zenocrate.
Sit up, and rest thee like a lovely queen.
So ; now she sits in pomp and majesty,
When these my sons, more precious in mine eyes
Than all the wealthy kingdoms I subdued,
Plac'd by her side, look on their mother's face.
But yet methinks their looks are amorous,
Not martial as the sons of Tamburlaine ;
Water and air, being symbolised in one,
Argue their want of courage and of wit ;
Their hair as white as milk and soft as down,
Which should be like the quills of porcupines,
As black as jet and hard as iron or steel,
Bewrays they are too dainty for the wars ;
Their fingers made to quaver on a lute,
Their arms to hang about a lady's neck,
Their legs to dance and caper in the air,
Would make me think them bastards, not my sons,
But that I know they issued from thy womb,
That never look'd on man but Tamburlaine.
Zenocrate. My gracious lord, they have their mother's
    looks,
But, when they list, their conquering father's heart.
This lovely boy, the youngest of the three,
Not long ago bestrid a Scythian steed,
Trotting the ring, and tilting at a glove,
Which when he tainted with his slender rod,
He rein'd him straight, and made him so curvet
As I cried out for fear he should have faln.

Tamburlaine. Well done, my boy ! thou shalt have
    shield and lance.
  Armour of proof, horse, helm, and curtle-axe,
  And I will teach thee how to charge thy foe,
  And harmless run among the deadly pikes.
  If thou wilt love the wars and follow me,
  Thou shalt be made a king and reign with me,
  Keeping in iron cages emperors.
  If thou exceed thy elder brothers' worth,
  And shine in complete virtue more than they,
  Thou shalt be king before them, and thy seed
  Shall issue crowned from their mother's womb.
Celebinus. Yes, father ; you shall see me, if I live,
  Have under me as many kings as you,
  And march with such a multitude of men
  As all the world shall tremble at their view.
Tamburlaine. These words assure me, boy, thou art my
    son.
  When I am old and cannot manage arms,
  Be thou the scourge and terror of the world.
Amyras. Why may not I, my lord, as well as he,
  Be term'd the scourge and terror of the world ?
Tamburlaine. Be all a scourge and terror to the world,
  Or else you are not sons of Tamburlaine.
Calyphas. But while my brothers follow arms, my lord,
  Let me accompany my gracious mother.
  They are enough to conquer all the world,
  And you have won enough for me to keep.
Tamburlaine. Bastardly boy, sprung from some coward's
    loins,

And not the issue of great Tamburlaine,
Of all the provinces I have subdued
Thou shalt not have a foot, unless thou bear
A mind courageous and invincible ;
For he shall wear the crown of Persia
Whose head hath deepest scars, whose breast most
    wounds,
Which, being wroth, sends lightning from his eyes,
And in the furrows of his frowning brows
Harbours revenge, war, death and cruelty ;
For in a field, whose superficies
Is covered with a liquid purple veil,
And sprinkled with the brains of slaughtered men,
My royal chair of state shall be advanc'd ;
And he that means to place himself therein,
Must armed wade up to the chin in blood.

Zenocrate. My lord, such speeches to our princely sons
  Dismays their minds before they come to prove
  The wounding troubles angry war affords.

Celebinus. No, madam, these are speeches fit for us ;
  For, if his chair were in a sea of blood,
  I would prepare a ship and sail to it,
  Ere I would lose the title of a king.

Amyras. And I would strive to swim through pools of
  blood,
  Or make a bridge of murdered carcasses,
  Whose arches should be fram'd with bones of Turks,
  Ere I would lose the title of a king.

Tamburlaine. Well, lovely boys, you shall be emperors
  both,

Stretching your conquering arms from east to west :
And, sirra, if you mean to wear a crown,
When we shall meet the Turkish deputy
And all his viceroys, snatch it from his head,
And cleave his pericranion with thy sword.
Calyphas. If any man will hold him, I will strike,
And cleave him to the channel with my sword,
Tamburlaine. Hold him, and cleave him too, or I'll
        cleave thee ;
For we will march against them presently.
Theridamas, Techelles and Casane
Promised to meet me on Larissa plains,
With hosts apiece against this Turkish crew ;
For I have sworn by sacred Mahomet
To make it parcel of my empery.
The trumpets sound ; Zenocrate, they come.

SCENE V

Enter [to them] THERIDAMAS, *and his train, with
        drums and trumpets.*

Tamburlaine. Welcome Theridamas, king of Argier.
Theridamas. My lord, the great and mighty Tambur-
        laine,
Arch-monarch of the world, I offer here
My crown, myself, and all the power I have,
In all affection at thy kingly feet.
Tamburlaine. Thanks, good Theridamas.

Theridamas. Under my colours march ten thousand
    Greeks,
  And of Argier and Afric's frontier towns
  Twice twenty thousand valiant men-at-arms ;
  All which have sworn to sack Natolia.
  Five hundred brigandines are under sail,
  Meet for your service on the sea, my lord,
  That, launching from Argier to Tripoly,
  Will quickly ride before Natolia,
  And batter down the castles on the shore.
Tamburlaine. Well said, Argier ! receive thy crown
    again.

SCENE VI

Enter TECHELLES *and* USUMCASANE *together.*

Tamburlaine. Kings of Moroccus and of Fesse, welcome.
Usumcasane. Magnificent and peerless Tamburlaine,
  I and my neighbour king of Fesse have brought,
  To aid thee in this Turkish expedition,
  A hundred thousand expert soldiers ;
  From Azamor to Tunis near the sea
  Is Barbary unpeopled for thy sake,
  And all the men in armour under me,
  Which with my crown I gladly offer thee.
Tamburlaine. Thanks, king of Moroccus : take your
    crown again.
Techelles. And, mighty Tamburlaine, our earthly god,
  Whose looks make this inferior world to quake,
  I here present thee with the crown of Fesse,

And with an host of Moors trained to the war,
Whose coal-black faces make their foes retire,
And quake for fear, as if infernal Jove,
Meaning to aid thee in these Turkish arms,
Should pierce the black circumference of hell,
With ugly Furies bearing fiery flags,
And millions of his strong tormenting spirits ;
From strong Tesella unto Biledull
All Barbary is unpeopled for thy sake.

Tamburlaine. Thanks, king of Fesse ; take here thy
crown again.
Your presence, loving friends and fellow kings,
Makes me to surfeit in conceiving joy ;
If all the crystal gates of Jove's high court
Were opened wide, and I might enter in
To see the state and majesty of heaven,
It could not more delight me than your sight.
Now will we banquet on these plains a while,
And after march to Turkey with our camp,
In number more than are the drops that fall
When Boreas rents a thousand swelling clouds ;
And proud Orcanes of Natolia
With all his viceroys shall be so afraid,
That, though the stones, as at Deucalion's flood,
Were turned to men, he should be overcome.
Such lavish will I make of Turkish blood,
That Jove shall send his winged messenger
To bid me sheathe my sword and leave the field ;
The sun, unable to sustain the sight,
Shall hide his head in Thetis' watery lap,

And leave his steeds to fair Böotes' charge ;
For half the world shall perish in this fight.
But now, my friends, let me examine ye ;
How have ye spent your absent time from me ?
Usumcasane. My lord, our men of Barbary have marched
Four hundred miles with armour on their backs,
And lain in leaguer fifteen months and more ;
For, since we left you at the Soldan's court,
We have subdued the southern Guallatia,
And all the land unto the coast of Spain ;
We kept the narrow Strait of Gibraltar,
And made Canarea call us kings and lords ;
Yet never did they recreate themselves,
Or cease one day from war and hot alarms ;
And therefore let them rest a while, my lord.
Tamburlaine. They shall, Casane, and 'tis time, i'faith.
Techelles. And I have march'd along the river Nile
To Machda, where the mighty Christian priest,
Call'd John the Great, sits in a milk-white robe,
Whose triple mitre I did take by force,
And made him swear obedience to my crown.
From thence unto Cazates did I march,
Where Amazonians met me in the field,
With whom, being women, I vouchsafed a league,
And with my power did march to Zanzibar,
The western part of Afric, where I view'd
The Ethiopian sea, rivers and lakes,
But neither man nor child in all the land.
Therefore I took my course to Manico,
Where, unresisted, I remov'd my camp ;

And, by the coast of Byather, at last
I came to Cubar, where the negroes dwell,
And, conquering that, made haste to Nubia.
There, having sacked Borno, the kingly seat,
I took the king and led him bound in chains
Unto Damasco, where I stayed before.

Tamburlaine. Well done, Techelles! What saith
Theridamas?

Theridamas. I left the confines and the bounds of Afric,
And made a voyage into Europe,
Where, by the river Tyros, I subdu'd
Stoka, Padolia, and Codemia;
Then crossed the sea and came to Oblia,
And Nigra Silva, where the devils dance,
Which, in despite of them, I set on fire.
From thence I crossed the gulf call'd by the name
Mare Majore of th' inhabitants.
Yet shall my soldiers make no period
Until Natolia kneel before your feet.

Tamburlaine. Then will we triumph, banquet, and
carouse;
Cooks shall have pensions to provide us cates,
And glut us with the dainties of the world;
Lachryma Christi and Calabrian wines
Shall common soldiers drink in quaffing bowls,
Ay, liquid gold, when we have conquer'd him,
Mingled with coral and with orient pearl.
Come, let us banquet and carouse the whiles.

Exeunt.

Finis Actus primi.

ACT II

SCENE I

SIGISMUND, FREDERICK, BALDWIN, *with their train.*

Sigismund. Now say, my lords of Buda and Bohemia,
   What motion is it that inflames your thoughts,
   And stirs your valours to such sudden arms ?
Frederick. Your majesty remembers, I am sure,
   What cruel slaughter of our Christian bloods
   These heathenish Turks and pagans lately made
   Betwixt the city Zula and Danubius ;
   How through the midst of Verna and Bulgaria,
   And almost to the very walls of Rome,
   They have, not long since, massacred our camp.
   It resteth now, then, that your majesty
   Take all advantages of time and power,
   And work revenge upon these infidels.
   Your highness knows, for Tamburlaine's repair,
   That strikes a terror to all Turkish hearts,
   Natolia hath dismissed the greatest part
   Of all his army, pitched against our power
   Betwixt Cutheia and Orminius' mount,
   And sent them marching up to Belgasar,

Acantha, Antioch, and Cæsarea,
To aid the kings of Soria and Jerusalem.
Now, then, my lord, advantage take hereof,
And issue suddenly upon the rest ;
That, in the fortune of their overthrow,
We may discourage all the pagan troop
That dare attempt to war with Christians.

Sigismund. But calls not, then, your grace to memory
The league we lately made with King Orcanes,
Confirm'd by oath and articles of peace,
And calling Christ for record of our truths ?
This should be treachery and violence
Against the grace of our profession.

Baldwin. No whit, my lord ; for with such infidels,
In whom no faith nor true religion rests,
We are not bound to those accomplishments
The holy laws of Christendom enjoin ;
But, as the faith which they profanely plight
Is not by necessary policy
To be esteem'd assurance for ourselves,
So what we vow to them should not infringe
Our liberty of arms and victory.

Sigismund. Though I confess the oaths they undertake
Breed little strength to our security,
Yet those infirmities that thus defame
Their faiths, their honours and their religion,
Should not give us presumption to the like.
Our faiths are sound, and must be consummate,
Religious, righteous, and inviolate.

Frederick. Assure your grace, 'tis superstition

To stand so strictly on dispensive faith
And, should we lose the opportunity
That God hath given to venge our Christians' death,
And scourge their foul blasphemous paganism,
As fell to Saul, to Balaam, and the rest,
That would not kill and curse at God's command,
So surely will the vengeance of the highest,
And jealous anger of his fearful arm,
Be pour'd with rigour on our sinful heads,
If we neglect this offered victory.

Sigismund. Then arm, my lords, and issue suddenly,
Giving commandment to our general host,
With expedition to assail the pagan,
And take the victory our God hath given.   *Exeunt.*

SCENE II

ORCANES, GAZELLUS [*Viceroy of* BYRON], URIBASSA,
with their train.

Orcanes. Gazellus, Uribassa, and the rest,
Now will we march from proud Orminius' mount
To fair Natolia, where our neighbour kings
Expect our power and our royal presence,
T' encounter with the cruel Tamburlaine,
That nigh Larissa sways a mighty host,
And with the thunder of his martial tools
Makes earthquakes in the hearts of men and heaven.

Byron. And now come we to make his sinews shake
With greater power than erst his pride hath felt.

An hundred kings, by scores, will bid him arms,
And hundred thousands subjects to each score :
Which, if a shower of wounding thunderbolts
Should break out of the bowels of the clouds,
And fall as thick as hail upon our heads,
In partial aid of that proud Scythian,
Yet should our courages and steeled crests,
And numbers, more than infinite, of men,
Be able to withstand and conquer him.

Uribassa. Methinks I see how glad the Christian king
Is made for joy of your admitted truce,
That could not but before be terrified
With unacquainted power of our host.

Enter a Messenger.

Messenger. Arm, dread sovereign, and my noble lords !
The treacherous army of the Christians,
Taking advantage of your slender power,
Comes marching on us, and determines straight
To bid us battle for our dearest lives.

Orcanes. Traitors, villains, damned Christians !
Have I not here the articles of peace
And solemn covenants we have both confirm'd,
He by his Christ, and I by Mahomet ?

Byron. Hell and confusion light upon their heads,
That with such treason seek our overthrow,
And cares so little for their prophet Christ !

Orcanes. Can there be such deceit in Christians,
Or treason in the fleshly heart of man,
Whose shape is figure of the highest God ?

Then, if there be a Christ, as Christians say,
But in their deeds deny him for their Christ,
If he be son to everliving Jove,
And hath the power of his outstretched arm,
If he be jealous of his name and honour
As is our holy prophet Mahomet,
Take here these papers as our sacrifice
And witness of thy servant's perjury !
Open, thou shining veil of Cynthia,
And make a passage from th' imperial heaven,
That he that sits on high and never sleeps,
Nor in one place is circumscriptible,
But everywhere fills every continent
With strange infusion of his sacred vigour,
May, in his endless power and purity,
Behold and venge this traitor's perjury !
Thou, Christ, that art esteem'd omnipotent,
If thou wilt prove thyself a perfect God,
Worthy the worship of all faithful hearts,
Be now reveng'd upon this traitor's soul,
And make the power I have left behind
Too little to defend our guiltless lives
Sufficient to discomfit and confound
The trustless force of those false Christians !
To arms, my lords ! on Christ still let us cry :
If there be Christ, we shall have victory.   *Exeunt.*

Sound to the battle, and SIGISMUND *comes out wounded.*

Sigismund. Discomfited is all the Christian host,
   And God hath thundered vengeance from on high,

For my accursed and hateful perjury.
O just and dreadful punisher of sin,
Let the dishonour of the pains I feel
In this my mortal well-deserved wound
End all my penance in my sudden death !
And let this death, wherein to sin I die,
Conceive a second life in endless mercy !

Enter ORCANES, GAZELLUS [*Viceroy of* BYRON],
URIBASSA, *with others.*

Orcanes. Now lie the Christians bathing in their bloods,
  And Christ or Mahomet hath been my friend.
Byron. See here the perjur'd traitor Hungary,
  Bloody and breathless for his villainy !
Orcanes. Now shall his barbarous body be a prey
  To beasts and fowls, and all the winds shall breathe
  Through shady leaves of every senseless tree,
  Murmurs and hisses for his heinous sin.
  Now scalds his soul in the Tartarian streams,
  And feeds upon the baneful tree of hell,
  That Zoacum, that fruit of bitterness,
  That in the midst of fire is ingraffed,
  Yet flourisheth as Flora in her pride,
  With apples like the heads of damned fiends.
  The devils there, in chains of quenchless flame
  Shall lead his soul through Orcus' burning gulf,
  From pain to pain, whose change shall never end.
  What sayst thou yet, Gazellus, to his foil,
  Which we referred to justice of his Christ

And to his power, which here appears as full
As rays of Cynthia to the clearest sight?

Byron. 'Tis but the fortune of the wars, my lord,
Whose power is often prov'd a miracle.

Orcanes. Yet in my thoughts shall Christ be honoured,
Not doing Mahomet an injury,
Whose power had share in this our victory;
And, since this miscreant hath disgrac'd his faith,
And died a traitor both to heaven and earth,
We will both watch and ward shall keep his trunk
Amidst these plains for fowls to prey upon.
Go, Uribassa, give it straight in charge.

Uribassa. I will, my lord.   *Exit Uribassa.*

Orcanes. And now, Gazellus, let us haste and meet
Our army, and our brothers of Jerusalem,
Of Soria, Trebizon, and Amasia,
And happily, with full Natolian bowls
Of Greekish wine, now let us celebrate
Our happy conquest and his angry fate.   *Exeunt.*

SCENE [III]

The arras is drawn, and ZENOCRATE *lies in her bed of state;*
    TAMBURLAINE *sitting by her; three* Physicians
    about her bed, tempering potions; THERIDAMAS,
    TECHELLES, USUMCASANE *and the three sons.*

Tamburlaine. Black is the beauty of the brightest day;
The golden ball of heaven's eternal fire,

That danc'd with glory on the silver waves,
Now wants the fuel that inflamed his beams,
And all with faintness and for foul disgrace,
He binds his temples with a frowning cloud,
Ready to darken earth with endless night.
Zenocrate, that gave him light and life,
Whose eyes shot fire from their ivory bowers,
And tempered every soul with lively heat,
Now by the malice of the angry skies,
Whose jealousy admits no second mate,
Draws in the comfort of her latest breath,
All dazzled with the hellish mists of death.
Now walk the angels on the walls of heaven,
As sentinels to warn th' immortal souls
To entertain divine Zenocrate :
Apollo, Cynthia, and the ceaseless lamps
That gently look'd upon this loathsome earth,
Shine downwards now no more, but deck the heavens
To entertain divine Zenocrate :
The crystal springs, whose taste illuminates
Refined eyes with an eternal sight,
Like tried silver run through Paradise
To entertain divine Zenocrate :
The cherubins and holy seraphins,
That sing and play before the King of Kings,
Use all their voices and their instruments
To entertain divine Zenocrate :
And in this sweet and curious harmony,
The god that tunes this music to our souls
Holds out his hand in highest majesty

To entertain divine Zenocrate.
Then let some holy trance convey my thoughts
Up to the palace of th' imperial heaven,
That this my life may be as short to me
As are the days of sweet Zenocrate.
Physicians, will no physic do her good ?

First Physician. My lord, your majesty shall soon per-
    ceive,
And if she pass this fit, the worst is past.

Tamburlaine. Tell me, how fares my fair Zenocrate ?

Zenocrate. I fare, my lord, as other empresses,
    That, when this frail and transitory flesh
    Hath sucked the measure of that vital air
    That feeds the body with his dated health,
    Wanes with enforced and necessary change.

Tamburlaine. May never such a change transform my
    love,
    In whose sweet being I repose my life,
    Whose heavenly presence, beautified with health,
    Gives light to Phœbus and the fixed stars,
    Whose absence makes the sun and moon as dark
    As when, oppos'd in one diameter,
    Their spheres are mounted on the serpent's head,
    Or else descended to his winding train.
    Live still, my love, and so conserve my life,
    Or, dying, be the author of my death.

Zenocrate. Live still, my lord ; O, let my sovereign
    live !
    And sooner let the fiery element
    Dissolve, and make your kingdom in the sky,

Than this base earth should shroud your majesty;
For, should I but suspect your death by mine,
The comfort of my future happiness,
And hope to meet your highness in the heavens,
Turn'd to despair, would break my wretched breast,
And fury would confound my present rest.
But let me die, my love; yet, let me die;
With love and patience let your true love die:
Your grief and fury hurts my second life.
Yet let me kiss my lord before I die,
And let me die with kissing of my lord.
But, since my life is lengthened yet a while,
Let me take leave of these my loving sons,
And of my lords, whose true nobility
Have merited my latest memory.
Sweet sons, farewell; in death resemble me,
And in your lives your father's excellency.
Some music, and my fit will cease, my lord.

They call music.

Tamburlaine. Proud fury and intolerable fit,
That dares torment the body of my love,
And scourge the scourge of the immortal God!
Now are those spheres, where Cupid used to sit,
Wounding the world with wonder and with love,
Sadly supplied with pale and ghastly death,
Whose darts do pierce the centre of my soul.
Her sacred beauty hath enchanted heaven,
And had she liv'd before the siege of Troy,
Helen, whose beauty summoned Greece to arms,
And drew a thousand ships to Tenedos,

Had not been nam'd in Homer's Iliads,
Her name had been in every line he wrote;
Or had those wanton poets, for whose birth
Old Rome was proud, but gazed a while on her,
Nor Lesbia nor Corinna had been nam'd,
Zenocrate had been the argument
Of every epigram or elegy.

> *The music sounds and she dies.*

What, is she dead? Techelles, draw thy sword,
And wound the earth, that it may cleave in twain,
And we descend into th' infernal vaults,
To hale the fatal Sisters by the hair,
And throw them in the triple moat of hell,
For taking hence my fair Zenocrate.
Casane and Theridamas, to arms!
Raise cavalieros higher than the clouds,
And with the cannon break the frame of heaven;
Batter the shining palace of the sun,
And shiver all the starry firmament,
For amorous Jove hath snatched my love from hence,
Meaning to make her stately queen of heaven.
What god soever holds thee in his arms,
Giving thee nectar and ambrosia,
Behold me here, divine Zenocrate,
Raving, impatient, desperate and mad,
Breaking my steeled lance, with which I burst
The rusty beams of Janus' temple doors,
Letting out death and tyrannising war,
To march with me under this bloody flag!
And, if thou pitiest Tamburlaine the Great,

Come down from heaven and live with me again !

Theridamas. Ah, good my lord, be patient ! she is dead,
And all this raging cannot make her live.
If words might serve, our voice hath rent the air ;
If tears, our eyes have watered all the earth ;
If grief, our murdered hearts have strained forth
    blood.
Nothing prevails, for she is dead, my lord.

Tamburlaine. For she is dead ! thy words do pierce my
    soul :
Ah, sweet Theridamas, say so no more ;
Though she be dead, yet let me think she lives,
And feed my mind that dies for want of her.
Where'er her soul be, thou shalt stay with me,
Embalm'd with cassia, ambergris, and myrrh,
Not lapt in lead, but in a sheet of gold,
And, till I die, thou shalt not be interr'd.
Then in as rich a tomb as Mausolus
We both will rest and have one epitaph
Writ in as many several languages
As I have conquered kingdoms with my sword.
This cursed town will I consume with fire,
Because this place bereft me of my love ;
The houses, burnt, will look as if they mourn'd ;
And here will I set up her stature
And march about it with my mourning camp,
Drooping and pining for Zenocrate.

                              The arras is drawn.

ACT III

SCENE I

Enter the KINGS OF TREBIZON *and* SORIA, *one bringing
a sword and another a sceptre; next,* [ORCANES,
King of] NATOLIA, *and* JERUSALEM *with the imperial crown; after,* CALLAPINE; *and, after him,
other* Lords *and* ALMEDA. ORCANES *and* JERUSALEM
crown [CALLAPINE], *and the other give him the sceptre.*

Orcanes. Callapinus Cyricelibes, otherwise Cybelius,
    son and successive heir to the late mighty
    emperor Bajazeth, by the aid of God and his
    friend Mahomet, Emperor of Natolia, Jeru-
    salem, Trebizon, Soria, Amasia, Thracia, Illyria,
    Carmonia, and all the hundred and thirty king-
    doms late contributory to his mighty father,—
    long live Callapinus, Emperor of Turkey !
Callapine. Thrice worthy kings of Natolia and the rest,
    I will requite your royal gratitudes
    With all the benefits my empire yields ;
    And, were the sinews of th' imperial seat
    So knit and strengthened as when Bajazeth,
    My royal lord and father, filled the throne,

Whose cursed fate hath so dismembered it,
Then should you see this thief of Scythia,
This proud usurping king of Persia,
Do us such honour and supremacy,
Bearing the vengeance of our father's wrongs,
As all the world should blot our dignities
Out of the book of base born infamies.
And now I doubt not but your royal cares
Hath so provided for this cursed foe,
That, since the heir of mighty Bajazeth
(An emperor so honoured for his virtues)
Revives the spirits of true Turkish hearts,
In grievous memory of his father's shame,
We shall not need to nourish any doubt,
But that proud Fortune, who hath followed long
The martial sword of mighty Tamburlaine,
Will now retain her old inconstancy,
And raise our honours to as high a pitch,
In this our strong and fortunate encounter ;
For so hath heaven provided my escape
From all the cruelty my soul sustained,
By this my friendly keeper's happy means,
That Jove, surcharg'd with pity of our wrongs,
Will pour it down in showers on our heads,
Scourging the pride of cursed Tamburlaine.

Orcanes. I have a hundred thousand men in arms ;
Some that, in conquest of the perjur'd Christian,
Being a handful to a mighty host,
Think them in number yet sufficient
To drink the river Nile or Euphrates,

And for their power ynow to win the world.

Jerusalem. And I as many from Jerusalem,
    Judæa, Gaza, and Scalonia's bounds,
    That on mount Sinai, with their ensigns spread,
    Look like the parti-coloured clouds of heaven
    That show fair weather to the neighbour morn.

Trebizon. And I as many bring from Trebizon,
    Chio, Famastro, and Amasia,
    All bordering on the Mare-Major sea ;
    Riso, Sancina, and the bordering towns
    That touch the end of famous Euphrates ;
    Whose courages are kindled with the flames
    The cursed Scythian sets on all their towns,
    And vow to burn the villain's cruel heart.

Soria. From Soria with seventy thousand strong,
    Ta'en from Aleppo, Soldino, Tripoly,
    And so unto my city of Damasco,
    I march to meet and aid my neighbour kings ;
    All which will join against this Tamburlaine,
    And bring him captive to your highness' feet.

Orcanes. Our battle, then, in martial manner pitched,
    According to our ancient use, shall bear
    The figure of the semicircled moon,
    Whose horns shall sprinkle through the tainted air
    The poisoned brains of this proud Scythian.

Callapine. Well then, my noble lords, for this my
       friend
    That freed me from the bondage of my foe,
    I think it requisite and honourable
    To keep my promise and to make him king,

That is a gentleman, I know, at least.

Almeda. That's no matter, sir, for being a king; for
    Tamburlaine came up of nothing.

Jerusalem. Your majesty may choose some 'pointed
    time,

    Performing all your promise to the full;

    'Tis naught for your majesty to give a kingdom.

Callapine. Then will I shortly keep my promise,
    Almeda.

Almeda. Why, I thank your majesty.   *Exeunt.*

SCENE II

TAMBURLAINE *with* USUMCASANE *and his three sons; four*
    bearing the hearse of ZENOCRATE, *and the drums*
    sounding a doleful march; the town burning.

Tamburlaine. So, burn the turrets of this cursed town,
    Flame to the highest region of the air,
    And kindle heaps of exhalations,
    That, being fiery meteors, may presage
    Death and destruction to th' inhabitants!
    Over my zenith hang a blazing star,
    That may endure till heaven be dissolv'd,
    Fed with the fresh supply of earthly dregs,
    Threatening a death and famine to this land!
    Flying dragons, lightning, fearful thunder-claps,
    Singe these fair plains, and make them seem as black

As is the island where the Furies mask,
Compassed with Lethe, Styx, and Phlegethon,
Because my dear Zenocrate is dead !

Calyphas. This pillar, plac'd in memory of her,
Where in Arabian, Hebrew, Greek, is writ,
This town, being burnt by Tamburlaine the Great,
Forbids the world to build it up again.

Amyras. And here this mournful streamer shall be
    plac'd,
Wrought with the Persian and Egyptian arms,
To signify she was a princess born,
And wife unto the monarch of the East.

Celebinus. And here this table as a register
Of all her virtues and perfections.

Tamburlaine. And here the picture of Zenocrate,
To show her beauty which the world admir'd ;
Sweet picture of divine Zenocrate,
That, hanging here, will draw the gods from heaven,
And cause the stars fixed in the southern arc,
Whose lovely faces never any viewed
That have not passed the centre's latitude,
As pilgrims travel to our hemisphere,
Only to gaze upon Zenocrate.
Thou shalt not beautify Larissa plains,
But keep within the circle of mine arms ;
At every town and castle I besiege,
Thou shalt be set upon my royal tent ;
And when I meet an army in the field,
Those looks will shed such influence in my camp,
As if Bellona, goddess of the war,

Threw naked swords and sulphur balls of fire
Upon the heads of all our enemies.
And now, my lords, advance your spears again ;
Sorrow no more, my sweet Casane, now :
Boys, leave to mourn ; this town shall ever mourn,
Being burnt to cinders for your mother's death.
Calyphas. If I had wept a sea of tears for her,
  It would not ease the sorrow I sustain.
Amyras. As is that town, so is my heart consum'd
  With grief and sorrow for my mother's death.
Celebinus. My mother's death hath mortified my mind,
  And sorrow stops the passage of my speech.
Tamburlaine. But now, my boys, leave off, and list to
        me,
  That mean to teach you rudiments of war.
  I'll have you learn to sleep upon the ground,
  March in your armour thorough watery fens,
  Sustain the scorching heat and freezing cold,
  Hunger and thirst, right adjuncts of the war ;
  And, after this, to scale a castle wall,
  Besiege a fort, to undermine a town,
  And make whole cities caper in the air.
  Then next, the way to fortify your men ;
  In champion grounds what figure serves you best,
  For which the quinque-angle form is meet,
  Because the corners there may fall more flat
  Whereas the fort may fittest be assailed,
  And sharpest where th' assault is desperate ;
  The ditches must be deep, the counterscarps
  Narrow and steep, the walls made high and broad,

The bulwarks and the rampiers large and strong,
With cavalieros and thick counterforts,
And room within to lodge six thousand men.
It must have privy ditches, countermines,
And secret issuings to defend the ditch ;
It must have high argins and covered ways
To keep the bulwark fronts from battery,
And parapets to hide the musketeers,
Casemates to place the great artillery,
And store of ordnance, that from every flank
May scour the outward curtains of the fort,
Dismount the cannon of the adverse part,
Murder the foe and save the walls from breach.
When this is learn'd for service on the land,
By plain and easy demonstration
I'll teach you how to make the water mount,
That you may dry-foot march through lakes and
　　pools,
Deep rivers, havens, creeks, and little seas,
And make a fortress in the raging waves,
Fenc'd with the concave of a monstrous rock,
Invincible by nature of the place.
When this is done, then are ye soldiers,
And worthy sons of Tamburlaine the Great.

Calyphas.　My lord, but this is dangerous to be done ;
We may be slain or wounded ere we learn.

Tamburlaine.　Villain, art thou the son of Tamburlaine,
And fear'st to die, or with a curtle-axe
To hew thy flesh, and make a gaping wound ?
Hast thou beheld a peal of ordnance strike

A ring of pikes, mingled with shot and horse,
Whose shattered limbs, being tossed as high as
    heaven,
Hang in the air as thick as sunny motes,
And canst thou, coward, stand in fear of death?
Hast thou not seen my horsemen charge the foe,
Shot through the arms, cut overthwart the hands,
Dying their lances with their streaming blood,
And yet at night carouse within my tent,
Filling their empty veins with airy wine,
That, being concocted, turns to crimson blood,
And wilt thou shun the field for fear of wounds?
View me, thy father, that hath conquered kings,
And with his host marched round about the earth,
Quite void of scars and clear from any wound,
That by the wars lost not a dram of blood,
And see him lance his flesh to teach you all.

                                    He cuts his arm.

A wound is nothing, be it ne'er so deep;
Blood is the god of war's rich livery.
Now look I like a soldier, and this wound
As great a grace and majesty to me,
As if a chair of gold enamelled,
Enchas'd with diamonds, sapphires, rubies,
And fairest pearl of wealthy India,
Were mounted here under a canopy,
And I sat down, cloth'd with the massy robe
That late adorn'd the Afric potentate,
Whom I brought bound unto Damascus' walls
Come, boys, and with your fingers search my wound,

And in my blood wash all your hands at once,
While I sit smiling to behold the sight.
Now, my boys, what think you of a wound?
Calyphas. I know not what I should think of it; me-
   thinks 'tis a pitiful sight.
Celebinus. 'Tis nothing. Give me a wound, father.
Amyras. And me another, my lord.
Tamburlaine. Come, sirrah, give me your arm.
Celebinus. Here, father, cut it bravely, as you did your
   own.
Tamburlaine. It shall suffice thou darst abide a wound;
   My boy, thou shalt not lose a drop of blood
   Before we meet the army of the Turk;
   But then run desperate through the thickest throngs,
   Dreadless of blows, of bloody wounds and death;
   And let the burning of Larissa walls,
   My speech of war, and this my wound you see,
   Teach you, my boys, to bear courageous minds,
   Fit for the followers of great Tamburlaine.
   Usumcasane, now come, let us march
   Towards Techelles and Theridamas,
   That we have sent before to fire the towns,
   The towers and cities of these hateful Turks,
   And hunt that coward faint-heart runaway,
   With that accursed traitor Almeda,
   Till fire and sword have found them at a bay.
Usumcasane. I long to pierce his bowels with my
      sword,
   That hath betrayed my gracious sovereign,
   That cursed and damned traitor Almeda.

Tamburlaine. Then let us see if coward Callapine
　　Dare levy arms against our puissance,
　　That we may tread upon his captive neck,
　　And treble all his father's slaveries.　　　　　*Exeunt.*

SCENE III

TECHELLES, THERIDAMAS, *and their train.*

Theridamas. Thus have we marched northward from
　　　　Tamburlaine,
　　Unto the frontier point of Soria ;
　　And this is Balsera, their chiefest hold,
　　Wherein is all the treasure of the land.
Techelles. Then let us bring our light artillery,
　　Minions, falc'nets, and sakers, to the trench,
　　Filling the ditches with the walls' wide breach,
　　And enter in to seize upon the gold.
　　How say ye, soldiers, shall we not ?
Soldiers. Yes, my lord, yes ; come, let's about it.
Theridamas. But stay a while ; summon a parley, drum.
　　It may be they will yield it quietly,
　　Knowing two kings, the friends to Tamburlaine,
　　Stand at the walls with such a mighty power.

　　　　Summon the battle.　Captain with his wife and son.

Captain. What require you, my masters ?
Theridamas. Captain, that thou yield up thy hold to us.

Captain. To you ! why, do you think me weary of it ?
Techelles. Nay, captain, thou art weary of thy life,
  If thou withstand the friends of Tamburlaine.
Theridamas. These pioners of Argier in Africa,
  Even in the cannon's face, shall raise a hill
  Of earth and faggots higher than thy fort,
  And, over thy argins and covered ways,
  Shall play upon the bulwarks of thy hold
  Volleys of ordinance, till the breach be made
  That with his ruin fills up all the trench ;
  And, when we enter in, not heaven itself
  Shall ransom thee, thy wife and family.
Techelles. Captain, these Moors shall cut the leaden
    pipes
  That bring fresh water to thy men and thee.
  And lie in trench before thy castle walls,
  That no supply of victual shall come in,
  Nor [any] issue forth but they shall die ;
  And therefore, captain, yield it quietly.
Captain. Were you, that are the friends of Tambur-
    laine,
  Brothers to holy Mahomet himself,
  I would not yield it ; therefore do your worst :
  Raise mounts, batter, intrench and undermine,
  Cut off the water, all convoys that can,
  Yet I am resolute : and so, farewell.   *Exeunt.*
Theridamas. Pioners, away ! and where I stuck the
    stake,
  Intrench with those dimensions I prescribed ;
  Cast up the earth towards the castle wall,

Which till it may defend you, labour low,
And few or none shall perish by their shot.
Pioners. We will, my lord.   [*Exeunt.*]
Techelles. A hundred horse shall scout about the plains,
    To spy what force comes to relieve the hold.
    Both we, Theridamas, will intrench our men,
    And with the Jacob's staff measure the height
    And distance of the castle from the trench,
    That we may know if our artillery
    Will carry full point blank unto their walls.
Theridamas. Then see the bringing of our ordinance
    Along the trench into the battery,
    Where we will have gabions of six foot broad,
    To save our cannoneers from musket shot ;
    Betwixt which shall our ordinance thunder forth,
    And with the breach's fall, smoke, fire and dust,
    The crack, the echo and the soldiers' cry,
    Make deaf the air and dim the crystal sky.
Techelles. Trumpets and drums, alarum presently !
    And, soldiers, play the men ; the hold is yours !
                                        [*Exeunt.*]

[SCENE IV]

Enter the Captain, *with* [Olympia] *his* Wife *and*
Son.

Olympia. Come, good my lord, and let us haste from
        hence,
    Along the cave that leads beyond the foe ;

No hope is left to save this conquered hold.
Captain. A deadly bullet gliding through my side,
  Lies heavy on my heart ; I cannot live.
  I feel my liver pierc'd and all my veins,
  That there begin and nourish every part,
  Mangled and torn, and all my entrails bath'd
  In blood that straineth from their orifex.
  Farewell, sweet wife ! sweet son, farewell ! I die.
Olympia. Death, whither art thou gone, that both we
      live ?
  Come back again, sweet death, and strike us both !
  One minute end our days, and one sepulchre
  Contain our bodies ! Death, why com'st thou not ?
  Well, this must be the messenger for thee.
  Now, ugly death, stretch out thy sable wings,
  And carry both our souls where his remains.
  Tell me, sweet boy, art thou content to die ?
  These barbarous Scythians, full of cruelty,
  And Moors, in whom was never pity found,
  Will hew us piecemeal, put us to the wheel,
  Or else invent some torture worse than that ;
  Therefore die by thy loving mother's hand,
  Who gently now will lance thy ivory throat,
  And quickly rid thee both of pain and life.
Son. Mother, despatch me, or I'll kill myself ;
  For think you I can live and see him dead ?
  Give me your knife, good mother, or strike home ;
  The Scythians shall not tyrannise on me :
  Sweet mother, strike, that I may meet my father.
                                    She stabs him.

Olympia. Ah, sacred Mahomet, if this be sin,
   Entreat a pardon of the God of heaven,
   And purge my soul before it come to thee !

Enter THERIDAMAS, TECHELLES, *and all their train.*

Theridamas. How now, Madam ! what are you doing ?
Olympia. Killing myself, as I have done my son,
   Whose body, with his father's, I have burnt,
   Lest cruel Scythians should dismember him.
Techelles. 'Twas bravely done, and like a soldier's wife.
   Thou shalt with us to Tamburlaine the Great,
   Who, when he hears how resolute thou wert,
   Will match thee with a viceroy or a king.
Olympia. My lord deceased was dearer unto me
   Than any viceroy, king, or emperor ;
   And for his sake here will I end my days.
Theridamas. But, lady, go with us to Tamburlaine,
   And thou shalt see a man greater than Mahomet,
   In whose high looks is much more majesty,
   Than from the concave superficies
   Of Jove's vast palace, the imperial orb,
   Unto the shining bower where Cynthia sits,
   Like lovely Thetis, in a crystal robe ;
   That treadeth fortune underneath his feet,
   And makes the mighty god of arms his slave ;
   On whom death and the fatal sisters wait
   With naked swords and scarlet liveries ;
   Before whom, mounted on a lion's back,
   Rhamnusia bears a helmet full of blood,

And strows the way with brains of slaughtered men ;
By whose proud side the ugly furies run,
Hearkening when he shall bid them plague the
    world ;
Over whose zenith, cloth'd in windy air,
And eagle's wings join'd to her feathered breast,
Fame hovereth, sounding of her golden trump,
That to the adverse poles of that straight line
Which measureth the glorious frame of heaven
The name of mighty Tamburlaine is spread ;
And him, fair, lady, shall thy eyes behold.
Come.

Olympia. Take pity of a lady's ruthful tears,
That humbly craves upon her knees to stay,
And cast her body in the burning flame
That feeds upon her son's and husband's flesh.

Techelles. Madam, sooner shall fire consume us both
Than scorch a face so beautiful as this,
In frame of which nature hath show'd more skill
Than when she gave eternal chaos form,
Drawing from it the shining lamps of heaven.

Theridamas. Madam, I am so far in love with you,
That you must go with us : no remedy.

Olympia. Then carry me, I care not, where you will,
And let the end of this my fatal journey
Be likewise end to my accursed life.

Techelles. No, madam, but the beginning of your joy :
Come willingly, therefore.

Theridamas. Soldiers, now let us meet the general,
Who by this time is at Natolia,

Ready to charge the army of the Turk.
The gold, the silver, and the pearl ye got,
Rifling this fort, divide in equal shares :
This lady shall have twice so much again
Out of the coffers of our treasury.   *Exeunt.*

SCENE V

CALLAPINE, ORCANES, JERUSALEM, TREBIZON,
SORIA, ALMEDA, *with their train.*

[*Enter a* Messenger.]

Messenger. Renowmed emperor, mighty Callapine,
God's great lieutenant over all the world,
Here at Aleppo, with an host of men,
Lies Tamburlaine, this king of Persia,
In number more than are the quivering leaves
Of Ida's forest, where your highness' hounds
With open cry pursues the wounded stag,
Who means to girt Natolia's walls with siege,
Fire the town and over-run the land.
Callapine. My royal army is as great as his,
That, from the bounds of Phrygia to the sea
Which washeth Cyprus with his brinish waves,
Covers the hills, the valleys and the plains.
Viceroys and peers of Turkey, play the men ;
Whet all your swords to mangle Tamburlaine,

His sons, his captains, and his followers :
By Mahomet, not one of them shall live !
The field wherein this battle shall be fought
For ever term the Persians' sepulchre,
In memory of this our victory.

Orcanes. Now he that calls himself the scourge of Jove,
The emperor of the world, and earthly god,
Shall end the warlike progress he intends,
And travel headlong to the lake of hell,
Where legions of devils, knowing he must die
Here in Natolia by your highness' hands,
All brandishing their brands of quenchless fire,
Stretching their monstrous paws, grin with their
    teeth,
And guard the gates to entertain his soul.

Callapine. Tell me, viceroys, the number of your men,
And what our army royal is esteem'd.

Jerusalem. From Palestina and Jerusalem,
Of Hebrews three score thousand fighting men
Are come, since last we showed your majesty.

Orcanes. So from Arabia Desert, and the bounds
Of that sweet land whose brave metropolis
Re-edified the fair Semiramis,
Came forty thousand warlike foot and horse,
Since last we numbered to your majesty.

Trebizon. From Trebizon in Asia the Less,
Naturalized Turks and stout Bithynains
Came to my bands, full fifty thousand more,
That, fighting, know not what retreat doth mean,
Nor e'er return but with the victory,

Since last we numbered to your majesty.

Soria. Of Sorians from Halla is repair'd,
    And neightbour cities of your highness' land,
    Ten thousand horse, and thirty thousand foot,
    Since last we numbered to your majesty ;
    So that the army royal is esteem'd
    Six hundred thousand valiant fighting men.

Callapine. Then welcome, Tamburlaine, unto thy
        death !
    Come, puissant viceroys, let us to the field,
    The Persians' sepulchre, and sacrifice
    Mountains of breathless men to Mahomet,
    Who now, with Jove, opens the firmament
    To see the slaughter of our enemies.

[*Enter*] TAMBURLAINE *with his three sons,* USUM-
        CASANE, *with other.*

Tamburlaine. How now, Casane ! see, a knot of kings,
    Sitting as if they were a-telling riddles.

Usumcasane. My lord, your presence makes them pale
        and wan :
    Poor souls, they look as if their deaths were near.

Tamburlaine. Why, so he is, Casane ; I am here.
    But yet I'll save their lives and make them slaves.
    Ye petty kings of Turkey, I am come,
    As Hector did into the Grecian camp,
    To overdare the pride of Græcia,
    And set his warlike person to the view
    Of fierce Achilles, rival of his fame.

I do you honour in the simile ;
For if I should, as Hector did Achilles,
(The worthiest knight that ever brandished sword,)
Challenge in combat any of you all,
I see how fearfully ye would refuse,
And fly my glove as from a scorpion.

Orcanes. Now, thou art fearful of thy army's strength,
    Thou wouldst with overmatch of person fight :
    But, shepherd's issue, base born Tamburlaine,
    Think of thy end ; this sword shall lance thy
       throat.

Tamburlaine. Villain, the shepherd's issue, at whose
    birth
    Heaven did afford a gracious aspect,
    And join'd those stars that shall be opposite
    Even till the dissolution of the world,
    And never meant to make a conqueror
    So famous as is mighty Tamburlaine,
    Shall so torment thee and that Callapine,
    That, like a roguish runaway, suborn'd
    That villain there, that slave, that Turkish dog,
    To false his service to his sovereign,
    As ye shall curse the birth of Tamburlaine.

Callapine. Rail not, proud Scythian : I shall now
    revenge
    My father's vile abuses and mine own.

Jerusalem. By Mahomet, he shall be tied in chains,
    Rowing with Christians in a brigandine
    About the Grecian isles to rob and spoil,
    And turn him to his ancient trade again ;

Methinks the slave should make a lusty thief.

Callapine. Nay, when the battle ends, all we will meet,
 And sit in council to invent some pain
 That most may vex his body and his soul.

Tamburlaine. Sirrah Callapine, I'll hang a clog about
       your neck for running away again ; you shall
       not trouble me thus to come and fetch you.
 But as for you, viceroy, you shall have bits,
 And, harnessed like my horses, draw my coach ;
 And, when ye stay, be lashed with whips of wire ;
 I'll have you learn to feed on provender,
 And in a stable lie upon the planks.

Orcanes. But, Tamburlaine, first thou shalt kneel to us,
 And humbly crave a pardon for thy life.

Trebizon. The common soldiers of our mighty host
 Shall bring thee bound unto the general's tent.

Soria. And all have jointly sworn thy cruel death,
 Or bind thee in eternal torments' wrath.

Tamburlaine. Well, sirs, diet yourselves ; you know I
       shall have occasion shortly to journey you.

Celebinus. See, father, how Almeda the jailor looks
       upon us !

Tamburlaine. Villain, traitor, damned fugitive,
 I'll make thee wish the earth had swallowed thee !
 Seest thou not death within my wrathful looks ?
 Go, villain, cast thee headlong from a rock,
 Or rip thy bowels, and rend out thy heart,
 T' appease my wrath ; or else I'll torture thee,
 Searing thy hateful flesh with burning irons
 And drops of scalding lead, while all thy joints

Be racked and beat asunder with the wheel ;
For, if thou livest, not any element
Shall shroud thee from the wrath of Tamburlaine.

Callapine. Well in despite of thee, he shall be king.
Come, Almeda ; receive this crown of me :
I here invest thee king of Ariadan,
Bordering on Mare Roso, near to Mecca.

Orcanes. What ! take it, man.

Almeda. Good my lord, let me take it.

Callapine. Dost thou ask him leave ? here ; take it.

Tamburlaine. Go to, sirrah ! take your crown, and
make up the half dozen. So, sirrah, now you
are a king, you must give arms.

Orcanes. So he shall, and wear thy head in his scutcheon.

Tamburlaine. No ; let him hang a bunch of keys on
his standard, to put him in remembrance he was
a jailor, that, when I take him, I may knock out
his brains with them, and lock you in the stable,
when you shall come sweating from my chariot.

Trebizon. Away ! let us to the field, that the villain
may be slain.

Tamburlaine. Sirrah, prepare whips, and bring my
chariot to my tent ; for, as soon as the battle
is done, I'll ride in triumph through the camp.

Enter THERIDAMAS, TECHELLES, *and their train.*

How now, ye pretty kings ? lo, here are bugs
Will make the hair stand upright on your heads,
And cast your crowns in slavery at their feet.

Welcome, Theridamas and Techelles, both :
See ye this rout, and know ye this same king ?

Theridamas. Ay, my lord ; he was Callapine's keeper.

Tamburlaine. Well now you see he is a king.   Look to
   him, Theridamas, when we are fighting, lest he
   hide his crown as the foolish king of Persia did.

Soria. No, Tamburlaine ; he shall not be put to that
   exigent, I warrant thee.

Tamburlaine. You know not, sir.
   But now, my followers and my loving friends,
   Fight as you ever did, like conquerors,
   The glory of this happy day is yours.
   My stern aspect shall make fair Victory,
   Hovering betwixt our armies, light on me,
   Loaden with laurel wreaths to crown us all.

Techelles. I smile to think how, when this field is
      fought
   And rich Natolia ours, our men shall sweat
   With carrying pearl and treasure on their backs.

Tamburlaine. You shall be princes all, immediately.
   Come, fight, ye Turks, or yield us victory.

Orcanes. No ; we will meet thee, slavish Tamburlaine.

                                        Exeunt.

ACT IV

SCENE I

Alarm. AMYRAS *and* CELEBINUS *issues from the tent where* CALYPHAS *sits asleep.*

[*Amyras.*] Now in their glories shine the golden crowns
  Of these proud Turks, much like so many suns
  That half dismay the majesty of heaven.
  Now, brother, follow we our father's sword,
  That flies with fury swifter than our thoughts,
  And cuts down armies with his conquering wings.
Celebinus. Call forth our lazy brother from the tent,
  For, if my father miss him in the field,
  Wrath, kindled in the furnace of his breast,
  Will send a deadly lightning to his heart.
Amyras. Brother, ho ! what, given so much to sleep,
  You cannot leave it, when our enemies' drums
  And rattling cannons thunder in our ears
  Our proper ruin and our father's foil ?
Calyphas. Away, ye fools ! my father needs not me,
  Nor you, in faith, but that you will be thought
  More childish valourous than manly wise.
  If half our camp should sit and sleep with me,

My father were enough to scare the foe ;
You do dishonour to his majesty,
To think our helps will do him any good.

Amyras. What, dar'st thou, then, be absent from the
　　　fight
Knowing my father hates thy cowardice,
And oft hath warn'd thee to be still in field,
When he himself amidst the thickest troops
Beats down our foes, to flesh our taintless swords ?

Calyphas. I know, sir, what it is to kill a man ;
It works remorse of conscience in me.
I take no pleasure to be murderous,
Nor care for blood when wine will quench my
　　　thirst.

Celebinus. O cowardly boy ! fie, for shame, come
　　　forth !
Thou dost dishonour manhood and thy house.

Calyphas. Go, go, tall stripling, fight you for us both ;
And take my other toward brother here,
For person like to prove a second Mars ;
'Twill please my mind as well to hear both you
Have won a heap of honour in the field,
And left your slender carcasses behind,
As if I lay with you for company.

Amyras. You will not go then ?

Calyphas. You say true.

Amyras. Were all the lofty mounts of Zona Mundi
That fill the midst of farthest Tartary
Turn'd into pearl and proffered for my stay,
I would not bide the fury of my father,

When, made a victor in these haughty arms,
He comes and finds his sons have had no shares
In all the honours he proposed for us.

Calyphas. Take you the honour, I will take my ease ;
My wisdom shall excuse my cowardice.
I go into the field before I need !

> *Alarm, and Amyras and Celebinus run in.*

The bullets fly at random where they list ;
And should I go and kill a thousand men,
I were as soon rewarded with a shot,
And sooner far than he that never fights ;
And should I go and do nor harm nor good,
I might have harm, which all the good I have,
Join'd with my father's crown, would never cure.
I'll to cards.—Perdicas !

Enter PERDICAS.

Perdicas. Here, my lord.

Calyphas. Come, thou and I will go to cards to drive
away the time.

Perdicas. Content, my lord : but what shall we play
for ?

Calyphas. Who shall kiss the fairest of the Turks'
concubines first, when my father hath conquered
them.

Perdicas. Agreed, i'faith.   *They play.*

Calyphas. They say I am a coward, Perdicas, and I fear
as little their taratantaras, their swords or their
cannons as I do a naked lady in a net of gold,

and, for fear I should be afraid, would put it
off and come to bed with me.

Perdicas. Such a fear, my lord, would never make ye
retire.

Calyphas. I would my father would let me be put in
the front of such a battle once, to try my valour !
(*Alarm.*) What a coil they keep ! I believe
there will be some hurt done anon amongst
them.   [*Exeunt into the tent.*]

 Enter TAMBURLAINE, THERIDAMAS, TECHELLES,
  USUMCASANE, AMYRAS, CELEBINUS *leading
  the* TURKISH KINGS.

Tamburlaine. See now, ye slaves, my children stoops
 your pride,
And leads your glories sheep-like to the sword !
Bring them, my boys, and tell me if the wars
Be not a life that may illustrate gods,
And tickle not your spirits with desire
Still to be train'd in arms and chivalry ?

Amyras. Shall we let go these kings again, my lord,
To gather greater numbers 'gainst our power,
That they may say, it is not chance doth this,
But matchless strength and magnanimity ?

Tamburlaine. No, no, Amyras ; tempt not Fortune so.
Cherish thy valour still with fresh supplies,
And glut it not with stale and daunted foes.
But where's this coward, villain, not my son,
But traitor to my name and majesty ?

    He goes in and brings [Calyphas] out.

Image of sloth, and picture of a slave,
The obloquy and scorn of my renown !
How may my heart, thus fired with mine eyes,
Wounded with shame and kill'd with discontent,
Shroud any thought may hold my striving hands
From martial justice on thy wretched soul ?

Theridamas. Yet pardon him, I pray your majesty.

Techelles and Usumcasane. Let all of us entreat your
　　highness' pardon.

Tamburlaine. Stand up, ye base, unworthy soldiers !
　Know ye not yet the argument of arms ?

Amyras. Good, my lord, let him be forgiven for once,
　And we will force him to the field hereafter.

Tamburlaine. Stand up, my boys, and I will teach ye
　　arms,
　And what the jealousy of wars must do.
　O Samarcanda, where I breathed first,
　And joy'd the fire of this martial flesh,
　Blush, blush, fair city, at thine honour's foil,
　And shame of nature, which Jaertis' stream,
　Embracing thee with deepest of his love,
　Can never wash from thy distained brows !
　Here, Jove, receive his fainting soul again ;
　A form not meet to give that subject essence
　Whose matter is the flesh of Tamburlaine,
　Wherein an incorporeal spirit moves,
　Made of the mould whereof thyself consists,
　Which makes me valiant, proud, ambitious,
　Ready to levy power against thy throne,
　That I might move the turning spheres of heaven ;

For earth and all this airy region
Cannot contain the state of Tamburlaine.

                              [*Stabs Calyphas.*]

By Mahomet, thy mighty friend, I swear,
In sending to my issue such a soul,
Created of the massy dregs of earth,
The scum and tartar of the elements,
Wherein was neither courage, strength or wit,
But folly, sloth, and damned idleness.
Thou hast procur'd a greater enemy
Than he that darted mountains at thy head,
Shaking the burden mighty Atlas bears,
Whereat thou trembling hidd'st thee in the air,
Cloth'd with a pitchy cloud for being seen.
And now, ye cankered curs of Asia,
That will not see the strength of Tamburlaine,
Although it shine as brightly as the sun,
Now you shall feel the strength of Tamburlaine,
And, by the state of his supremacy,
Approve the difference 'twixt himself and you.

Orcanes. Thou showest the difference 'twixt ourselves
          and thee,
In this thy barbarous damned tyranny.
Jerusalem. Thy victories are grown so violent,
That shortly heaven, filled with the meteors
Of blood and fire thy tyrannies have made,
Will pour down blood and fire on thy head,
Whose scalding drops will pierce thy seething brains,
And with our bloods revenge our bloods on thee.
Tamburlaine. Villains, these terrors and these tyrannies

                              177

(If tyrannies war's justice ye repute),
I execute, enjoin'd me from above,
To scourge the pride of such as Heaven abhors ;
Nor am I made arch-monarch of the world,
Crown'd and invested by the hand of Jove,
For deeds of bounty or nobility ;
But since I exercise a greater name,
The scourge of God and terror of the world,
I must apply myself to fit those terms,
In war, in blood, in death, in cruelty,
And plague such peasants as resist in me
The power of heaven's eternal majesty.
Theridamas, Techelles and Casane,
Ransack the tents and the pavilions
Of these proud Turks and take their concubines,
Making them bury this effeminate brat ;
For not a common soldier shall defile
His manly fingers with so faint a boy :
Then bring those Turkish harlots to my tent,
And I'll dispose them as it likes me best.
Meanwhile, take him in.

Soldiers. We will, my lord.

            [*Exeunt with the body of Calyphas.*]

Jerusalem. O damned monster, nay, a fiend of hell,
   Whose cruelties are not so harsh as thine,
   Nor yet imposed with such a bitter hate !

Orcanes. Revenge it, Rhadamanth and Æacus,
   And let your hates, extended in his pains,
   Expel the hate wherewith he pains our souls !

Trebizon. May never day give virtue to his eyes,

Whose sight, composed of fury and of fire,
Doth send such stern affections to his heart !
Soria. May never spirit, vein or artier feed
  The cursed substance of that cruel heart ;
  But, wanting moisture and remorseful blood,
  Dry up with anger, and consume with heat !
Tamburlaine. Well, bark, ye dogs ; I'll bridle all your
      tongues,
  And bind them close with bits of burnished steel,
  Down to the channels of your hateful throats ;
  And, with the pains my rigour shall inflict,
  I'll make ye roar, that earth may echo forth
  The far resounding torments ye sustain ;
  As when an herd of lusty Cimbrian bulls
  Run mourning round about the females' miss,
  And, stung with fury of their following,
  Fill all the air with troublous bellowing.
  I will, with engines never exercised,
  Conquer, sack and utterly consume
  Your cities and your golden palaces,
  And with the flames that beat against the clouds,
  Incense the heavens and make the stars to melt,
  As if they were the tears of Mahomet
  For hot consumption of his country's pride ;
  And, till by vision or by speech I hear
  Immortal Jove say " Cease, my Tamburlaine,"
  I will persist a terror to the world,
  Making the meteors, that, like armed men,
  Are seen to march upon the towers of heaven,
  Run tilting round about the firmament,

And break their burning lances in the air,
For honour of my wondrous victories,
Come, bring them in to our pavilion.   *Exeunt.*

SCENE [II]

OLYMPIA *alone.*

Olympia. Distressed Olympia, whose weeping eyes,
   Since thy arrival here, beheld no sun,
   But, closed within the compass of a tent,
   Hath stain'd thy cheeks, and made thee look like
     death,
   Devise some means to rid thee of thy life,
   Rather than yield to his detested suit,
   Whose drift is only to dishonour thee ;
   And since this earth, dew'd with thy brinish tears,
   Affords no herbs whose taste may poison thee,
   Nor yet this air, beat often with thy sighs,
   Contagious smells and vapours to infect thee,
   Nor thy close cave a sword to murder thee,
   Let this invention be the instrument.

Enter THERIDAMAS.

Theridamas. Well met, Olympia ; I sought thee in my
    tent,
   But when I saw the place obscure and dark,

Which with thy beauty thou wast wont to light,
Enrag'd, I ran about the fields for thee,
Supposing amorous Jove had sent his son,
The winged Hermes, to convey thee hence ;
But now I find thee, and that fear is past,
Tell me, Olympia, wilt thou grant my suit ?

Olympia. My lord and husband's death, with my sweet
            son's,
With whom I buried all affections
Save grief and sorrow, which torment my heart,
Forbids my mind to entertain a thought
That tends to love, but meditate on death,
A fitter subject for a pensive soul.

Theridamas. Olympia, pity him in whom thy looks
Have greater operation and more force
Than Cynthia's in the watery wilderness ;
For with thy view my joys are at the full,
And ebb again as thou departst from me.

Olympia. Ah, pity me, my lord, and draw your sword,
Making a passage for my troubled soul,
Which beats against this prison to get out,
And meet my husband and my loving son !

Theridamas. Nothing but still thy husband and thy
              son ?
Leave this, my love, and listen more to me ;
Thou shalt be stately queen of fair Argier ;
And, cloth'd in costly cloth of massy gold,
Upon the marble turrets of my court
Sit like to Venus in her chair of state,
Commanding all thy princely eye desires ;

And I will cast off arms and sit with thee,
Spending my life in sweet discourse of love.
Olympia. No such discourse is pleasant in mine ears,
But that where every period ends with death,
And every line begins with death again.
I cannot love, to be an emperess.
Theridamas. Nay lady, then, if nothing will prevail,
I'll use some other means to make you yield.
Such is the sudden fury of my love,
I must and will be pleased, and you shall yield.
Come to the tent again.
Olympia. Stay, good my lord and, will you save my
    honour,
I'll give your grace a present of such price
As all the world can not afford the like.
Theridamas. What is it?
Olympia. An ointment which a cunning alchemist
Distilled from the purest balsamum
And simplest extracts of all minerals,
In which the essential form of marble stone,
Tempered by science metaphysical,
And spells of magic from the mouths of spirits,
With which if you but 'noint your tender skin,
Nor pistol, sword, nor lance can pierce your flesh.
Theridamas. Why, madam, think ye to mock me thus
    palpably?
Olympia. To prove it, I will 'noint my naked throat,
Which when you stab, look on your weapon's point,
And you shall see't rebated with the blow.
Theridamas. Why gave you not your husband some of it,

If you lov'd him, and it so precious ?

Olympia. My purpose was, my lord, to spend it so,
But was prevented by his sudden end ;
And for a present easy proof hereof,
That I dissemble not, try it on me.

Theridamas. I will, Olympia, and will keep it for
The richest present of this eastern world.

She 'noints her throat.

Olympia. Now stab, my lord, and mark your weapon's
point,
That will be blunted if the blow be great.

Theridamas. Here, then, Olympia.   [*Stabs her.*]
What, have I slain her ? Villain, stab thyself !
Cut off this arm that murdered my love,
In whom the learned Rabbis of this age
Might find as many wondrous miracles
As in the theoria of the world !
Now hell is fairer than Elisian ;
A greater lamp than that bright eye of heaven,
From whence the stars do borrow all their light,
Wanders about the black circumference ;
And now the damned souls are free from pain,
For every Fury gazeth on her looks ;
Infernal Dis is courting of my love,
Inventing masks and stately shows for her,
Opening the doors of his rich treasury
To entertain this queen of chastity ;
Whose body shall be tomb'd with all the pomp
The treasure of my kingdom may afford.

Exit, taking her away.

SCENE [III]

TAMBURLAINE, *drawn in his chariot by* TREBIZON
    and SORIA, *with bits in their mouths, reins in his*
    left hand, and in his right hand a whip with which he
    scourgeth them; TECHELLES, THERIDAMAS, USUM-
    CASANE, AMYRAS, CELEBINUS; [ORCANES, *King of*]
    NATOLIA *and* JERUSALEM, *led by five or six common*
    Soldiers.

Tamburlaine. Holla, ye pampered jades of Asia !
    What, can ye draw but twenty miles a day,
    And have so proud a chariot at your heels,
    And such a coachman as great Tamburlaine,
    But from Asphaltis, where I conquered you,
    To Byron here, where thus I honour you ?
    The horse that guide the golden eye of heaven,
    And blow the morning from their nostrils,
    Making their fiery gait above the clouds,
    Are not so honoured in their governor
    As you, ye slaves, in mighty Tamburlaine.
    The headstrong jades of Thrace Alcides tam'd,
    That King Ægeus fed with human flesh,
    And made so wanton that they knew their strengths,
    Were not subdu'd with valour more divine
    Than you by this unconquered arm of mine.
    To make you fierce, and fit my appetite,
    You shall be fed with flesh as raw as blood,
    And drink in pails the strongest muscadel ;

If you can live with it, then live and draw
My chariot swifter than the racking clouds ;
If not, then die like beasts, and fit for naught
But perches for the black and fatal ravens.
Thus am I right the scourge of highest Jove ;
And see the figure of my dignity,
By which I hold my name and majesty.

Amyras. Let me have coach, my lord, that I may ride,
And thus be drawn with these two idle kings.

Tamburlaine. Thy youth forbids such ease, my kingly
    boy ;
They shall to-morrow draw my chariot,
While these their fellow kings may be refreshed.

Orcanes. O thou that swayest the region under earth,
And art a king as absolute as Jove,
Come as thou didst in fruitful Sicily,
Surveying all the glories of the land,
And as thou took'st the fair Proserpina,
Joying the fruit of Ceres' garden plot,
For love, for honour, and to make her queen,
So, for just hate, for shame, and to subdue
This proud contemner of thy dreadful power,
Come once in fury, and survey his pride,
Haling him headlong to the lowest hell !

Theridamas. Your majesty must get some bits for
    these,
To bridle their contemptuous cursing tongues,
That, like unruly never broken jades,
Break through the hedges of their hateful mouths,
And pass their fixed bounds exceedingly.

Techelles. Nay, we will break the hedges of their
          mouths,
     And pull their kicking colts out of their pastures.
Usumcasane. Your majesty already hath devised
     A mean, as fit as may be, to restrain
     These coltish coach-horse tongues from blasphemy.
Celebinus. How like you that, sir king ? why speak
          you not ?
Jerusalem. Ah, cruel brat, sprung from a tyrant's loins
     How like his cursed father he begins
     To practice taunts and bitter tyrannies !
Tamburlaine. Ay, Turk, I tell thee, this same boy is he
     That must, advanced in higher pomp than this,
     Rifle the kingdoms I shall leave unsacked,
     If Jove, esteeming me too good for earth,
     Raise me to match the fair Aldeboran,
     Above the threefold astracism of heaven,
     Before I conquer all the triple world.
     Now fetch me out the Turkish concubines ;
     I will prefer them for the funeral
     They have bestowed on my abortive son.
                              The Concubines are brought in
     Where are my common soldiers now, that fought
     So lion-like upon Asphaltis' plains ?
Soldiers. Here, my lord.
Tamburlaine. Hold ye, tall soldiers, take ye queens
          piece,
     I mean such queens as were kings' concubines ;
     Take them ; divide them, and their jewels too,
     And let them equally serve all your turns.

Soldiers. We thank your majesty.

Tamburlaine. Brawl not, I warn you, for your lechery ;
  For every man that so offends shall die.

Orcanes. Injurious tyrant, wilt thou so defame
  The hateful fortunes of thy victory,
  To exercise upon such guiltless dames
  The violence of thy common soldiers' lust ?

Tamburlaine. Live continent, then, ye slaves, and meet
      not me
  With troops of harlots at your slothful heels.

Concubines. O pity us, my lord, and save our honours !

Tamburlaine. Are ye not gone, ye villains, with your
      spoils ?   *They run away with the ladies.*

Jerusalem. O merciless, infernal cruelty !

Tamburlaine. Save your honours ! 'twere but time
      indeed,
  Lost long before you knew what honour meant.

Theridamas. It seems they meant to conquer us, my
      lord,
  And make us jesting pageants for their trulls.

Tamburlaine. And now themselves shall make our
      pageant,
  And common soldiers jest with all their trulls.
  Let them take pleasure soundly in their spoils,
  Till we prepare our march to Babylon,
  Whether we next make expedition.

Techelles. Let us not be idle, then, my lord,
  But presently be prest to conquer it.

Tamburlaine. We will, Techelles. Forward, then, ye
      jades !

Now crouch, ye kings of greatest Asia,
And tremble when ye hear this scourge will come
That whips down cities and controlleth crowns,
Adding their wealth and treasure to my store.
The Euxine sea, north to Natolia ;
The Terrene, west ; the Caspian, north north-east ;
And on the south, Sinus Arabicus ;
Shall all be loaden with the martial spoils
We will convey with us to Persia.
Then shall my native city Samarcanda,
And crystal waves of fresh Jaertis' stream,
The pride and beauty of her princely seat,
Be famous through the furthest continents ;
For there my palace royal shall be plac'd,
Whose shining turrets shall dismay the heavens,
And cast the fame of Ilion's tower to hell ;
Thorough the streets, with troops of conquered
     kings,
I'll ride in golden armour like the sun ;
And in my helm a triple plume shall spring,
Spangled with diamonds, dancing in the air,
To note me emperor of the three-fold world ;
Like to an almond tree ymounted high
Upon the lofty and celestial mount
Of ever green Selinus, quaintly decked
With blooms more white than Herycina's brows,
Whose tender blossoms tremble every one
At every little breath that thorough heaven is blown.
Then in my coach, like Saturn's royal son
Mounted his shining chariot gilt with fire,

And drawn with princely eagles through the path
Pav'd with bright crystal and enchas'd with stars,
When all the gods stand gazing at his pomp,
So will I ride through Samarcanda streets,
Until my soul, dissevered from this flesh,
Shall mount the milk-white way, and meet him
      there.
To Babylon, my lords, to Babylon !   *Exeunt.*

Finis Actus Quarti.

ACT V

SCENE I

Enter the GOVERNOR OF BABYLON [*and* MAXIMUS]
upon the walls with others.

Governor. What saith Maximus?
Maximus. My lord, the breach the enemy hath made
  Gives such assurance of our overthrow,
  That little hope is left to save our lives,
  Or hold our city from the conqueror's hands.
  Then hang out flags, my lord, of humble truce,
  And satisfy the people's general prayers,
  That Tamburlaine's intolerable wrath
  May be suppressed by our submission.
Governor. Villain, respects thou more thy slavish life
  Than honour of thy country or thy name?
  Is not my life and state as dear to me,
  The city and my native country's weal,
  As any thing of price with thy conceit?
  Have we not hope, for all our battered walls,
  To live secure and keep his forces out,
  When this our famous lake of Limnasphaltis
  Makes walls afresh with every thing that falls

Into the liquid substance of his stream,
More strong than are the gates of death or hell ?
What faintness should dismay our courages,
When we are thus defenc'd against our foe,
And have no terror but his threatening looks ?

Enter another [Citizen], *kneeling to the* GOVERNOR.

itizen. My lord, if ever you did deed of ruth,
And now will work a refuge to our lives,
Offer submission, hang up flags of truce,
That Tamburlaine may pity our distress,
And use us like a loving conqueror.
Though this be held his last day's dreadful siege,
Wherein he spareth neither man nor child,
Yet are there Christians of Georgia here,
Whose state he ever pitied and reliev'd,
Will get his pardon, if your grace would send.
overnor. How is my soul environed !
And this eternised city Babylon
Fill'd with a pack of faint-heart fugitives
That thus entreat their shame and servitude !
nother. My lord, if ever you will win our hearts,
Yield up the town, save our wives and children ;
For I will cast myself from off these walls,
Or die some death of quickest violence,
Before I bide the wrath of Tamburlaine.
overnor. Villains, cowards, traitors to our state !
Fall to the earth, and pierce the pit of hell, .
That legions of tormenting spirits may vex

Your slavish bosoms with continual pains !
I care not, nor the town will never yield
As long as any life is in my breast.

Enter THERIDAMAS *and* TECHELLES, *with other*
Soldiers.

[*Theridamas.*] Thou desperate governor of Babylon,
  To save thy life, and us a little labour,
  Yield speedily the city to our hands,
  Or else be sure thou shalt be forc'd with pains
  More exquisite than ever traitor felt.
Governor. Tyrant, I turn the traitor in thy throat,
  And will defend it in despite of thee.
  Call up the soldiers to defend these walls.
Techelles. Yield, foolish governor ; we offer more
  Than ever yet we did to such proud slaves
  As durst resist us till our third day's siege.
  Thou seest us prest to give the last assault,
  And that shall bide no more regard of parlie.
Governor. Assault and spare not ; we will never yield
                Alarm ; and they scale the walls.

Enter TAMBURLAINE, *with* USUMCASANE, AMYRAS
  and CELEBINUS [*etc., the kings drawing his chariot
  as before*]; *with others, the two spare kings.*

Tamburlaine. The stately buildings of fair Babylon,
  Whose lofty pillars, higher than the clouds,
  Were wont to guide the seaman in the deep,

Being carried thither by the cannon's force,
Now fill the mouth of Limnasphaltis' lake,
And make a bridge unto the battered walls.
Where Belus, Ninus and great Alexander
Have rode in triumph, triumphs Tamburlaine,
Whose chariot wheels have burst th' Assyrians' bones,
Drawn with these kings on heaps of carcasses.
Now in the place where fair Semiramis,
Courted by kings and peers of Asia,
Hath trod the measures, do my soldiers march ;
And in the streets, where brave Assyrian dames
Have rid in pomp like rich Saturnia,
With furious words and frowning visages
My horsemen brandish their unruly blades.

Enter THERIDAMAS *and* TECHELLES, *bringing the*
GOVERNOR OF BABYLON.

Who have ye there, my lords ?
Theridamas. The sturdy governor of Babylon,
  That made us all the labour for the town,
  And used such slender reckoning of your majesty.
Tamburlaine. Go, bind the villain ; he shall hang in
    chains
Upon the ruins of this conquered town.—
Sirrah, the view of our vermilion tents,
Which threatened more than if the region
Next underneath the element of fire
Were full of comets and of blazing stars,
Whose flaming trains should reach down to the earth,

Could not affright you ; no, nor I myself,
The wrathful messenger of mighty Jove,
That with his sword hath quail'd all earthly kings,
Could not persuade you to submission,
But still the ports were shut : villain, I say,
Should I but touch the rusty gates of hell,
The triple headed Cerberus would howl,
And wake black Jove to crouch and kneel to me ;
But I have sent volleys of shot to you,
Yet could not enter till the breach was made.

Governor. Nor, if my body could have stopt the breach
Shouldst thou have entered, cruel Tamburlaine.
'Tis not thy bloody tents can make me yield,
Nor yet thyself, the anger of the highest ;
For, though thy cannon shook the city walls,
My heart did never quake, or courage faint.

Tamburlaine. Well, now I'll make it quake.   Go draw
him up,
Hang him in chains upon the city walls,
And let my soldiers shoot the slave to death.

Governor. Vile monster, born of some infernal hag,
And sent from hell to tyrannise on earth,
Do all thy worst ; nor death, nor Tamburlaine,
Torture, or pain, can daunt my dreadless mind.

Tamburlaine. Up with him, then ! his body shall be
scarred.

Governor. But, Tamburlaine, in Limnasphaltis' lake
There lies more gold than Babylon is worth,
Which, when the city was besieg'd, I hid :
Save but my life, and I will give it thee.

amburlaine. Then, for all your valour, you would save
    your life ?
Whereabout lies it ?

overnor. Under a hollow bank, right opposite
Against the western gate of Babylon.

amburlaine. Go thither, some of you, and take his
    gold :—
The rest forward with execution.
Away with him hence, let him speak no more.
I think I make your courage something quail.
When this is done, we'll march from Babylon,
And make our greatest haste to Persia.
These jades are broken winded and half tir'd ;
Unharness them, and let me have fresh horse.
So ; now their best is done to honour me,
Take them and hang them both up presently.

rebizon. Vild tyrant ! barbarous, bloody Tambur-
    laine !

amburlaine. Take them away, Theridamas ; see them
    despatched.

heridamas. I will, my lord.

                    [Exit with TREBIZON and SORIA.]

amburlaine. Come, Asian viceroys ; to your tasks a
    while,
And take such fortune as your fellows felt.

rcanes. First let thy Scythian horse tear both our
    limbs,
Rather than we should draw thy chariot,
And, like base slaves, abject our princely minds
To vile and ignominious servitude.

Jerusalem. Rather lend me thy weapon, Tamburlaine,
  That I may sheathe it in this breast of mine.
  A thousand deaths could not torment our hearts
  More than the thought of this doth vex our souls.
Amyras. They will talk still, my lord, if you do no
  bridle them.
Tamburlaine. Bridle them, and let me to my coach.

> *They bridle them.—*[*The* GOVERNOR OF BABYLO
>   *appears hanging in chains on the walls.—Re-ent*
>   THERIDAMAS.]

Amyras. See now, my lord, how brave the captai
  hangs.
Tamburlaine. 'Tis brave indeed, my boy : well done
  Shoot first, my lord, and then the rest shall follow.
Theridamas. Then have at him, to begin withal.

> *Theridamas shoot*

Governor. Yet save my life, and let this wound appeas
  The mortal fury of great Tamburlaine !
Tamburlaine. No, though Asphaltis' lake were liqui
  gold,
  And offer'd me as ransom for thy life,
  Yet shouldst thou die.—Shoot at him all at once.

> *They shoo*

  So, now he hangs like Bagdet's governor,
  Having as many bullets in his flesh
  As there be breaches in her battered wall.
  Go now, and bind the burghers hand and foot,
  And cast them headlong in the city's lake.

Tartars and Persians shall inhabit there ;
And, to command the city, I will build
A citadel, that all Africa,
Which hath been subject to the Persian king,
Shall pay me tribute for, in Babylon.

echelles. What shall be done with their wives and
        children, my lord ?

amburlaine. Techelles, drown them all, man, woman
        and child ;
Leave not a Babylonian in the town.

echelles. I will about it straight.   Come, soldiers.

                                                Exit.

amburlaine. Now, Casane, where's the Turkish
        Alcaron,
And all the heaps of superstitious books
Found in the temples of that Mahomet
Whom I have thought a god ? they shall be burnt.

sumcasane. Here they are, my lord.

amburlaine. Well said.   Let there be a fire presently.
                                        [*They light a fire.*]
In vain, I see, men worship Mahomet :
My sword hath sent millions of Turks to hell,
Slew all his priests, his kinsmen and his friends,
And yet I live untouched by Mahomet.
There is a God, full of revenging wrath,
From whom the thunder and the lightning breaks,
Whose scourge I am, and him will I obey.
So, Casane ; fling them in the fire.
                                        [*They burn the books.*]
Now, Mahomet, if thou have any power,

Come down thyself and work a miracle.
Thou art not worthy to be worshipped
That suffers flames of fire to burn the writ
Wherein the sum of thy religion rests.
Why send'st thou not a furious whirlwind down,
To blow thy Alcaron up to thy throne,
Where men report thou sitt'st by God himself,
Or vengeance on the head of Tamburlaine
That shakes his sword against thy majesty,
And spurns the abstracts of thy foolish laws?
Well soldiers, Mahomet remains in hell;
He cannot hear the voice of Tamburlaine:
Seek out another godhead to adore;
The God that sits in heaven, if any god,
For he is God alone, and none but he.

[*Re-enter* TECHELLES.]

Techelles. I have fulfill'd your highness' will, my lord
    Thousands of men, drown'd in Asphaltis' lake,
    Have made the water swell above the banks,
    And fishes, fed by human carcasses,
    Amazed, swim up and down upon the waves,
    As when they swallow assafitida,
    Which makes them fleet aloft and gasp for air.
Tamburlaine. Well, then, my friendly lords, what now
        remains,
    But that we leave sufficient garrison,
    And presently depart to Persia,
    To triumph after all our victories?

Theridamas. Ay, good my lord, let us in haste to
      Persia ;
  And let this captain be remov'd the walls
  To some high hill about the city here.
Tamburlaine. Let it be so ; about it, soldiers.
  But stay ; I feel myself distempered suddenly.
Techelles. What is it dares distemper Tamburlaine ?
Tamburlaine. Something, Techelles ; but I know not
      what.
  But, forth, ye vassals ! whatsoe'er it be,
  Sickness or death can never conquer me.   *Exeunt.*

SCENE II

Enter CALLAPINE, AMASIA, *with drums and trumpets.*

Callapine. King of Amasia, now our mighty host
  Marcheth in Asia Major, where the streams
  Of Euphrates and Tigris swiftly runs ;
  And here may we behold great Babylon,
  Circled about with Limnasphaltis' lake,
  Where Tamburlaine with all his army lies,
  Which being faint and weary with the siege,
  We may lie ready to encounter him
  Before his host be full from Babylon,
  And so revenge our latest grievous loss,
  If God or Mahomet send any aid.
Amasia. Doubt not, my lord, but we shall conquer him ;

The monster that hath drunk a sea of blood,
And yet gapes still for more to quench his thirst,
Our Turkish swords shall headlong send to hell ;
And that vile carcass, drawn by warlike kings,
The fowls shall eat ; for never sepulchre
Shall grace that base-born tyrant Tamburlaine.

Callapine. When I record my parents' slavish life,
Their cruel death, mine own captivity,
My viceroys' bondage under Tamburlaine,
Methinks I could sustain a thousand deaths,
To be reveng'd of all his villany.
Ah, sacred Mahomet, thou that hast seen
Millions of Turks perish by Tamburlaine,
Kingdoms made waste, brave cities sacked and burnt,
And but one host is left to honour thee,
Aid thy obedient servant Callapine,
And make him, after all these overthrows,
To triumph over cursed Tamburlaine !

Amasia. Fear not, my lord : I see great Mahomet,
Clothed in purple clouds, and on his head
A chaplet brighter than Apollo's crown,
Marching about the air with armed men,
To join with you against this Tamburlaine.
Renowned general, mighty Callapine,
Though God himself and holy Mahomet
Should come in person to resist your power,
Yet might your mighty host encounter all,
And pull proud Tamburlaine upon his knees
To sue for mercy at your highness' feet.

Callapine. Captain, the force of Tamburlaine is great

His fortune greater, and the victories
Wherewith he hath so sore dismayed the world
Are greatest to discourage all our drifts ;
Yet when the pride of Cynthia is at full,
She wanes again ; and so shall his, I hope ;
For we have here the chief selected men
Of twenty several kingdoms at the least ;
Nor ploughman, priest, nor merchant stays at home ;
All Turkey is in arms with Callapine ;
And never will we sunder camps and arms
Before himself or his be conquered :
This is the time that must eternise me
For conquering the tyrant of the world.
Come, soldiers, let us lie in wait for him,
And if we find him absent from his camp,
Or that it be rejoin'd again at full,
Assail it, and be sure of victory.   *Exeunt.*

SCENE III

THERIDAMAS, TECHELLES, USUMCASANE.

Theridamas.] Weep, heavens, and vanish into liquid
      tears !
Fall, stars that govern his nativity,
And summon all the shining lamps of heaven
To cast their bootless fires to the earth,
And shed their feeble influence in the air ;

Muffle your beauties with eternal clouds,
For hell and darkness pitch their pitchy tents,
And Death, with armies of Cimmerian spirits,
Gives battle 'gainst the heart of Tamburlaine.
Now, in defiance of that wonted love
Your sacred virtues pour'd upon his throne,
And made his state an honour to the heavens,
These cowards invisibly assail his soul,
And threaten conquest on our sovereign ;
But if he die, your glories are disgrac'd,
Earth droops and says that hell in heaven is plac'd.

Techelles. O, then, ye powers that sway eternal seats,
And guide this massy substance of the earth,
If you retain desert of holiness,
As your supreme estates instruct our thoughts,
Be not inconstant, careless of your fame,
Bear not the burden of your enemies' joys,
Triumphing in his fall whom you advanc'd ;
But as his birth, life, health and majesty
Were strangely blest and governed by heaven,
So honour, heaven, till heaven dissolved be,
His birth, his life, his health and majesty !

Usumcasane. Blush, heaven, to lose the honour of thy
    name,
To see thy footstool set upon thy head ;
And let no baseness in thy haughty breast
Sustain a shame of such inexcellence,
To see the devils mount in angels' thrones,
And angels dive into the pools of hell.
And, though they think their painful date is out,

And that their power is puissant as Jove's,
Which makes them manage arms against thy state,
Yet make them feel the strength of Tamburlaine,
Thy instrument and note of majesty,
Is greater far than they can thus subdue ;
For, if he die, thy glory is disgrac'd,
Earth droops and says that hell in heaven is plac'd.

[*Enter* TAMBURLAINE, *drawn by the captive kings,*
    AMYRAS, CELEBINUS, *and* Physicians.]

Tamburlaine. What daring god torments my body thus,
  And seeks to conquer mighty Tamburlaine ?
  Shall sickness prove me now to be a man,
  That have been term'd the terror of the world ?
  Techelles and the rest, come, take your swords,
  And threaten him whose hand afflicts my soul :
  Come, let us march against the powers of heaven,
  And set black streamers in the firmament,
  To signify the slaughter of the gods.
  Ah, friends, what shall I do ? I cannot stand.
  Come, carry me to war against the gods,
  That thus envy the health of Tamburlaine.
Theridamas. Ah, good my lord, leave these impatient
        words,
  Which add much danger to your malady !
Tamburlaine. Why, shall I sit and languish in this pain ?
  No, strike the drums, and, in revenge of this,
  Come, let us charge our spears, and pierce his breast
  Whose shoulders bear the axis of the world,

That, if I perish, heaven and earth may fade.
Theridamas, haste to the court of Jove ;
Will him to send Apollo hither straight,
To cure me, or I'll fetch him down myself.

Techelles. Sit still, my gracious lord ; this grief will
    cease,
And cannot last, it is so violent.

Tamburlaine. Not last, Techelles ! no, for I shall die.
See, where my slave, the ugly monster death,
Shaking and quivering, pale and wan for fear,
Stands aiming at me with his murdering dart,
Who flies away at every glance I give,
And, when I look away, comes stealing on !
Villain, away, and hie thee to the field !
I and mine army come to load thy bark
With souls of thousand mangled carcasses.
Look, where he goes ! but, see, he comes again,
Because I stay ! Techelles, let us march,
And weary Death with bearing souls to hell.

Physician. Pleaseth your majesty to drink this potion,
Which will abate the fury of your fit,
And cause some milder spirits govern you.

Tamburlaine. Tell me, what think you of my sickness
    now ?

First Physician. I view'd your urine, and the hypostasis,
Thick and obscure, both make your danger great ;
Your veins are full of accidental heat,
Whereby the moisture of your blood is dried :
The humidum and calor, which some hold
Is not a parcel of the elements,

But of a substance more divine and pure,
Is almost clean extinguished and spent ;
Which, being the cause of life, imports your death.
Besides, my lord, this day is critical,
Dangerous to those whose crisis is as yours :
Your artiers, which alongst the veins convey
The lively spirits which the heart engenders,
Are parched and void of spirit, that the soul,
Wanting those organons by which it moves,
Cannot endure, by argument of art.
Yet, if your majesty may escape this day,
No doubt but you shall soon recover all.

Tamburlaine. Then will I comfort all my vital parts,
And live, in spite of death, above a day.

Alarm within.

[*Enter a* Messenger.]

Messenger. My lord, young Callapine, that lately fled
        from your majesty, hath now gathered a fresh
        army, and, hearing your absence in the field,
        offers to set upon us presently.

Tamburlaine. See, my physicians, now, how Jove hath
        sent
A present medicine to recure my pain !
My looks shall make them fly ; and, might I
        follow,
There should not one of all the villain's power
Live to give offer of another fight.

Usumcasane. I joy, my lord, your highness is so strong,
        That can endure so well your royal presence,

Which only will dismay the enemy.

Tamburlaine. I know it will, Casane.   Draw, you
  slaves !

In spite of death, I will go show my face.

  *Alarm.   Tamburlaine goes in and comes out again
    with all the rest.*

Tamburlaine. Thus are the villains, cowards fled for
  fear,

Like summer's vapours vanished by the sun ;
And, could I but a while pursue the field,
That Callapine should be my slave again.
But I perceive my martial strength is spent :
In vain I strive and rail against those powers
That mean t' invest me in a higher throne,
As much too high for this disdainful earth.
Give me a map ; then let me see how much
Is left for me to conquer all the world,
That these, my boys, may finish all my wants.

One brings a map.

Here I began to march towards Persia,
Along Armenia and the Caspian Sea,
And thence unto Bithynia, where I took
The Turk and his great empress prisoners.
Then marched I into Egypt and Arabia ;
And here, nor far from Alexandria,
Whereas the Terrene and the Red Sea meet,
Being distant less than full a hundred leagues,
I meant to cut a channel to them both,
That men might quickly sail to India.
From thence to Nubia near Borno lake,

And so along the Ethiopian sea,
Cutting the tropic line of Capricorn,
I conquered all as far as Zanzibar.
Then, by the northern part of Africa,
I came at last to Græcia, and from thence
To Asia, where I stay against my will ;
Which is from Scythia, where I first began,
Backward and forwards near five thousand leagues.
Look here, my boys ; see what a world of ground
Lies westward from the midst of Cancer's line
Unto the rising of this earthly globe,
Whereas the sun, declining from our sight,
Begins the day with our Antipodes !
And shall I die, and this unconquered ?
Lo, here, my sons, are all the golden mines,
Inestimable drugs and precious stones,
More worth than Asia and the world beside ;
And from th'Antarctic Pole eastward behold
As much more land, which never was descried,
Wherein are rocks of pearl that shine as bright
As all the lamps that beautify the sky !
And shall I die, and this unconquered ?
Here, lovely boys, what death forbids my life,
That let your lives command in spite of death.

Amyras. Alas, my lord, how should our bleeding
     hearts,
Wounded and broken with your highness' grief,
Retain a thought of joy or spark of life ?
Your soul gives essence to our wretched subjects,
Whose matter is incorporate in your flesh.

Celebinus. Your pains do pierce our souls ; no hop
    survives,
  For by your life we entertain our lives.
Tamburlaine. But sons, this subject, not of force
    enough
  To hold the fiery spirit it contains,
  Must part, imparting his impressions
  By equal portions into both your breasts ;
  My flesh, divided in your precious shapes,
  Shall still retain my spirit, though I die,
  And live in all your seeds immortally.
  Then now remove me, that I may resign
  My place and proper title to my son.
  First, take my scourge and my imperial crown,
  And mount my royal chariot of estate,
  That I may see thee crown'd before I die.
  Help me, my lords, to make my last remove.
Theridamas. A woeful change, my lord, that daunts our
    thoughts
  More than the ruin of our proper souls.
Tamburlaine. Sit up, my son, let me see how well
  Thou wilt become thy father's majesty.

                          They crown him.
Amyras. With what a flinty bosom should I joy
  The breath of life and burden of my soul,
  If not resolv'd into resolved pains,
  My body's mortified lineaments
  Should exercise the motions of my heart,
  Pierc'd with the joy of any dignity !
  O father, if the unrelenting ears

Of death and hell be shut against my prayers,
And that the spiteful influence of heaven
Deny my soul fruition of her joy,
How should I step or stir my hateful feet
Against the inward powers of my heart,
Leading a life that only strives to die,
And plead in vain unpleasing sovereignty ?

Tamburlaine. Let not thy love exceed thine honour, son,
Nor bar thy mind that magnanimity
That nobly must admit necessity.
Sit up, my boy, and with those silken reins
Bridle the steeled stomachs of those jades.

Theridamas. My lord, you must obey his majesty,
Since fate commands and proud necessity.

Amyras. Heavens witness me with what a broken
heart
And damned spirit I ascend this seat,
And send my soul, before my father die,
His anguish and his burning agony !

Tamburlaine. Now fetch the hearse of fair Zenocrate ;
Let it be plac'd by this my fatal chair,
And serve as parcel of my funeral.

Usumcasane. Then feels your majesty no sovereign ease,
Nor may our hearts, all drown'd in tears of blood,
Joy any hope of your recovery ?

Tamburlaine. Casane, no ; the monarch of the earth,
And eyeless monster that torments my soul,
Cannot behold the tears ye shed for me,
And therefore still augments his cruelty.

Techelles. Then let some god oppose his holy power

Against the wrath and tyranny of death,
That his tear-thirsty and unquenched hate
May be upon himself reverberate !

> *They bring in the hearse.*

Tamburlaine. Now, eyes, enjoy your latest benefit,
And, when my soul hath virtue of your sight,
Pierce through the coffin and the sheet of gold,
And glut your longings with a heaven of joy.
So reign, my son ; scourge and control those slaves,
Guiding thy chariot with thy father's hand.
As precious is the charge thou undertak'st
As that which Clymene's brain-sick son did guide
When wandering Phœbe's ivory cheeks were
    scorched,
And all the earth, like Ætna, breathing fire.
Be warned by him, then ; learn with awful eye
To sway a throne as dangerous as his ;
For, if thy body thrive not full of thoughts
As pure and fiery as Phyteus' beams,
The nature of these proud rebelling jades
Will take occasion by the slenderest hair,
And draw thee piecemeal, like Hippolytus,
Through rocks more steep and sharp than Caspian
    clifts :
The nature of thy chariot will not bear
A guide of baser temper than myself,
More than heaven's coach the pride of Phaeton.
Farewell, my boys ! my dearest friends, farewell !
My body feels, my soul doth weep to see
Your sweet desires depriv'd my company,

For Tamburlaine, the scourge of God, must die.

Amyras. Meet heaven and earth, and here let all things
      end,
For earth hath spent the pride of all her fruit,
And heaven consum'd his choicest living fire !
Let earth and heaven his timeless death deplore,
For both their worths will equal him no more.

FINIS

THE TRAGICAL HISTORY OF
DOCTOR FAUSTUS

" *Doctor Faustus* " was written between 1588 and 1592. It may have been published in 1601, eight years after Marlowe's death, but the earliest extant edition is the Quarto of 1604. Another version, half as long again, appeared in 1616. Both versions are corrupt and mutilated, and both contain a good deal of matter which is not Marlowe's. The relationship of the two versions and the attempt to distinguish Marlowe's own work constitute one of the most complicated problems in English textual criticism, which the student will find fully discussed in the invaluable edition by Dr. F. S. Boas. That the comic scenes are crude and discordant is no proof that they are not the work of Marlowe.

The present edition follows very closely the earliest extant edition. The editor has worked from the photographic facsimile of the Quarto of 1604, Students' Facsimile Edition, issued by John S. Farmer in 1920, and has used as the basis of the text his own expurgated acting edition in " *The Nelson Playbooks.*" Spelling, punctuation, and use of capitals have been modernized, and minor emendations have been made without notice, but nothing has been omitted and all editorial additions have been enclosed in " square " brackets.

Johann Faust was a vagabond conjurer who lived in Germany about 1488–1541, and whose doings grew into legends which were recorded in the famous " Faustbuch," the " Historia von D. Johann Fausten," published at Frankfort-on-the-Main in 1587. The English translation, from which Marlowe took his material, probably appeared in 1588, although there is no extant edition earlier than 1592, when " The Historie of the damnable life and deserved death of Doctor John Faustus " was " imprinted at London."

THE
TRAGICALL
History of D. Faustus.

As it hath bene Acted by the Right
Honorable the Earle of Nottingham his seruants.

Written by Ch. Marl.

LONDON
Printed by V.S. for Thomas Bushell. 1604.

[CHARACTERS

Chorus.

Doctor Faustus.
Valdes, } Friends of Faustus.
Cornelius, }
Wagner, Faustus' servant.
Robin.
Ralph.
A Clown.
A Vintner.
A Horse-Courser.
First Scholar.
Second Scholar.
Third Scholar.
The Pope.
The Cardinal of Lorraine.
The Emperor.
A Knight of the Emperor's Train.
The Duke of Vanholt.
The Duchess of Vanholt.
An Old Man.
    Attendants, Friars, etc.

Mephistophilis.
Lucifer.
Belzebub.
Good Angel.
Evil Angel.
Devils.
The Seven Deadly Sins.
    Spirits taking the form of Alexander the Great, his
    Paramour, and Helen of Troy.]

The Tragical History of Doctor Faustus

Enter CHORUS.

Not marching now in fields of Thrasimene,
Where Mars did mate the Carthaginians;
Nor sporting in the dalliance of love,
In courts of kings where state is overturn'd;
Nor in the pomp of proud audacious deeds,
Intends our Muse to vaunt his heavenly verse:
Only this, gentlemen,—we must perform
The form of Faustus' fortunes, good or bad:
To patient judgments we appeal for plaud,
And speak for Faustus in his infancy.
Now is he born, his parents base of stock,
In Germany, within a town call'd Rhodes:
Of riper years, to Wertenberg he went,
Whereas his kinsmen chiefly brought him up.
So soon he profits in divinity,
The fruitful plot of scholarism grac'd,
That shortly he was grac'd with doctor's name,
Excelling all whose sweet delight disputes
In heavenly matters of theology;
Till swoln with cunning, of a self-conceit,

His waxen wings did mount above his reach,
And, melting, heavens conspired his overthrow ;
For, falling to a devilish exercise,
And glutted now with learning's golden gifts,
He surfeits upon cursèd necromancy ;
Nothing so sweet as magic is to him,
Which he prefers before his chiefest bliss :
And this the man that in his study sits.   *Exit.*

[ACT I

SCENE I]

Enter FAUSTUS *in his study.*

Faustus. Settle thy studies, Faustus, and begin
To sound the depth of that thou wilt profess :
Having commenced, be a divine in show,
Yet level at the end of every art,
And live and die in Aristotle's works.
Sweet Analytics, 'tis thou hast ravish'd me !
Bene disserere est finis logices.[1]
Is, to dispute well, logic's chiefest end ?
Affords this art no greater miracle ?

---

[1] *Bene . . . logices,* Translated in the next line. All Latin passages not explained in footnotes are so translated.

Then read no more ; thou hast attain'd that end.
A greater subject fitteth Faustus' wit :
Bid Economy farewell ; Galen come ;
Seeing, *Ubi desinit philosophus ibi incipit medicus* : [1]
Be a physician, Faustus ; heap up gold,
And be etèrnised for some wondrous cure !
Summum bonum medicinæ sanitas,
The end of physic is our body's health.
Why, Faustus, hast thou not attain'd that end ?
Is not thy common talk found aphorisms ?
Are not thy bills hung up as monuments,
Whereby whole cities have escap'd the plague,
And thousand desp'rate maladies been eas'd ?
Yet art thou still but Faustus, and a man.
Couldst thou make men to live eternally,
Or, being dead, raise them to life again,
Then this profession were to be esteem'd.
Physic, farewell !   Where is Justinian ?

                        [Turning to the book.]

" *Si una eademque res legatur duobus, alter rem, alter valorem rei,*" *etc.* [2]

A pretty case of paltry legacies !   *[Reading again.]*
" *Exhæreditare filium non potest pater nisi,*" *etc.* [3]
Such is the subject of the institute,
And universal body of the law :
His study fits a mercenary drudge,
Who aims at nothing but external trash ;

---

[1] *Ubi . . . medicus,* Where the philosopher ends the doctor begins.
[2] *Si una . . . rei, etc.,* If one and the same thing is bequeathed to two persons, one shall have the thing and the other the value of the thing.
[3] *Exhæreditare . . . nisi,* A father cannot disinherit his son unless . . .

Too servile and illiberal for me.
When all is done, divinity is best :
Jeromë's Bible, Faustus ; view it well.

> [*He takes the Bible and opens it.*]

" *Stipendium peccati mors est.*"   Ha !   " *Stipendium peccati mors est.*"
The reward of sin is death : that's hard.
" *Si peccasse negamus fallimur et nulla est in nobis veritas.*"
If we say that we have no sin, we deceive ourselves, and there's no truth in us.
Why, then, belike we must sin, and so consequently die :
Ay, we must die an everlasting death.
What doctrine call you this, " *Che sera, sera* " :
What will be, shall be ?   Divinity, adieu !

> [*He closes the Bible and turns to books of magic.*]

These metaphysics of magicians,
And necromantic books are heavenly ;
Lines, circles, scenes, letters, and characters ;
Ay, these are those that Faustus most desires.
O, what a world of profit and delight,
Of power, of honour, of omnipotence,
Is promised to the studious artisan !
All things that move between the quiet poles
Shall be at my command : emperors and kings
Are but obeyèd in their several provinces,
Nor can they raise the wind, or rend the clouds ;
But his dominion that exceeds in this,
Stretcheth as far as doth the mind of man ;

A sound magician is a mighty god :
Here, Faustus, try thy brains to gain a deity !

Enter WAGNER.

Wagner, commend me to my dearest friends.
The German Valdes and Cornelius ;
Request them earnestly to visit me.
Wagner. I will, sir.   *Exit.*
Faustus. Their conference will be a greater help to me
  Than all my labours, plod I ne'er so fast.

Enter the GOOD ANGEL *and the* EVIL ANGEL.

Good Angel. O, Faustus, lay that damnèd book aside,
  And gaze not on it, lest it tempt thy soul,
  And heap God's heavy wrath upon thy head !
  Read, read the Scriptures :—that is blasphemy.
Evil Angel. Go forward, Faustus, in that famous art
  Wherein all Nature's treasure is contain'd :
  Be thou on earth as Jove is in the sky,
  Lord and commander of these elements.   *Exeunt.*
Faustus. How am I glutted with conceit of this !
  Shall I make spirits fetch me what I please,
  Resolve me of all ambiguities,
  Perform what desperate enterprise I will ?
  I'll have them fly to India for gold,
  Ransack the ocèan for orient pearl,
  And search all corners of the new-found world
  For pleasant fruits and princely delicates ;

I'll have them read me strange philosophy,
And tell the secrets of all foreign kings ;
I'll have them wall all Germany with brass,
And make swift Rhine circle fair Wertenberg,
I'll have them fill the public schools with silk,
Wherewith the students shall be bravely clad ;
I'll levy soldiers with the coin they bring,
And chase the Prince of Parma from our land,
And reign sole king of all our provinces ;
Yea, stranger engines for the brunt of war,
Than was the fiery keel at Antwerp's bridge,
I'll make my servile spirits to invent.
Come, German Valdes, and Cornelius,
And make me blest with your sage conference !

Enter VALDES *and* CORNELIUS.

Valdes, sweet Valdes, and Cornelius,
Know that your words have won me at the last
To practise magic and concealèd arts :
Yet not your words only, but mine own fantasy,
That will receive no object for my head,
But ruminates on necromantic skill.
Philosophy is odious and obscure ;
Both law and physic are for petty wits ;
Divinity is basest of the three,
Unpleasant, harsh, contemptible, and vile :
'Tis magic, magic, that hath ravish'd me.
Then, gentle friends, aid me in this attempt ;
And I, that have with concise syllogisms

Gravell'd the pastors of the German church,
And made the flowering pride of Wertenberg
Swarm to my problems, as the infernal spirits
On sweet Musæus when he came to hell,
Will be as cunning as Agrippa was,
Whose shadows made all Europe honour him.

Valdes. Faustus,
These books, thy wit, and our experience
Shall make all nations to canònize us.
As Indian Moors obey their Spanish lords,
So shall the subjects of every element
Be always serviceable to us three ;
Like lions shall they guard us when we please ;
Like Almain rutters with their horsemen's staves,
Or Lapland giants, trotting by our sides ;
Sometimes like women, or unwedded maids,
Shadowing more beauty in their airy brows
Than have the white breasts of the queen of love :
From Venice shall they drag huge argosies,
And from America the golden fleece
That yearly stuffs old Philip's treasury ;
If learnèd Faustus will be resolute.

Faustus. Valdes, as resolute am I in this
As thou to live : therefore object it not.

Cornelius. The miracles that magic will perform
Will make thee vow to study nothing else.
He that is grounded in astrology,
Enrich'd with tongues, well seen in minerals,
Hath all the principles magic doth require :
Then doubt not, Faustus, but to be renown'd,

And more frequented for this mystery
Than heretofore the Delphian oracle.
The spirits tell me they can dry the sea,
And fetch the treasure of all foreign wrecks,
Ay, all the wealth that our forefathers hid
Within the massy entrails of the earth :
Then tell me, Faustus, what shall we three want ?

Faustus. Nothing, Cornelius. O, this cheers my soul !
Come, show me some demonstrations magical,
That I may conjure in some lusty grove,
And have these joys in full possession.

Valdes. Then haste thee to some solitary grove,
And bear wise Bacon's and Albanus' works,
The Hebrew Psalter, and New Testament ;
And whatsoever else is requisite
We will inform thee ere our conference cease.

Cornelius. Valdes, first let him know the words of art ;
And then, all other ceremonies learn'd,
Faustus may try his cunning by himself.

Valdes. First I'll instruct thee in the rudiments,
And then wilt thou be perfecter than I.

Faustus. Then come and dine with me, and, after meat,
We'll canvass every quiddity thereof ;
For, ere I sleep, I'll try what I can do :
This night I'll conjure, though I die therefore.

Exeunt.

[SCENE II

Before FAUSTUS' *house*]

Enter two Scholars.

First Scholar. I wonder what's become of Faustus, that was wont to make our schools ring with *sic probo.*[1]

Second Scholar. That shall we know; for see, here comes his boy.

Enter WAGNER [*carrying bottles of wine*].

First Scholar. How now, sirrah! where's thy master?

Wagner. God in heaven knows.

Second Scholar. Why, dost not thou know?

Wagner. Yes, I know; but that follows not.

First Scholar. Go to, sirrah! leave your jesting, and tell us where he is.

Wagner. That follows not necessary by force of argument, that you, being licentiate, should stand upon 't: therefore acknowledge your error, and be attentive.

Second Scholar. Why, didst thou not say thou knewest?

Wagner. Have you any witness on 't?

First Scholar. Yes, sirrah, I heard you.

Wagner. Ask my fellow if I be a thief.

Second Scholar. Well, you will not tell us?

Wagner [*solemnly imitating learned methods of argument*].

---

[1] *Sic probo,* Thus I prove it.

Yes, sir, I will tell you: yet, if you were not dunces, you would never ask me such a question: for is not he *corpus naturale* ?[1] and is not that *mobile* ?[2] then wherefore should you ask me such a question? But that I am by nature phlegmatic, slow to wrath, and prone to lechery (to love, I should say), it were not for you to come within forty foot of the place of execution, although I do not doubt to see you both hanged the next sessions. Thus having triumphed over you, I will set my countenance like a precisian, and begin to speak thus:—[*In a sanctimonious manner*] Truly, my dear brethren, my master is within at dinner, with Valdes and Cornelius, as this wine, if it could speak, it would inform your worships: and so, the Lord bless you, preserve you, and keep you, my dear brethren, my dear brethren!   *Exit.*

First Scholar. Nay, then, I fear he is fallen into that damned art for which they two are infamous through the world.

Second Scholar. Were he a stranger, and not allied to me, yet should I grieve for him. But, come, let us go and inform the Rector, and see if he by his grave counsel can reclaim him.

First Scholar. O, but I fear me nothing can reclaim him!

Second Scholar. Yet let us try what we can do. (*Exeunt.*)

---

[1] *Corpus naturale*, Natural body.   [2] *Mobile*, Able to move.

[SCENE III

A grove]

Enter FAUSTUS *to conjure.*

Faustus. Now that the gloomy shadow of the earth,
Longing to view Orion's drizzling look,
Leaps from th' antarctic world unto the sky,
And dims the welkin with her pitchy breath,
Faustus, begin thine incantations,
And try if devils will obey thy hest,
Seeing thou hast pray'd and sacrificed to them.
   [*He begins to trace a magic circle on the ground with his
        wand.*]
Within this circle is Jehovah's name,
Forward and backward anagrammatiz'd,
The breviated names of holy saints,
Figures of every adjunct to the heavens,
And characters of signs and erring stars,
By which the spirits are enforc'd to rise :
Then fear not, Faustus, but be resolute,
And try the uttermost magic can perform.
" *Sint mihi Dei Acherontis propitii !   Valeat numen
     triplex Jehovæ !   Ignis, aeris, aquæ, terræ spiritus,
     salvete !   Orientis princeps Belzebub, inferni arden-
     tis monarcha, et Demogorgon, propitiamus vos, ut
     appareat et surgat Mephistophilis.   Quid tu
     moraris ?   per Jehovam, Gehennam, et consecratam*

aquam quam nunc spargo, signumque crucis quod
nunc facio, et per vota nostra, ipse nunc surgat nobis
dicatus Mephistophilis ! " [1]

Enter a Devil [MEPHISTOPHILIS].

[*Faustus.*] I charge thee to return, and change thy
    shape ;
Thou art too ugly to attend on me :
Go, and return an old Franciscan friar ;
That holy shape becomes a devil best.   *Exit Devil.*
I see there's virtue in my heavenly words :
Who would not be proficient in this art ?
How pliant is this Mephistophilis,
Full of obedience and humility !
Such is the force of magic and my spells :
Now, Faustus, thou art conjuror laureate,
That canst command great Mephistophilis :
Quin regis Mephistophilis fratris imagine. [2]

Enter MEPHISTOPHILIS [*as a Franciscan friar.*]

Mephistophilis. Now, Faustus, what would'st thou have
    me do ?
Faustus. I charge thee wait upon me whilst I live,

[1] *Sint mihi . . . Mephistophilis,* " May the gods of Acheron be propitious to me ! May the threefold deity of Jehovah prevail. Spirits of fire,
air, water, and earth, hail ! Belzebub, Prince of the East, Monarch of
Burning Hell, and Demogorgon, we propiciate you, that Mephistophilis
may appear and arise. Why dost thou tarry ? By Jehovah, Gehenna, and
the consecrated water which I now pour, and by the sign of the cross
which I now make, and by our prayers, may Mephistophilis whom we
have summoned now arise ! "
[2] *Quin . . . imagine,* For in the shape of thy brother Mephistophilis
thou hast dominion.

    To do whatever Faustus shall command,
    Be it to make the moon drop from her sphere,
    Or the ocean to overwhelm the world.

Mephistophilis. I am a servant to great Lucifer,
    And may not follow thee without his leave ;
    No more than he commands must we perform.

Faustus. Did not he charge thee to appear to me ?

Mephistophilis. No, I came hither of mine own accord.

Faustus. Did not my conjuring speeches raise thee ?
    speak.

Mephistophilis. That was the cause, but yet *per accidens* ;
    For, when we hear one rack the name of God,
    Abjure the Scriptures and his Saviour Christ,
    We fly, in hope to get his glorious soul ;
    Nor will we come, unless he use such means
    Whereby he is in danger to be damn'd.
    Therefore the shortest cut for conjuring
    Is stoutly to abjure the Trinity,
    And pray devoutly to the prince of hell.

Faustus. So Faustus hath
    Already done ; and holds this principle,
    There is no chief but only Belzebub,
    To whom Faustus doth dedicate himself.
    This word " damnation " terrifies not him,
    For he confounds hell in Elysium :
    His ghost be with the old philosophers !
    But, leaving these vain trifles of men's souls,
    Tell me what is that Lucifer thy lord ?

Mephistophilis. Arch-regent and commander of all
    spirits.

Faustus. Was not that Lucifer an angel once ?

Mephistophilis. Yes, Faustus, and most dearly lov'd of
    God.

Faustus. How comes it then that he is prince of
    devils ?

Mephistophilis. O, by aspiring pride and insolence ;
  For which God threw him from the face of heaven.

Faustus. And what are you that live with Lucifer ?

Mephistophilis. Unhappy spirits that fell with Lucifer,
  Conspired against our God with Lucifer,
  And are for ever damn'd with Lucifer.

Faustus. Where are you damn'd ?

Mephistophilis. In hell.

Faustus. How comes it then that thou art out of
    hell ?

Mephistophilis. Why, this is hell, nor am I out of it :
  Think'st thou that I, who saw the face of God,
  And tasted the eternal joys of heaven,
  Am not tormented with ten thousand hells,
  In being depriv'd of everlasting bliss ?
  O, Faustus, leave these frivolous demands,
  Which strike a terror to my fainting soul !

Faustus. What, is great Mephistophilis so passionate
  For being deprivèd of the joys of heaven ?
  Learn thou of Faustus manly fortitude,
  And scorn those joys thou never shalt possess.
  Go bear these tidings to great Lucifer :
  Seeing Faustus hath incurr'd eternal death
  By desp'rate thoughts against Jove's deity,
  Say, he surrenders up to him his soul,

So he will spare him four-and-twenty years,
Letting him live in all voluptuousness ;
Having thee ever to attend on me,
To give me whatsoever I shall ask,
To tell me whatsoever I demand,
To slay mine enemies, and aid my friends,
And always be obedient to my will.
Go and return to mighty Lucifer,
And meet me in my study at midnight,
And then resolve me of thy master's mind.

Mephistophilis. I will, Faustus.   *Exit.*

Faustus. Had I as many souls as there be stars,
I'd give them all for Mephistophilis.
By him I'll be great emp'ror of the world,
And make a bridge thorough the moving air,
To pass the ocean with a band of men ;
I'll join the hills that bind the Afric shore,
And make that country continent to Spain,
And both contributory to my crown :
The Emperor shall not live but by my leave,
Nor any potentate of Germany.
Now that I have obtain'd what I desired,
I'll live in speculation of this art,
Till Mephistophilis return again.   *Exit.*

[SCENE IV

A Street]

Enter WAGNER *and the* Clown.

Wagner. Sirrah boy, come hither !

Clown. How, boy ! 'Swowns, boy ! I hope you have
seen many boys with such pickadevaunts as I
have. Boy, quotha !

Wagner. Tell me, sirrah, hast thou any comings in ?

Clown. Ay, and goings out too. You may see else.

Wagner. Alas, poor slave ! See how poverty jesteth
in his nakedness ! The villain is bare and out
of service, and so hungry that I know he would
give his soul to the Devil for a shoulder of
mutton, though it were blood raw !

Clown. How, my soul to the Devil for a shoulder of
mutton though 'twere blood-raw ? Not so,
good friend. By'r Lady, I had need have it
well roasted, and good sauce to it, if I pay so
dear.

Wagner. Well, wilt thou serve me, and I'll make the
go like *Qui mihi discipulus* ?

Clown. How, in verse ?

Wagner. No, sirrah, in beaten silk and stavesacre.

Clown. How, how, knave's acre ? Ay, I thought that
was all the land his father left him. Do ye

hear ? I would be sorry to rob you of your living.

Wagner. Sirrah, I say in stavesacre.

Clown. Oho, oho, stavesacre ! Why then, belike, if I were your man, I should be full of vermin.

Wagner. So thou shalt, whether thou beest with me or no. But sirrah, leave your jesting and bind yourself presently unto me for seven years, or I'll turn all the lice about thee into familiars and they shall tear thee in pieces.

Clown. Do you hear, sir ? You may save that labour ; they are too familiar with me already. Swowns, they are as bold with my flesh as if they had paid for my meat and drink.

Wagner. Well, do you hear, sirrah ? Hold, take these guilders.

Clown. Gridirons, what be they ?

Wagner. Why, French crowns.

Clown. Mass, but for the name of French crowns a man were as good have as many English counters; and what should I do with these ?

Wagner. Why now, sirrah, thou art at an hour's warning, whensoever or wheresoever the devil shall fetch thee.

Clown. No, no. Here, take your gridirons again.

Wagner. Truly, I'll none of them.

Clown. Truly, but you shall.

Wagner. Bear witness, I gave them him.

Clown. Bear witness I give them you again.

Wagner. Well, I will cause two devils presently to
fetch thee away. Baliol and Belcher.

Clown. Let your Baliol and your Belcher come here,
and I'll knock them, they were never so
knocked since they were devils. Say I should
kill one of them, what would folks say? "Do
ye see yonder tall fellow in the round slop, he
has killed the devil." So should I be called
Kill-devil all the parish over.

*Enter two Devils, and the Clown runs up and down,
crying.*

Wagner. Baliol and Belcher! Spirits, away! *Exeunt.*

Clown. What, are they gone? A vengeance on them!
They have vile long nails! There was a he-
devil and a she-devil. I'll tell you how you
shall know them; all he-devils has horns and all
she-devils has clifts and cloven feet.

Wagner. Well, sirrah, follow me.

Clown. But, do you hear,—if I should serve you, would
you teach me to raise up Banios and Belcheos?

Wagner. I will teach thee to turn thyself to anything;
to a dog or a cat, or a mouse or a rat, or anything.

Clown. How, a Christian fellow to a dog or a cat,
a mouse or a rat! No, no, sir! If you turn
me into anything let it be in the likeness of a
little, pretty, frisking flea, that I may be here
and there and everywhere. Oh, I'll tickle the
pretty wenches' plackets; I'll be amongst them,
i'faith.

Wagner. Well, sirrah, come.

Clown. But do you hear, Wagner?

Wagner. How! [*calling*] Baliol and Belcher!

Clown. O Lord! I pray, sir, let Banio and Belcher go
 sleep.

Wagner. Villain, call me Master Wagner, and let thy
 left eye be diametarily fixed upon my right heel,
 with *quasi vestigiis nostris insistere.*   *Exit.*

Clown. God forgive me, he speaks Dutch fustian.
 Well, I'll follow him. I'll serve him. That's
 flat.   *Exit.*

[ACT II

SCENE I]

Enter FAUSTUS *in his study.*

Faustus. Now, Faustus, must thou needs be damned,
    And canst thou not be sav'd !
    What boots it them to think of God or heaven ?
    Away with such vain fancies, and despair ;
    Despair in God, and trust in Belzebub :
    Now go not backward ; no, Faustus, be resolute :
    Why waver'st thou ? O, something soundeth in
        mine ears,
    " Abjure this magic, turn to God again ! "
    Ay, and Faustus will turn to God again.
    To God ? he loves thee not ;
    The God thou serv'st is thine own appetite,
    Wherein is fix'd the love of Belzebub :
    To him I'll build an altar and a church,
    And offer lukewarm blood of new-born babes.

Enter GOOD ANGEL *and* EVIL.

Good Angel. Sweet Faustus, leave that execrable art.
Faustus. Contrition, prayer, repentance—what of
    them ?

236

Good Angel. O, they are means to bring thee unto
        heaven !
Evil Angel. Rather illusions, fruits of lunacy,
    That make men foolish that do trust them most.
Good Angel. Sweet Faustus, think of heaven and
        heavenly things.
Evil Angel. No, Faustus ; think of honour and of
        wealth.   *Exeunt.*
Faustus. Of wealth !
    Why, the signiory of Emden shall be mine.
    When Mephistophilis shall stand by me,
    What God can hurt thee, Faustus ? thou art safe :
    Cast no more doubts.—Come, Mephistophilis,
    And bring glad tidings from great Lucifer ;—
    Is't not midnight ?—come, Mephistophilis,
    Veni, veni, Mephistophile !

Enter MEPHISTOPHILIS.

    Now tell [me] what says Lucifer, thy lord ?
Mephistophilis. That I shall wait on Faustus while he
        lives,
    So he will buy my service with his soul.
Faustus. Already Faustus hath hazarded that for thee.
Mephistophilis. But, Faustus, thou must bequeath it
        solemnly,
    And write a deed of gift with thine own blood ;
    For that security craves great Lucifer.
    If thou deny it, I will back to hell.
Faustus. Stay, Mephistophilis, and tell me, what good
    Will my soul do thy lord ?

Mephistophilis. Enlarge his kingdom.

Faustus. Is that the reason why he tempts us thus ?

Mephistophilis. " *Solamen miseris socios habuisse doloris.*" [1]

Faustus. [Why], have you any pain that torture
    others ?

Mephistophilis. As great as have the human souls of men.
  But tell me, Faustus, shall I have thy soul ?
  And I will be thy slave, and wait on thee,
  And give thee more than thou hast wit to ask.

Faustus. Ay, Mephistophilis, I give it thee.

Mephistophilis. Then, Faustus, stab thine arm courage-
    ously.
  And bind thy soul, that at some certain day
  Great Lucifer may claim it as his own ;
  And then be thou as great as Lucifer.

Faustus. Lo, Mephistophilis, for love of thee,
  I cut mine arm, and with my proper blood
  Assure my soul to be great Lucifer's,
  Chief lord and regent of perpetual night !
  View here the blood that trickles from mine arm,
  And let it be propitious for my wish.

Mephistophilis. But, Faustus, thou must
  Write it in manner of a deed of gift.

Faustus. Ay, so I will.   *[He takes a scroll and writes.]*
      But, Mephistophilis,
  My blood congeals, and I can write no more.

Mephistophilis. I'll fetch thee fire to dissolve it straight.
                                   Exit.

---

[1] *Solamen . . . doloris,* It is solace to the wretched to have companions
in their misery.

Faustus. What might the staying of my blood portend?
  Is it unwilling I should write this bill?
  Why streams it not, that I may write afresh?
  " Faustus gives to thee his soul "; ah, there it
     stay'd!
  Why shouldst thou not? is not thy soul thine own?
  Then write again, " Faustus gives to thee his soul."

    Enter MEPHISTOPHILIS *with a chafer of coals.*

Mephistophilis. Here's fire; come, Faustus, set it on.
Faustus. So, now the blood begins to clear again;
  Now will I make an end immediately.   [*He writes.*]
Mephistophilis [*aside*]. O, what will not I do to obtain
  his soul?
Faustus. Consummatum est; this bill is ended,
  And Faustus hath bequeath'd his soul to Lucifer.
  But what is this inscription on mine arm?
  " *Homo, fuge!* " Whither should I fly?
  If unto God, he'll throw me down to hell.
  My senses are deceiv'd; here's nothing writ:—
  I see it plain; here in this place is writ,
  " *Homo, fuge!* " Yet shall not Faustus fly.
Mephistophilis [*aside*]. I'll fetch him somewhat to delight
  his mind.   *Exit.*

    Enter [MEPHISTOPHILIS] *with* Devils, *giving crowns
    and rich apparel to* FAUSTUS, *and dance, and then
    depart.*

Faustus. Speak, Mephistophilis, what means this
  show?

Mephistophilis. Nothing, Faustus, but to delight thy
    mind withal,
  And to show thee what magic can perform.
Faustus. But may I raise up spirits when I please ?
Mephistophilis. Ay, Faustus, and do greater things than
    these.
Faustus. Then there's enough for a thousand souls.
  Here, Mephistophilis, receive this scroll,
  A deed of gift of body and of soul :
  But yet conditionally that thou perform
  All articles prescrib'd between us both.
Mephistophilis. Faustus, I swear by hell and Lucifer
  To effect all promises between us made !
Faustus. Then hear me read them :—

  On these conditions following.
      *First, that Faustus may be a spirit in form and sub-
  stance.*
      *Secondly, that Mephistophilis shall be his servant, and
  at his command.*
      *Thirdly, that Mephistophilis shall do for him, and
  bring him whatsoever.*
      *Fourthly, that he shall be in his chamber or house
  invisible.*
      *Lastly, that he shall appear to the said John Faustus
  at all times, in what form or shape soever he please.*
      *I, John Faustus, of Wertenberg, Doctor, by these
  presents, do give both body and soul to Lucifer, Prince
  of the East, and his minister Mephistophilis, and
  furthermore grant unto them that, twenty-four years*

*being expired, the articles above written inviolate, full
power to fetch or carry the said John Faustus, body and
soul, flesh, blood, or goods, into their habitation wheresoever.*   By me JOHN FAUSTUS.

Mephistophilis. Speak, Faustus, do you deliver this as
    your deed?

Faustus. Ay, take it, and the devil give thee good on't!

Mephistophilis. Now, Faustus, ask what thou wilt.

Faustus. First will I question with thee about hell.
  Tell me, where is the place that men call hell?

Mephistophilis. Under the heavens.

Faustus. Ay, but whereabout?

Mephistophilis. Within the bowels of these elements,
  Where we are tortur'd and remain for ever:
  Hell hath no limits, nor is circumscrib'd
  In one self place; for where we are is hell,
  And where hell is, [there] must we ever be:
  And, to conclude, when all the world dissolves,
  And every creature shall be purified,
  All places shall be hell that is not heaven.

Faustus. Come, I think hell's a fable.

Mephistophilis. Ay, think so, till experience change thy
    mind.

Faustus. Why, think'st thou, then, that Faustus shall
    be damn'd?

Mephistophilis. Ay, of necessity, for here's the scroll,
  Wherein thou hast given thy soul to Lucifer.

Faustus. Ay, and body too: but what of that?
  Think'st thou that Faustus is so fond to imagine

That, after this life, there is any pain ?

Tush, these are trifles and mere old wives' tales.

Mephistophilis. But, Faustus, I am an instance to prove
    the contrary ;

For I am damnèd, and am now in hell.

Faustus. How ? Now in hell ?

Nay, an this be hell, I'll willingly be damned here.

What !—walking, disputing——

But leaving off this, let me have a wife,

The fairest maid in Germany, for I

Am wanton and lascivious, and cannot

Live without a wife.

Mephistophilis. How, a wife ?

I prithee, Faustus, talk not of a wife.

Faustus. Nay, sweet Mephistophilis, fetch me one,

For I will have one.

Mephistophilis. Well, thou wilt have one. Sit there till
    I come,

I'll fetch thee a wife in the devil's name.

Enter with a Devil *dressed like a woman, with fireworks.*

Mephistophilis. Tell, Faustus, how dost thou like thy
    wife ?

Faustus. A plague on her for a hot whore.

Mephistophilis. Tut, Faustus,

Marriage is but a ceremonial toy,

If thou lovest me, think no more of it.

I'll cull thee out the fairest courtesans

And bring them every morning to thy bed :

She whom thine eye shall like, thy heart shall have,
Be she as chaste as was Penelope,
As wise as Saba, or as beautiful
As was bright Lucifer before his fall.
Hold, take this book, peruse it thoroughly :
> [*He lays it open on the table before Faustus.*]

The iterating of these lines brings gold ;
The framing of this circle on the ground
Brings whirlwinds, tempests, thunder, and lightning;
Pronounce this thrice devoutly to thyself,
And men in armour shall appear to thee,
Ready to execute what thou desir'st.

Faustus. Thanks, Mephistophilis ; yet fain would I have
A book wherein I might behold all spells
And incantations, that I might raise up
Spirits when I please.

Mephistophilis. Here they are in this book.
> (*There turn to them.*)

Faustus. Now would I have a book where I might see
all characters and planets of the heavens, that
I might know their motions and dispositions.

Mephistophilis. Here they are too.   (*Turn to them.*)

Faustus. Nay, let me have one book more,—and then
I have done,—wherein I might see all plants,
herbs, and trees, that grow upon the earth.

Mephistophilis. Here they be.

Faustus. O, thou art deceived.

Mephistohilis. Tut, I warrant thee.   (*Turn to them.*)

[SCENE II¹

Faustus' Study. FAUSTUS *and* MEPHISTOPHILIS,
the former at the window]

Faustus. When I behold the heavens, then I repent,
  And curse thee, wicked Mephistophilis,
  Because thou hast depriv'd me of those joys.
Mephistophilis. Why, Faustus.
  Thinkest thou heaven is such a glorious thing?
  I tell thee, [Faustus,] 'tis not half so fair
  As thou, or any man that breathes on earth.
Faustus. How prov'st thou that?
Mephistophilis. 'Twas made for man, therefore is man
      more excellent.
Faustus. If it were made for man, 'twas made for me:
  I will renounce this magic and repent.

(*Enter* GOOD ANGEL *and* EVIL ANGEL.)

Good Angel. Faustus, repent; yet God will pity thee.
Evil Angel. Thou art a spirit; God cannot pity thee.
Faustus. Who buzzeth in mine ears, I am a spirit?
  Be I a devil, yet God may pity me;
  Ay, God will pity me, if I repent.
Evil Angel. Ay, but Faustus never shall repent.

(*Exeunt.*)

Faustus. My heart's so harden'd, I cannot repent:

¹ The quarto of 1604 shows no break between this scene and the pre-
ceding, but a passage of time is evidently required, and there are indica-
tions that a comedy scene has dropped out.

Scarce can I name salvation, faith, or heaven,
But fearful echoes thunder in mine ears,
" Faustus, thou art damn'd ! "   Then swords, and
    knives,
Poison, guns, halters, and envenom'd steel
Are laid before me to despatch myself ;
And long ere this I should have slain myself,
Had not sweet pleasure conquer'd deep despair.
Have not I made blind Homer sing to me
Of Alexander's love and Oenon's death ?
And hath not he, that built the walls of Thebes,
With ravishing sound of his melodious harp,
Made music with my Mephistophilis ?
Why should I die, then, or basely despair ?
I am resolv'd ; Faustus shall ne'er repent.—
Come, Mephistophilis, let us dispute again,
And argue of divine astrology.
Tell me, are there many heavens above the moon ?
Are all celestial bodies but one globe,
As is the substance of this centric earth ?

Mephistophilis. As are the elements, such are the
    spheres,
Mutually folded in each other's orb,
And, Faustus,
All jointly move upon one axletree,
Whose terminine is term'd the world's wide pole ;
Nor are the names of Saturn, Mars, or Jupiter
Feign'd, but are erring stars.

Faustus. But, tell me, have they all one motion, both
    situ et tempore ?

Mephistophilis. All jointly move from east to west in
   twenty-four hours upon the poles of the world;
   but differ in their motion upon the poles of the
   zodiac.

Faustus. Tush,
   These slender trifles Wagner can decide:
   Hath Mephistophilis no greater skill?
   Who knows not the double motion of the planets?
   The first is finish'd in a natural day;
   The second thus: as Saturn in thirty years; Jupiter
   in twelve; Mars in four; the Sun, Venus, and
   Mercury in a year; the Moon in twenty-eight
   days. Tush, these are freshmen's suppositions.
   But, tell me, hath every sphere a dominion or
   intelligentia?

Mephistophilis. Ay.

Faustus. How many heavens or spheres are there?

Mephistophilis. Nine; the seven planets, the firmament,
   and the empyreal heaven.

Faustus. Well, resolve me in this question: why have
   we not conjunctions, oppositions, aspects,
   eclipses, all at one time, but in some years we
   have more, in some less?

Mephistophilis. *Per inaequalem motum respectu totius.*[1]

Faustus. Well, I am answered. Tell me who made the
   world?

Mephistophilis. I will not.

Faustus. Sweet Mephistophilis, tell me.

---

[1] *Per . . . totius*, Because of their unequal motion with regard to the
whole.

Mephistophilis. Move me not, for I will not tell thee.

Faustus. Villain, have I not bound thee to tell me any thing ?

Mephistophilis. Ay, that is not against our kingdom ; but this is.

Think thou on hell, Faustus, for thou art damned.

Faustus. Think, Faustus, upon God that made the world.

Mephistophilis. Remember this. (*Exit.*)

Faustus. Ay, go, accursèd spirit, to ugly hell !

'Tis thou hast damn'd distressèd Faustus' soul.

Is't not too late ?

Enter GOOD ANGEL *and* EVIL.

Evil Angel. Too late.

Good Angel. Never too late, if Faustus can repent.

Evil Angel. If thou repent, devils shall tear thee in pieces.

Good Angel. Repent, and they shall never raze thy skin. *Exeunt.*

Faustus. Ay, Christ, my Saviour,

Seek to save distressèd Faustus' soul !

Enter LUCIFER, BELZEBUB, *and* MEPHISTOPHILIS.

Lucifer. Christ cannot save thy soul, for he is just :

There's none but I have interest in the same.

Faustus. O, who art thou that look'st so terrible ?

Lucifer. I am Lucifer.

And this is my companion Prince in hell.

Faustus. O, Faustus, they are come to fetch away thy
    soul !

Lucifer. We come to tell thee thou dost injure us ;
    Thou talk'st of Christ, contráry to thy promise ;
    Thou shouldst not think of God : think of the
        devil.
    And of his dame too.

Faustus. Nor will I henceforth : pardon me in this,
    And Faustus vows never to look to heaven,
    Never to name God, or to pray to him,
    To burn his Scriptures, slay his ministers,
    And make my spirits pull his churches down.

Lucifer. Do so, and we will highly gratify thee.
    Faustus, we are come from hell to show thee
    some pastime : sit down, and thou shalt see
    all the Seven Deadly Sins appear in their proper
    shapes.

Faustus. That sight will be as pleasing unto me,
    As Paradise was to Adam, the first day
    Of his creation.

Lucifer. Talk not of Paradise nor creation ; but mark
    this show : talk of the devil, and nothing else.
    —Come away !

Enter the Seven Deadly Sins.

[*Lucifer.*] Now, Faustus, examine them of their several
    names and dispositions.

Faustus. What art thou, the first ?

Pride. I am Pride. I disdain to have any parents.
    I am like Ovid's flea ; I can creep into every

corner of a wench ; sometimes, like a periwig,
I sit upon her brow ; or like a fan of feathers,
I kiss her lips. Indeed I do—what do I not ?
But, fie, what a scent is here ! I'll not speak
another word, except the ground were perfumed,
and covered with cloth of arras.

Faustus. What art thou, the second ?

Covetousness. I am Covetousness, begotten of an old
churl in an old leathern bag : and, might I have
my wish, I would desire that this house and all
the people in it were turned to gold, that I
might lock you up in my good chest. O my
sweet gold !

Faustus. What art thou, the third ?

Wrath. I am Wrath. I had neither father nor mother :
I leapt out of a lion's mouth when I was scarce
half an hour old ; and ever since I have run up
and down the world with this case of rapiers,
wounding myself when I had nobody to fight
withal. I was born in hell ; and look to it, for
some of you shall be my father.

Faustus. What art thou, the fourth ?

Envy. I am Envy, begotten of a chimney-sweeper and
an oyster-wife. I cannot read, and therefore
wish all books were burnt. I am lean with
seeing others eat. O, that there would come a
famine through all the world, that all might die,
and I live alone, then thou shouldst see how
fat I would be ! But must thou sit, and I
stand ? Come down with a vengeance !

Faustus. Away, envious rascal ! —What art thou, the fifth ?

Gluttony. Who, I, sir ? I am Gluttony. My parents are all dead, and the devil a penny they have left me, but a bare pension, and that is thirty meals a day and ten bevers,—a small trifle to suffice nature. O, I come of a royal parentage ! My grandfather was a Gammon of Bacon, my grandmother a Hogshead of Claret-wine. My godfathers were these, Peter Pickle-herring and Martin Martlemas-beef. O, but my godmother, she was a jolly gentlewoman, and well beloved in every good town and city ; her name was Mistress Margery Marchbeer. Now, Faustus, thou hast heard all my progeny ; wilt thou bid me to supper ?

Faustus. No, I'll see thee hanged ; thou wilt eat up all my victuals.

Gluttony. Then the devil choke thee.

Faustus. Choke thyself, glutton !—What art thou, the sixth ?

Sloth. I am Sloth. I was begotten on a sunny bank, where I have lain ever since ; and you have done me great injury to bring me from thence : let me be carried thither again by Gluttony and Lechery. I'll not speak another word for a king's ransom.

Faustus. What are you, Mistress Minx, the seventh and last ?

Lechery. Who, I, sir ? I am one that loves an inch of

raw mutton better than an ell of fried stock fish, and the first letter of my name begins with Lechery.

Lucifer. Away, to hell, to hell !   *Exeunt the Sins.*
  Now, Faustus, how dost thou like this ?

Faustus. O, this feeds my soul !

Lucifer. Tut, Faustus, in hell is all manner of delight.

Faustus. O, might I see hell, and return again,
  How happy were I then !

Lucifer. Thou shalt ; I will send for thee at midnight.
  In meantime take this book ; peruse it throughly,
  And thou shalt turn thyself into what shape thou wilt.

Faustus. Great thanks, mighty Lucifer !
  This will I keep as chary as my life.

Lucifer. Farewell, Faustus, and think on the devil.

Faustus. Farewell, great Lucifer. Come, Mephistophilis.   *Exeunt omnes.*

[ACT III

PROLOGUE]

Enter WAGNER, *solus.*

Wagner. Learnèd Faustus,
  To know the secrets of astronomy
  Graven in the book of Jove's high firmament,
  Did mount himself to scale Olympus' top,
  Being seated in a chariot burning bright,
  Drawn by the strength of yoky dragons' necks,
  [He views the clouds, the planets, and the stars,
  The tropic zones, and quarters of the sky,
  From the bright circle of the hornèd moon,
  E'en to the height of *Primum Mobile* :
  And whirling round with this circumference,
  Within the concave compass of the pole,
  From east to west his dragons swiftly glide,
  And in eight days did bring him home again.
  Not long he stayed within his quiet house,
  To rest his bones after his weary toil,
  But new exploits do hale him out again,
  And mounted then upon a dragon's back,
  That with his wings did part the subtle air],

The lines enclosed in square brackets are taken from the quarto of 1616.

He now is gone to prove cosmography,
[That measures coasts, and kingdoms of the earth :]
And, as I guess, will first arrive at Rome,
To see the Pope and manner of his court,
And take some part of holy Peter's feast,
That to this day is highly solemniz'd.

                               Exit Wagner.

[SCENE I

Rome. The Pope's Palace]

Enter FAUSTUS *and* MEPHISTOPHILIS.

Faustus. Having now, my good Mephistophilis,
  Pass'd with delight the stately town of Trier,
  Environ'd round with airy mountain-tops,
  With walls of flint, and deep entrenchèd lakes,
  Not to be won by any conquering prince ;
  From Paris next, coasting the realm of France,
  We saw the river Maine fall into Rhine,
  Whose banks are set with groves of fruitful vines.
  Then up to Naples, rich Campania,
  Whose buildings fair and gorgeous to the eye,
  The streets straight forth, and paved with finest
    brick,
  Quarters the town in four equivalents ;
  There saw we learnèd Maro's golden tomb,
  The way he cut, an English mile in length,

Thorough a rock of stone, in one night's space ;
From thence to Venice, Padua, and the rest,
In one of which a sumptuous temple stands,
That threats the stars with her aspiring top.
Thus hitherto hath Faustus spent his time :
But tell me now, what resting-place is this ?
Hast thou, as erst I did command,
Conducted me within the walls of Rome ?

Mephistophilis. Faustus, I have ; and, because we will
  not be unprovided, I have taken up his Holiness'
  privy-chamber for our use.

Faustus. I hope his Holiness will bid us welcome.

Mephistophilis. Tut, 'tis no matter, man ; we'll be
  bold with his good cheer.

And now, my Faustus, that thou may'st perceive
What Rome containeth to delight thee with,
Know that this city stands upon seven hills
That underprop the groundwork of the same :
Over the which four stately bridges lean,
That make safe passage to each part of Rome :
Upon the bridge called Ponte Angelo
Erected is a castle passing strong,
Within whose walls such store of ordnance are,
And double cannons framed of carvèd brass,
As match the days within one cómplete year :
Besides the gates, and high pyrámidës,
Which Julius Cæsar brought from Africa.

Faustus. Now, by the kingdoms of infernal rule,
  Of Styx, of Acheron, and the fiery lake
  Of ever-burning Phlegethon, I swear

That I do long to see the monuments
And situation of bright-splendent Rome :
Come, therefore, let's away.

Mephistophilis. Nay, Faustus, stay ; I know you'd fain
    see the Pope,
And take some part of holy Peter's feast,
Where thou shalt see a troupe of bald-pate friars,
Whose *summum bonum* is in belly-cheer.

Faustus. Well, I am content to compass then some
    sport,
And by their folly make us merriment.
Then charm me, that I may be invisible to do what I
    please
Unseen of any whilst I stay in Rome.

Mephistophilis [making magical passes]. So, Faustus ; now
Do what thou wilt, thou shalt not be discerned.

    (*Sound a sennet. Enter the* POPE *and the* CARDINAL
       OF LORRAINE *to the banquet, with* Friars
       attending.)

Pope. My Lord of Lorraine, wilt please you draw near ?
Faustus. Fall to, and the Devil choke you an you
    spare.
Pope. How now ? Who's that which spake ? Friars,
    look about.
Friars [searching busily]. Here's nobody, if it like your
    Holiness.
Pope. My Lord, here is a dainty dish
    Was sent me from the Bishop of Milan.
Faustus. I thank you, sir.   *Snatch it.*

Pope. How now ?

Who's that which snatched the meat from me ?

Will no man look ?—My Lord, this dish was sent
me.

From the Cardinal of Florence.

Faustus. You say true, I'll ha't.   [*He snatches the dish.*

Pope. What, again ?—My Lord, I'll drink to your
grace.

Faustus. I'll pledge your Grace.   [*He snatches the cup.*

Lorraine. My Lord, it may be some ghost newly crept
out of Purgatory come to beg a pardon of your
Holiness.

Pope. It may be so.   Friars, prepare a dirge

To lay the fury of this ghost.   Once again, my Lord,
fall to.   *The Pope crosseth himself.*

Faustus. What, are you crossing of yourself ?

Well, use that trick no more, I would advise you.

Cross again.

Faustus. Well, there's the second time.   Aware the
third.

I give you fair warning.

*Cross again, and Faustus hits him a box of the ear,
and they all run away.*

Faustus. Come on, Mephistophilis, what shall we
do ?

Mephistophilis. Nay, I know not.   We shall be curst
with bell, book, and candle.

Faustus. How ! bell, book, and candle—candle, book,
and bell,—

Forward and backward, to curse Faustus to hell !

Anon you shall hear a hog grunt, a calf bleat, and an
    ass bray,
Because it is Saint Peter's holiday.

Enter all the Friars *to sing the Dirge.*

irst Friar. Come, brethren, let's about our business
    with good devotion.

Sing this.

*Cursed be he that stole away his Holiness' meat from the
    table !*
    Maledicat Dominus !
Cursed be he that struck his Holiness a blow on the face !
    Maledicat Dominus !
Cursed be he that took Friar Sandelo a blow on the pate !
    Maledicat Dominus !
Cursed be he that disturbeth our holy dirge !
    Maledicat Dominus !
Cursed be he that took away his Holiness' wine !
    Maledicat Dominus !
      Et omnes Sancti !   Amen !

[*Mephistophilis and Faustus*] *beat the* Friars, *and fling
    fireworks among them ; and so exeunt.*

[SCENE II

An Inn-yard]

Enter ROBIN *the Ostler with a book in his hand.*

Robin. O, this is admirable ! here I ha' stolen one of
Dr. Faustus's conjuring books, and i' faith I
mean to search some circles for my own use.
Now will I make all the maidens in our parish
dance at my pleasure, stark naked before me;
and so by that means I shall see more than e'er
I felt or saw yet.

Enter RALPH, *calling* ROBIN.

Ralph. Robin, prithee come away ; there's a gentleman tarries to have his horse, and he would
have his things rubbed and made clean. He
keeps such a chafing with my mistress about it;
and she has sent me to look thee out. Prithee
come away.

Robin. Keep out, keep out, or else you are blown up,
you are dismembered, Ralph. Keep out, for I
am about a roaring piece of work.

Ralph. Come, what dost thou with that same book?
thou can'st not read.

Robin. Yes, my master and mistress shall find that

can read, he for his forehead, she for her private study. She's born to bear with me, or else my art fails.

alph. Why, Robin, what book is that ?

obin. What book ! why the most intolerable book for conjuring that e'er was invented by any brimstone devil.

alph. Can'st thou conjure with it ?

obin. I can do all these things easily with it. First, I can make thee drunk with ippocras at any tabern in Europe for nothing ; that's one of my conjuring works.

alph. Our Master Parson says that's nothing.

obin. True, Ralph ; and more, Ralph, if thou hast any mind to Nan Spit, our kitchenmaid, then turn her and wind her to thy own use as often as thou wilt, and at midnight.

alph. O brave Robin, shall I have Nan Spit, and to mine own use ? On that condition I'd feed thy devil with horsebread as long as he lives, of free cost.

Robin. No more, sweet Ralph. Let's go and make clean our boots, which lie foul upon our hands, and then to our conjuring in the Devil's name.

                             Exeunt.

[SCENE III] [1]

Enter ROBIN *and* RALPH *with a silver goblet.*

Robin. Come, Ralph, did not I tell thee we were fo
ever made by this Doctor Faustus' book ? *ecc
signum*, here's a simple purchase for horsekeepers
our horses shall eat no hay as long as this lasts.
Ralph. But, Robin, here comes the vintner.
Robin. Hush ! I'll gull him supernaturally.

Enter Vintner.

Drawer, I hope all is paid : God be with you ; come
Ralph.
Vintner. Soft, sir ; a word with you. I must yet hav
a goblet paid from you, ere you go.
Robin. I, a goblet, Ralph ! I, a goblet ! I scorn you
and you are but a — —, &c. I, a goblet ! searcl
me.
Vintner. I mean so, sir, with your favour.
                                            [*Searches him.*
Robin. How say you now ?
Vintner. I must say somewhat to your fellow. You
sir !
Ralph. Me, sir ! me, sir ! search your fill. [*Vintne
searches him.*] Now, sir, you may be ashamed t
burden honest men with a matter of truth.

[1] Either Scene II. or Scene III. appears to be misplaced. The forme
might follow Act II., Scene II.

Vintner. Well, t'one of you hath this goblet about you.

Robin [*aside*]. You lie, drawer, 'tis afore me—Sirrah
   you, I'll teach you to impeach honest men ;—
   stand by ;—I'll scour you for a goblet !—stand
   aside you had best, I charge you in the name of
   Belzebub. [*Aside to Ralph.*] Look to the goblet,
   Ralph.

Vintner. What mean you, sirrah ?

Robin. I'll tell you what I mean. [*Reads from the book.*]
   Sanctobulorum Periphrasticon—Nay, I'll tickle you,
   Vintner. [*Aside to Ralph.*] Look to the goblet,
   Ralph.—*Polypragmos Belseborams framanto pacosti-*
   phos tostu, Mephistophilis, &c.

   Enter MEPHISTOPHILIS, *sets squibs at their backs*,
   [*and then exit.*] *They run about.*

Vintner. *O nomine Domini !* what meanest thou, Robin ?
   thou hast no goblet.

Ralph. *Peccatum peccatorum !* Here's thy goblet, good
   Vintner. [*Gives it to him.   Exit Vintner.*]

Robin. *Misericordia pro nobis !* What shall I do ? Good
   Devil, forgive me now, and I'll never rob thy
   library more.

   Enter to them MEPHISTOPHILIS.

Mephistophilis. Monarch of hell, under whose black
   survey
  Great potentates do kneel with awful fear,

Upon whose altars thousand souls do lie,
How am I vexèd with these villains' charms ?
From Constantinople am I hither come
Only for pleasure of these damnèd slaves.

Robin. How, from Constantinople ! You have had
    great journey : will you take sixpence in you
    purse to pay for your supper, and begone ?

Mephistophilis. Well, villains, for your presumption,
    transform thee into an ape, and thee into a dog
    and so begone.   *Exi*

Robin. How, into an ape ; that's brave ! I'll have fin
    sport with the boys. I'll get nuts and apple
    enow.

Ralph. And I must be a dog.

Robin. I'faith thy head will never be out of the pottag
    pot.   *Exeunt*

[ACT IV

PROLOGUE.]

Enter CHORUS.

When Faustus had with pleasure ta'en the view
Of rarest things, and royal courts of kings,
He stay'd his course, and so returnèd home ;
Where such as bear his absence but with grief,
I mean his friends and near'st companions,
Did gratulate his safety with kind words,
And in their conference of what befell,
Touching his journey through the world and air,
They put forth questions of astrology,
Which Faustus answer'd with such learnèd skill
As they admired and wonder'd at his wit.
Now is his fame spread forth in every land :
Amongst the rest the Emperor is one,
Carolus the Fifth, at whose palace now
Faustus is feasted 'mongst his noblemen.
What there he did, in trial of his art,
I leave untold ; your eyes shall see perform'd. *Exit.*

In the Quarto this Prologue precedes Act. III., Scene II.

[SCENE I]

[The Emperor's Palace.]

(*Enter the* EMPEROR, FAUSTUS, *and a* Knight, *with*
Attendants.)

The Emperor. Master Doctor Faustus, I have heard
strange report of thy knowledge in the Black
Art, how that none in my Empire, nor in the
whole world, can compare with thee for the rare
effects of magic. They say thou hast a familiar
spirit, by whom thou canst accomplish what
thou list. This therefore is my request, that
thou let me see some proof of thy skill, that
mine eyes may be witnesses to confirm what
mine ears have heard reported ; and here I
swear to thee, by the honour of mine imperial
crown, that whatever thou doest thou shalt be
no ways prejudiced or indamaged.

Knight (*aside*). I' faith, he looks much like a conjurer.

Faustus. My gracious sovereign, though I must confess myself far inferior to the report men have
published, and nothing answerable to the
honour of your Imperial Majesty ; yet, for that
love and duty binds me thereunto, I am content
to do whatsoever your Majesty shall command
me.

The Emperor. Then, Doctor Faustus, mark what I shall
say.

     As I was sometime solitary set

Within my closet, sundry thoughts arose
About the honour of mine ancestors,
How they had won by prowess such exploits,
Got such riches, subdued so many kingdoms,
As we that do succeed, or they that shall
Hereafter possess our throne, shall
(I fear me) never attain to that degree
Of high renown and great authority :
Amongst which kings is Alexander the Great,
Chief spectacle of the world's pre-eminence,
The bright shining of whose glorious acts
Lightens the world with his reflecting beams,
As when I hear but motion made of him,
It grieves my soul I never saw the man :
If, therefore, thou, by cunning of thine art,
Canst raise this man from hollow vaults below,
Where lies entomb'd this famous conqueror,
And bring with him his beauteous paramour,
Both in their right shapes, gesture, and attire
They used to wear during their time of life,
Thou shalt both satisfy my just desire,
And give me cause to praise thee whilst I live.

Faustus. My gracious Lord, I am ready to accomplish
      your request, so far forth as by art and power of
      my spirit I am able to perform.

Knight (aside). I' faith, that's just nothing at all.

Faustus. But if it like your Grace, it is not in my
      ability to present before your eyes the true sub-
      stantial bodies of those two deceased princes.
      which long since are consumed to dust.

Knight (aside). Ay, marry, Master Doctor, now there's
    a sign of grace in you when you will confess the
    truth.

Faustus. But such spirits as can lively resemble
    Alexander and his paramour shall appear before
    your Grace, in that manner that they best lived
    in, in their most flourishing estate ; which I
    doubt not shall sufficiently content your Im-
    perial Majesty.

The Emperor. Go to, Master Doctor ; let me see them
    presently.

Knight. Do you hear, Master Doctor ? You bring
    Alexander and his paramour before the Emperor ?

Faustus. How then, sir ?

Knight. I' faith, that's as true as Diana turned me to
    a stag.

Faustus. No, sir, but when Actæon died he left the
    horns for you. Mephistophilis, begone.

Exit Mephistophilis.

Knight. Nay, an you go to conjuring, I'll be gone.

Exit Knight.

Faustus. I'll meet with you anon for interrupting me
    so.—Here they are, my gracious Lord.

(*Enter* MEPHISTOPHILIS, *with* Alexander *and his*
    Paramour.)

The Emperor. Master Doctor, I heard this lady, while
    she lived, had a wart or mole in her neck. How
    shall I know whether it be so, or no ?

Faustus. Your Highness may boldly go and see.

> [*The Emperor does so.*] *Exit Alexander* [*and the Lady*].

The Emperor. Sure, these are no spirits, but the true substantial bodies of those two deceased princes.

Faustus. Wilt please your Highness now to send for the Knight that was so pleasant with me here of late ?

The Emperor. One of you, call him forth.

> *Enter the* Knight *with a pair of horns on his head.*

The Emperor. How now, sir Knight ? Why, I had thought thou hadst been a bachelor, but now I see thou hast a wife that not only gives thee horns but makes thee wear them. Feel on thy head.

Knight [*to Faustus*]. Thou damned wretch, and execrable dog,

Bred in the concave of some monstrous rock ;

How darest thou thus abuse a Gentleman ?

Villain, I say, undo what thou hast done.

Faustus. Oh, not so fast, sir ; there's no haste. But good, are you remembered how you crossed me in my conference with the Emperor ? I think I have met with you for it.

The Emperor. Good Master Doctor, at my entreaty release him ; he hath done penance sufficient.

Faustus. My Gracious Lord, not so much for the injury he offered me here in your presence, as to

delight you with some mirth, hath Faustus
worthily requited this injurious knight ; which
being all I desire, I am content to release him
of his horns. And, sir Knight, hereafter speak
well of scholars. Mephistophilis, transform
him straight. [*Mephistophilis removes the horns.*]
Now, my good Lord, having done my duty, I
humbly take my leave.

The Emperor. Farewell, Master Doctor. Yet ere you
go

Expect from me a bounteous reward. *Exit Emperor.*

Faustus. Now, Mephistophilis, the restless course
That time doth run with calm and silent foot,
Short'ning my days and thread of vital life,
Calls for the payment of my latest years :
Therefore, sweet Mephistophilis, let us
Make haste to Wertenberg.

Mephistophilis. What, will you go on horse-back or on
foot ?

Faustus. Nay, till I'm past this fair and pleasant green
I'll walk on foot.

[SCENE II

Faustus' House]

Enter a Horse-Courser.

Horse-Courser. I have been all this day seeking one
Master Fustian.

[*Enter* FAUSTUS *and* MEPHISTOPHILIS.]

Mass, see where he is ! God save you, Master
    Doctor !

Faustus. What, horse-courser ! You are well met.

Horse-Courser. Do you hear, sir ? I have brought you
    forty dollars for your horse.

Faustus. I cannot sell him so : if thou likest him for
    fifty, take him.

Horse-Courser. Alas, sir, I have no more.—I pray you
    speak for me.

Mephistophilis. I pray you let him have him : he is an
    honest fellow, and he has a great charge, neither
    wife nor child.

Faustus. Well, come, give me your money. [*He does so.*]
    My boy will deliver him to you. But I must
    tell you one thing before you have him ; ride
    him not into the water at any hand.

Horse-Courser. Why, sir, will he not drink of all
    waters ?

Faustus. O yes, he will drink of all waters, but ride
    him not into the water : ride him over hedge or
    ditch, or where thou wilt, but not into the
    water.

Horse-Courser. Well, sir.—[*Aside.*] Now am I made
    man for ever : I'll not leave my horse for twice
    forty : if he had but the quality of hey-ding-
    ding, hey-ding-ding, I'd make a brave living
    on him : he has a buttock as slick as an eel.—
    Well, God b' wi' ye, sir, your boy will deliver

him me. But hark you, sir, if my horse be sic'
or ill at ease, if I bring his water to you, you'
tell me what it is ?

Faustus. Away, you villain ; what, dost think I am
     horse-doctor ?   *Exit Horse-Courser*

    What art thou, Faustus, but a man condemned t
     die ?

    Thy fatal time doth draw to final end ;

    Despair doth drive distrust unto my thoughts :

    Confound these passions with a quiet sleep :

    Tush, Christ did call the thief upon the cross ;

    Then rest thee, Faustus, quiet in conceit.

                     Sleeps in his chair

     Enter Horse-Courser, *all wet, crying.*

Horse-Courser. Alas, alas ! Doctor Fustian quotha
    mass, Doctor Lopus was never such a doctor
    has given me a purgation has purged me of forty
    dollars ; I shall never see them more. But yet
    like an ass as I was, I would not be ruled by him
    for he bade me I should ride him into no water :
    now I, thinking my horse had had some rare
    quality that he would not have had me knowr
    of, I, like a venturous youth, rid him into the
    deep pond at the town's end. I was no sooner
    in the middle of the pond, but my horse
    vanished away, and I sat upon a bottle of hay,
    never so near drowning in my life. But I'll seek
    out my Doctor, and have my forty dollars again,

or I'll make it the dearest horse !—O, yonder is
his snipper-snapper.—Do you hear ? you hey-
pass, where's your master ?

Mephistophilis. Why, sir, what would you ? You cannot
speak with him.

Horse-Courser. But I will speak with him.

Mephistophilis. Why, he's fast asleep. Come some other
time.

Horse-Courser. I'll speak with him now, or I'll break his
glass windows about his ears.

Mephistophilis. I tell thee he has not slept this eight
nights.

Horse-Courser. An he have not slept this eight weeks
I'll speak with him.

Mephistophilis. See where he is, fast asleep.

Horse-Courser. Ay, this is he. God save you, Master
Doctor, Master Doctor, Master Doctor Fustian !
—Forty dollars, forty dollars for a bottle of
hay !

Mephistophilis. Why, thou seest he hears thee not.

Horse-Courser. So ho, ho !—so ho, ho ! (*Holla in his
ear.*) No, will you not wake ? I'll make you
wake ere I go. (*Pull him by the leg, and pull it
away.*) Alas, I am undone ! What shall I do ?

Faustus. O my leg, my leg ! Help, Mephistophilis !
call the officers. My leg, my leg !

Mephistophilis. Come, villain, to the constable.

Horse-Courser. O lord, sir, let me go, and I'll give you
forty dollars more.

Mephistophilis. Where be they ?

Horse-Courser. I have none about me. Come to my
    ostry and I'll give them you.

Mephistophilis. Begone quickly. *Horse-Courser runs away.*

Faustus. What, is he gone? Farewell he! Faustus has
    his leg again, and the horse-courser, I take it, a
    bottle of hay for his labour. Well, this trick
    shall cost him forty dollars more.

Enter WAGNER.

How now, Wagner, what's the news with thee?

Wagner. Sir, the Duke of Vanholt doth earnestly
    entreat your company.

Faustus. The Duke of Vanholt! an honourable gentle-
    man, to whom I must be no niggard of my
    cunning. Come, Mephistophilis, let's away
    to him.   *Exeunt.*

[SCENE III

The Duke of Vanholt's Palace

FAUSTUS *and* MEPHISTOPHILIS.] *Enter to them the*
    DUKE *and the* DUCHESS. *The* DUKE *speaks.*

Duke. Believe me, Master Doctor, this merriment hath
    much pleased me.

Faustus. My gracious lord, I am glad it contents you

so well. But it may be, madam, you take no
delight in this. I have heard that great bellied
women do long for some dainties or other: what
is it, madam? tell me, and you shall have it.

Duchess. Thanks, good Master Doctor: and, for I see
your courteous intent to pleasure me, I will not
hide from you the thing my heart desires; and,
were it now summer, as it is January, and the
dead time of winter, I would desire no better
meat than a dish of ripe grapes.

Faustus. Alas, madam, that's nothing.—[*Aside*] Mephistophilis, begone. (*Exit Mephistophilis.*) Were
it a greater thing than this, so it would content you, you should have it.

(*Enter* MEPHISTOPHILIS *with grapes.*)

[*Faustus.*] Here they be, madam: will't please you
taste on them?

Duke. Believe me, Master Doctor, this makes me
wonder above the rest, that being in the dead
time of winter and in the month of January,
how you should come by these grapes.

Faustus. If it like your grace, the year is divided into
two circles over the whole world, that, when it
is here winter with us, in the contrary circle it
is summer with them, as in India, Saba, and
farther countries in the east; and by means of
a swift spirit that I have I had them brought
hither, as you see.—How do you like them,
madam? be they good?

Duchess. Believe me, Master Doctor, they be the best
    grapes that e'er I tasted in my life before.
Faustus. I am glad they content you so, madam.
Duke. Come, madame, let us in, where you must well
    reward this learned man for the great kindness
    he hath shewed to you.
Duchess. And so I will, my lord, and whilst I live
  Rest beholding for this courtesy.
Faustus. I humbly thank your Grace.
Duke. Come, Master Doctor, follow us and receive
    your reward.   *Exeunt.*

[ACT V

SCENE I

Faustus' Study]

Enter WAGNER, *solus.*

Wagner. I think my master means to die shortly,
  For he hath given to me all his goods :
  And yet, methinks, if that death were near,
  He would not banquet, and carouse, and swill
  Amongst the students, as even now he doth,
  Who are at supper with such belly-cheer
  As Wagner ne'er beheld in all his life.
  See, where they come ! belike the feast is ended.
                          [Exit Wagner.]

Enter FAUSTUS *with two or three* Scholars [*and*
            MEPHISTOPHILIS.]

First Scholar. Master Doctor Faustus,
  Since our conference about fair ladies,
  Which was the beautiful'st in all the world,
  We have determined with ourselves that Helen

Of Greece was the admirablest lady that ever lived.
Therefore, Master Doctor, if you will do us that
    favour,
As to let us see that peerless dame of Greece,
Whom all the world admires for majesty,
We should think ourselves much beholding unto
    you.

Faustus. Gentlemen,
For that I know your friendship is unfeign'd,
And Faustus' custom is not to deny
The just requests of those that wish him well,
You shall behold that peerless dame of Greece,
No otherways for pomp and majesty
Than when Sir Paris crossed the seas with her,
And brought the spoils to rich Dardania.
Be silent, then, for danger is in words.

            Music sounds, and Helen passeth over the stage.

Third Scholar. Too simple is my wit to tell her praise,
Whom all the world admires for majesty.

Second Scholar. No marvel though the angry Greeks
    pursued
With ten years' war the rape of such a queen,
Whose heavenly beauty passeth all compare.

First Scholar. Since we have seen the pride of Nature's
    works,
And only paragon of excellence,

            Enter an Old Man.

Let us depart ; and for this glorious deed
Happy and blest be Faustus evermore !

Faustus. Gentlemen, farewell: the same I wish to
    you.   *Exeunt Scholars.*

Old Man. Ah, Doctor Faustus, that I might prevail
  To guide thy steps unto the way of life,
  By which sweet path thou mayst attain the goal
  That shall conduct thee to celestial rest.
  Break heart, drop blood, and mingle it with tears !—
  Tears falling from repentant heaviness
  Of thy most vile and loathsome filthiness,—
  The stench whereof corrupts the inward soul
  With such flagitious crimes of heinous sins
  As no commiseration may expel,
  But mercy, Faustus, of thy Saviour sweet,
  Whose blood alone must wash away thy guilt.

Faustus. Where are thou, Faustus ? wretch, what hast
    thou done ?
  Damn'd art thou, Faustus, damn'd ! despair and die !
  Hell calls for right, and with a roaring voice
  Says, " Faustus, come ; thine hour is come " ;
  And Faustus now will come to do thee right.
               Mephistophilis gives him a dagger.

Old Man. Ah, stay, good Faustus, stay thy desperate
    steps !
  I see an angel hovers o'er thy head,
  And, with a vial full of precious grace,
  Offers to pour the same into thy soul :
  Then call for mercy, and avoid despair.

Faustus. Ay, my sweet friend, I feel
  Thy words to comfort my distressèd soul !
  Leave me a while to ponder on my sins.

Old Man. I go, sweet Faustus ; but with heavy cheer,
 Fearing the ruin of thy hopeless soul.

           [Exit Old Man.]

Faustus. Accursèd Faustus, where is mercy now ?
 I do repent ; and yet I do despair :
 Hell strives with grace for conquest in my breast :
 What shall I do to shun the snares of death ?

Mephistophilis. Thou traitor, Faustus, I arrest thy
  soul
 For disobedience to my sovereign lord :
 Revolt, or I'll in piecemeal tear thy flesh.

Faustus. Sweet Mephistophilis, entreat thy lord
 To pardon my unjust presumption,
 And with my blood again I will confirm
 My former vow I made to Lucifer.

Mephistophilis. Do it, then, quickly, with unfeignèd
  heart,
 Lest greater danger do attend thy drift.

Faustus. Torment, sweet friend, that base and crooked
  age,[1]
 That durst dissuade me from thy Lucifer,
 With greatest torments that our hell affords.

Mephistophilis. His faith is great ; I cannot touch his
  soul ;
 But what I may afflict his body with
 I will attempt, which is but little worth.

Faustus. One thing, good servant, let me crave of
  thee,
 To glut the longing of my heart's desire,

     [1] *Age*, Old man.

That I may have unto my paramour
That heavenly Helen which I saw of late
Whose sweet embracings may extinguish clean
These thoughts that do dissuade me from my vow,
And keep mine oath I made to Lucifer.

Mephistophilis. Faustus, this, or what else thou shalt
    desire,
    Shall be perform'd in twinkling of an eye.

(*Enter* Helen.)

Faustus. Was this the face that launch'd a thousand
    ships,
    And burnt the topless towers of Ilium ?—
    Sweet Helen, make me immortal with a kiss.—
    Her lips suck forth my soul : see where it flees !—
    Come, Helen, come, give me my soul again.
    Here will I dwell, for heaven is in these lips,
    And all is dross that is not Helena.

Enter Old Man.

I will be Paris, and for love of thee,
Instead of Troy, shall Wertenberg be sack'd ;
And I will combat with weak Menelaus,
And wear thy colours on my plumèd crest ;
Yea, I will wound Achilles in the heel,
And then return to Helen for a kiss.
O, thou art fairer than the evening air
Clad in the beauty of a thousand stars ;
Brighter art thou than flaming Jupiter

When he appear'd to hapless Semele :
More lovely than the monarch of the sky
In wanton Arethusa's azured arms ;
And none but thou shalt be my paramour !

                             Exeunt.

Old Man. Accursèd Faustus, miserable man,
    That from thy soul exclud'st the grace of Heaven,
    And fly'st the throne of his tribunal-seat !

               Enter the Devils.

Satan begins to sift me with his pride :
As in this furnace God shall try my faith,
My faith, vile hell, shall triumph over thee.
         [*He defies the Devils, who shrink from him.*]
Ambitious fiends, see how the heavens smile
At your repulse, and laugh your state to scorn !
Hence, hell ! for hence I fly unto my God.   *Exeunt.*

[SCENE II

Faustus' Study]

Enter FAUSTUS *with the* Scholars.

Faustus. Ah, gentlemen !
First Scholar. What ails Faustus ?
Faustus. Ah, my sweet chamber-fellow, had I lived
       with thee, then had I lived still ! but now I die

    eternally. [*In horror.*] Look, comes he not?
    comes he not?

Second Scholar. What means Faustus?

Third Scholar. Belike he is grown into some sickness
    by being over solitary.

First Scholar. If it be so, we'll have physicians to cure
    him.—'Tis but a surfeit; never fear, man.

Faustus. A surfeit of deadly sin, that hath damned
    both body and soul.

Second Scholar. Yet, Faustus, look up to heaven;
    remember God's mercies are infinite.

Faustus. But Faustus' offence can ne'er be pardoned.
    The serpent that tempted Eve may be saved,
    but not Faustus. Ah, gentlemen, hear me with
    patience, and tremble not at my speeches.
    Though my heart pants and quivers to remember
    that I have been a student here these thirty
    years, O, would I had never seen Wertenberg,
    never read book: and what wonders I have
    done, all Germany can witness, yea, all the
    world; for which Faustus hath lost both
    Germany and the world; yea, heaven itself,—
    heaven, the seat of God, the throne of the
    blessed, the kingdom of joy; and must remain
    in hell for ever,—hell, ah, hell for ever! Sweet
    friends, what shall become of Faustus, being in
    hell for ever?

Third Scholar. Yet, Faustus, call on God.

Faustus. On God, whom Faustus hath abjured! on
    God, whom Faustus hath blasphemed! Ah,

my God, I would weep! but the devil draws
in my tears.   Gush forth blood, instead of
tears! yea, life and soul—O, he stays my
tongue! I would lift up my hands; but see,
they hold them, they hold them!

All. Who, Faustus?

Faustus. Lucifer and Mephistophilis. Ah, gentlemen,
I gave them my soul for my cunning!

All. God forbid!

Faustus. God forbade it, indeed; but Faustus hath
done it: for vain pleasure of twenty-four years
hath Faustus lost eternal joy and felicity. I
writ them a bill with mine own blood: the
date is expired; the time will come, and he will
fetch me.

First Scholar. Why did not Faustus tell us of this
before, that divines might have prayed for
thee?

Faustus. Oft have I thought to have done so, but the
devil threatened to tear me in pieces, if I named
God; to fetch both body and soul, if I once
gave ear to divinity: and now 'tis too late.
Gentlemen, away, lest you perish with me.

Second Scholar. O, what shall we do to [save] Faustus?

Faustus. Talk not of me, but save yourselves, and
depart.

Third Scholar. God will strengthen me; I will stay
with Faustus.

First Scholar. Tempt not God, sweet friend; but let
us into the next room, and there pray for him.

Faustus. Ay, pray for me, pray for me ; and what
     noise soever ye hear, come not unto me, for
     nothing can rescue me.

Second Scholar. Pray thou, and we will pray that God
     may have mercy upon thee.

Faustus. Gentlemen, farewell : if I live till morning,
  I'll visit you ; if not, Faustus is gone to hell.

All. Faustus, farewell.   *Exeunt Scholars.*
                       The clock strikes eleven.

Faustus. Ah, Faustus,
  Now hast thou but one bare hour to live,
  And then thou must be damn'd perpetually !
  Stand still, you ever-moving spheres of heaven,
  That time may cease, and midnight never come ;
  Fair Nature's eye, rise, rise again, and make
  Perpetual day ; or let this hour be but
  A year, a month, a week, a natural day,
  That Faustus may repent and save his soul !
  O lente, lente currite, noctis equi ! [1]
  The stars move still, time runs, the clock will strike,
  The devil will come, and Faustus must be damn'd.
  O, I'll leap up to my God !—Who pulls me down ?—
  See, see, where Christ's blood streams in the
     firmament !
  One drop would save my soul, half a drop : ah, my
     Christ !—
  Rend not my heart for naming of my Christ !
  Yet will I call on him : O, spare me, Lucifer !—
  Where is it now ? 'tis gone : and see, where God

[1] *O lente . . . equi,* O run slowly, slowly, ye horses of the night.

Stretcheth out his arm, and bends his ireful brows !
Mountains and hills, come, come, and fall on me,
And hide me from the heavy wrath of God !
No, no !
Then will I headlong run into the earth :
Earth, gape ! O, no, it will not harbour me !
You stars that reign'd at my nativity,
Whose influence hath allotted death and hell,
Now draw up Faustus, like a foggy mist,
Into the entrails of yon lab'ring clouds,
That, when you vomit forth into the air,
My limbs may issue from your smoky mouths,
So that my soul may but ascend to heaven !

                         The watch strikes.

Ah, half the hour is past ! 'twill all be passed anon.
O God,
If thou wilt not have mercy on my soul,
Yet for Christ's sake, whose blood hath ransom'd me
Impose some end to my incessant pain ;
Let Faustus live in hell a thousand years,
A hundred thousand, and at last be saved !
Oh, no end is limited to damnèd souls !
Why wert thou not a creature wanting soul ?
Or why is this immortal that thou hast ?
Ah, Pythagoras' metempsychosis,
Were that true,
This soul should fly from me, and I be changed
Unto some brutish beast ! all beasts are happy,
For, when they die,
Their souls are soon dissolved in elements ;

But mine must live still to be plagued in hell.
Cursed be the parents that engender'd me!
No, Faustus, curse thyself, curse Lucifer
That hath deprived thee of the joys of heaven.

The clock striketh twelve.

O, it strikes, it strikes! Now, body, turn to air,
Or Lucifer will bear thee quick to hell!

Thunder and lightning.

O soul, be changed into little water-drops,
And fall into the ocean, ne'er be found!

Enter Devils.

My God, my God, look not so fierce on me!
Adders and serpents, let me breathe a while!
Ugly hell, gape not!—Come not, Lucifer!—
I'll burn my books!—Ah, Mephistophilis!

Exeunt with him.

Enter CHORUS.

Cut is the branch that might have grown full
        straight,
And burnèd is Apollo's laurel-bough,
That sometime grew within this learnèd man.
Faustus is gone: regard his hellish fall,
Whose fiendful fortune may exhort the wise,
Only to wonder at unlawful things,
Whose deepness doth entice such forward wits
To practise more than heavenly power permits.

Terminat hora diem; terminat auctor opus.

EDWARD THE SECOND

"*Edward II.*" was probably written and first performed about 1591-92. Marlowe's name appeared on all the early editions, and the whole play is generally accepted as his. It is based almost entirely on the "*Chronicles of England, Scotland, and Ireland,*" by Raphael Holinshed (1577), from which Shakespeare drew so much material for his " histories."

The earliest known edition was published in octavo in 1594, but there was probably an edition in 1593. The octavo of 1594 is the editio princeps from which all subsequent editions have been derived, and it has been followed very closely by the present editor, who has used the type-facsimile prepared by W. W. Greg, Malone Society Reprints, 1925. Spelling, punctuation, and use of capitals have been modernized, and minor emendations have been made without notice, but nothing has been omitted, and all editorial additions have been enclosed in "square" brackets.

The troublesome

raigne and lamentable death of
Edward *the second*, *K*ing of
England : with the tragicall
fall of proud Mortimer:

As it was sundrie times publiquely acted
in the honourable citie of London , *by the*
right honourable the Earle of Pem-
brooke *his seruants.*

Written by Chri. Marlow *Gent.*

Imprinted at London for. *William Iones,*
dwelling neere Holbourne conduit at the
signe of the Gunne. 1594

[DRAMATIS PERSONÆ

KING EDWARD THE SECOND.
PRINCE EDWARD, *his Son, afterwards* KING EDWARD THE THIRD.
EARL OF KENT, *Brother of King Edward the Second.*
GAVESTON.
WARWICK.
LANCASTER.
PEMBROKE.
ARUNDEL.
LEICESTER.
BERKELEY.
MORTIMER *senior.*
MORTIMER *junior, his Nephew.*
SPENCER *senior.*
SPENCER *junior, his Son.*
ARCHBISHOP OF CANTERBURY.
BISHOP OF COVENTRY.
BISHOP OF WINCHESTER.
BALDOCK.
BEAUMONT.
TRUSSEL.
GURNEY.
MATREVIS.
LIGHTBORN.
SIR JOHN OF HAINAULT.
LEVUNE.
RICE AP HOWEL.
*Abbot, Monks, Herald, Lords, Poor Men, James, Mower, Champion,
    Messengers, Soldiers, and Attendants.*
QUEEN ISABELLA, *Wife of King Edward the Second.*
NIECE TO KING EDWARD THE SECOND, *daughter of the Duke of
    Gloucester.*
Ladies.]

The Troublesome Reign and Lamentable Death of Edward the Second, King of England : with the tragical fall of proud Mortimer.

[ACT I

SCENE I

A Street in London]

Enter GAVESTON, *reading on a letter that was brought him from the King.*

Gaveston. " My father is deceas'd. Come, Gaveston,
And share the kingdom with thy dearest friend."
Ah, words that make me surfeit with delight !
What greater bliss can hap to Gaveston
Than live and be the favourite of a king ?
Sweet prince, I come ; these, these thy amorous lines
Might have enforc'd me to have swum from France,
And, like Leander, gasp'd upon the sand,
So thou wouldst smile, and take me in thy arms.
The sight of London to my exil'd eyes
Is as Elysium to a new-come soul ;
Not that I love the city, or the men,

But that it harbours him I hold so dear,
The king, upon whose bosom let me die,
And with the world be still at enmity.
What need the arctic people love starlight,
To whom the sun shines both by day and night ?
Farewell base stooping to the lordly peers.
My knee shall bow to none but to the king.
As for the multitude that are but sparks,
Rak'd up in embers of their poverty—
Tanti ; I'll fawn first on the wind
That glanceth at my lips, and flieth away.
But how now, what are these ?

Enter three Poor Men.

Poor Men. Such as desire your worship's service.

Gaveston. What canst thou do ?

1st Poor [*Man*]. I can ride.

Gaveston. But I have no horses. What art thou ?

2nd Poor [*Man*]. A traveller.

Gaveston. Let me see—thou wouldst do well
    To wait at my trencher and tell me lies at dinner-
      time ;
    And as I like your discoursing, I'll have you.
    And what art thou ?

3rd Poor [*Man*]. A soldier, that hath served against the
    Scot.

Gaveston. Why, there are hospitals for such as you ;
    I have no war, and therefore, sir, be gone.

[*3rd Poor Man*]. Farewell, and perish by a soldier's
      hand,

That wouldst reward them with an hospital.

Gaveston [*aside*]. Ay, ay, these words of his move me as
    much
As if a goose should play the porpintine,
And dart her plumes, thinking to pierce my breast.
But yet it is no pain to speak men fair ;
I'll flatter these and make them live in hope.—
You know that I came lately out of France,
And yet I have not view'd my lord the king.
If I speed well, I'll entertain you all.

Omnes. We thank your worship.

Gaveston. I have some business ; leave me to myself.

Omnes. We will wait here about the court.   [*Exeunt.*

Gaveston. Do ; these are not men for me :
I must have wanton poets, pleasant wits,
Musicians, that with touching of a string
May draw the pliant king which way I please.
Music and poetry is his delight ;
Therefore I'll have Italian masques by night,
Sweet speeches, comedies, and pleasing shows ;
And in the day, when he shall walk abroad,
Like sylvan nymphs my pages shall be clad ;
My men, like satyrs grazing on the lawns,
Shall with their goat-feet dance an antic hay.
Sometime a lovely boy in Dian's shape,
With hair that gilds the water as it glides,
Crownets of pearl about his naked arms,
And in his sportful hands an olive-tree,
To hide those parts which men delight to see,
Shall bathe him in a spring ; and there hard by,

One, like Actæon peeping through the grove,
Shall by the angry goddess be transform'd,
And running in the likeness of an hart
By yelping hounds pull'd down, and seem to die ;—
Such things as these best please his majesty.

                                            [*Starting.*

My lord ! Here comes the king, and the nobles
From the parliament. I'll stand aside.   [*Retires.*

Enter the KING, LANCASTER, MORTIMER *senior*
    MORTIMER *junior,* EDMUND, *Earl of Kent*
    GUY, *Earl of Warwick, etc.*

Edward. Lancaster !
Lancaster. My lord.
Gaveston [*aside*]. That Earl of Lancaster do I abhor.
Edward [*aside to Lancaster*]. Will you not grant me this
        In spite of them
    I'll have my will ; and these two Mortimers,
    That cross me thus, shall know I am displeased.
Mortimer sen. If you love us, my lord, hate Gaveston.
Gaveston [*aside*]. That villain Mortimer ! I'll be hi:
        death.
Mortimer jun. Mine uncle here, this Earl, and
        myself,
    Were sworn to your father at his death,
    That he should ne'er return into the realm :
    And know, my lord, ere I will break my oath,
    This sword of mine, that should offend your foes,
    Shall sleep within the scabbard at thy need,

And underneath thy banners march who will,
For Mortimer will hang his armour up.

Gaveston [*aside*]. *Mort Dieu !*

Edward. Well, Mortimer, I'll make thee rue these
     words.
Beseems it thee to contradict thy king ?
Frownst thou thereat, aspiring Lancaster ?
The sword shall plane the furrows of thy brows,
And hew these knees that now are grown to stiff.
I will have Gaveston ; and you shall know
What danger 'tis to stand against your king.

Gaveston [*aside*]. Well done, Ned !

Lancaster. My lord, why do you thus incense your peers,
     That naturally would love and honour you
     But for that base and obscure Gaveston ?
Four earldoms have I besides Lancaster,
Derby, Salisbury, Lincoln, Leicester ;
These will I sell to give my soldiers pay,
Ere Gaveston shall stay within the realm ;
Therefore, if he be come, expel him straight.

Kent.] Barons and earls, your pride hath made me
     mute ;
But now I'll speak, and to the proof, I hope.
I do remember, in my father's days,
Lord Percy of the north, being highly mov'd,
Brav'd Mowbery in presence of the king ;
For which, had not his highness lov'd him well,
He should have lost his head ; but with his look
The undaunted spirit of Percy was appeas'd,
And Mowbery and he were reconcil'd :

Yet dare you brave the king unto his face.
Brother, revenge it, and let these their heads
Preach upon poles, for trespass of their tongues.
Warwick. O, our heads !
Edward. Ay, yours ; and therefore I would wish you
    grant—
Warwick. Bridle thy anger, gentle Mortimer.
Mortimer jun. I cannot, nor I will not : I must speak.
    Cousin, our hands I hope shall fence our heads,
    And strike off his that makes you threaten us.
    Come, uncle, let us leave the brain-sick king,
    And henceforth parley with our naked swords.
Mortimer sen. Wiltshire hath men enough to save our
    heads.
Warwick. All Warwickshire will love him for my sake.
Lancaster. And northward Gaveston hath many friends.
    Adieu, my lord, and either change your mind,
    Or look to see the throne, where you should sit,
    To float in blood ; and at thy wanton head,
    The glozing head of thy base minion thrown.
              Exeunt nobles [except the Earl of Kent].
Edward. I cannot brook these haughty menaces ;
    Am I a king, and must be overrul'd ?
    Brother, display my ensigns in the field ;
    I'll bandy with the barons and the earls,
    And either die, or live with Gaveston.
Gaveston [coming forward]. I can no longer keep me from
    my lord.
Edward. What, Gaveston ! welcome !—Kiss not my
    hand,

Embrace me, Gaveston, as I do thee.
Why shouldst thou kneel ? knowest thou not who
     I am ?
Thy friend, thyself, another Gaveston !
Not Hylas was more mourn'd of Hercules,
Than thou hast been of me since thy exile.

Gaveston. And since I went from hence, no soul in hell
     Hath felt more torment than poor Gaveston.

Edward. I know it. [*To Kent.*] Brother, welcome home
     my friend.
Now let the treacherous Mortimers conspire,
And that high-minded Earl of Lancaster.
I have my wish, in that I joy thy sight ;
And sooner shall the sea o'erwhelm my land,
Than bear the ship that shall transport thee hence.
I here create thee Lord High Chamberlain,
Chief Secretary to the state and me,
Earl of Cornwall, King and Lord of Man.

Gaveston. My lord, these titles far exceed my worth.

Kent. Brother, the least of these may well suffice
     For one of greater birth than Gaveston.

Edward. Cease, brother : for I cannot brook these
     words.—
Thy worth, sweet friend, is far above my gifts,
Therefore, to equal it, receive my heart.
If for these dignities thou be envied,
I'll give thee more ; for but to honour thee
Is Edward pleased with kingly regiment.
Fearst thou thy person ? thou shalt have a guard :
Wantest thou gold ? go to my treasury :

Wouldst thou be lov'd and fear'd? receive my seal;
Save or condemn, and in our name command
Whatso thy mind affects, or fancy likes.

Gaveston. It shall suffice me to enjoy your love,
Which whiles I have, I think myself as great
As Caesar riding in the Roman street,
With captive kings at his triumphant car.

Enter the BISHOP *of* COVENTRY.

Edward. Whither goes my lord of Coventry so fast?
Bishop. To celebrate your father's exequies.
But is that wicked Gaveston return'd?
Edward. Ay, priest, and lives to be reveng'd on thee,
That wert the only cause of his exile.
Gaveston. 'Tis true; and but for reverence of these
robes,
Thou shouldst not plod one foot beyond this place.
Bishop. I did no more than I was bound to do;
And, Gaveston, unless thou be reclaim'd,
As then I did incense the parliament,
So will I now and thou shalt back to France.
Gaveston [*seizing the Bishop*]. Saving your reverence,
you must pardon me.
Edward. Throw off his golden mitre, rend his stole,
And in the channel christen him anew.
Kent. Ah, brother, lay not violent hands on him!
For he'll complain unto the See of Rome.
Gaveston. Let him complain unto the See of Hell;
I'll be reveng'd on him for my exile.

Edward. No, spare his life, but seize upon his goods :
  Be thou lord bishop and receive his rents,
  And make him serve thee as thy chaplain :
  I give him thee—here, use him as thou wilt.

Gaveston. He shall to prison, and there die in bolts.

Edward. Ay, to the Tower, the Fleet, or where thou
  wilt.

Bishop. For this offence, be thou accurst of God !

Edward [*turning to attendants*]. Who's there ?   Convey
  this priest to the Tower.

                     [*They take him in charge.*]

Bishop. True, true.

Edward. But in the meantime, Gaveston, away,
  And take possession of his house and goods.
  Come, follow me, and thou shalt have my guard
  To see it done, and bring thee safe again.

Gaveston. What should a priest do with so fair a
  house ?
  A prison may beseem his holiness.   [*Exeunt omnes.*]

[SCENE II

Near the King's Palace]

Enter [*on one side*] *both the* MORTIMERS [*; on the
other*], WARWICK *and* LANCASTER.

Warwick. 'Tis true, the Bishop is in the Tower,
  And goods and body given to Gaveston.

Lancaster. What ! will they tyrannise upon the church ?
  Ah, wicked king ! accursed Gaveston !
  This ground, which is corrupted with their steps,
  Shall be their timeless sepulchre, or mine.

Mortimer jun. Well, let that peevish Frenchman guard
      him sure ;
  Unless his breast be sword-proof he shall die.

Mortimer sen. How now ! why droops the Earl of
      Lancaster ?

Mortimer jun. Wherefore is Guy of Warwick dis-
      content ?

Lancaster. That villain Gaveston is made an earl.

Mortimer sen. An earl !

Warwick. Ay, and besides Lord Chamberlain of the
      realm,
  And Secretary too, and Lord of Man.

Mortimer sen. We may not, nor we will not suffer this.

Mortimer jun. Why post we not from hence to levy
      men ?

Lancaster. " My Lord of Cornwall " now at every
      word !
  And happy is the man whom he vouchsafes,
  For vailing of his bonnet, one good look.
  Thus arm in arm the king and he doth march :
  Nay more, the guard upon his lordship waits,
  And all the court begins to flatter him.

Warwick. Thus leaning on the shoulder of the king,
  He nods, and scorns, and smiles at those that pass.

Mortimer sen. Doth no man take exceptions at the
      slave ?

Lancaster. All stomach him, but none dare speak a
  word.

Mortimer jun. Ah, that bewrays their baseness, Lancaster !

 Were all the earls and barons of my mind,

 We'll hale him from the bosom of the king

 And at the court-gate hang the peasant up,

 Who, swoln with venom of ambitious pride,

 Will be the ruin of the realm and us.

Enter the BISHOP *of* CANTERBURY [*and an* Attendant].

Warwick. Here comes my lord of Canterbury's grace.

Lancaster. His countenance bewrays he is displeas'd.

[*Canterbury.*] First were his sacred garments rent and
  torn,

 Then laid they violent hands upon him ; next

 Himself imprison'd, and his goods asseiz'd.—

 This certify the Pope ; away, take horse.

          [*Exit Attendant.*]

Lancaster. My lord, will you take arms against the
  king ?

[*Canterbury.*] What need I ?   God himself is up in
  arms,

 When violence is offer'd to the church.

Mortimer jun. Then will you join with us that be his
  peers,

 To banish or behead that Gaveston ?

[*Canterbury.*] What else, my lords ? for it concerns me
  near ;

 The Bishopric of Coventry is his.

Enter the QUEEN.

Mortimer jun. Madam, whither walks your majesty so
    fast ?

Queen. Unto the forest, gentle Mortimer,
    To live in grief and baleful discontent ;
    For now my lord the king regards me not,
    But doats upon the love of Gaveston.
    He claps his cheeks, and hangs about his neck,
    Smiles in his face, and whispers in his ears ;
    And when I come, he frowns, as who should say,
    Go whither thou wilt, seeing I have Gaveston.

Mortimer sen. Is it not strange, that he is thus be-
    witch'd ?

Mortimer jun. Madam, return unto the court again :
    That sly inveighling Frenchman we'll exile,
    Or lose our lives ; and yet, ere that day come,
    The king shall lose his crown, for we have power,
    And courage too, to be reveng'd at full.

[*Canterbury.*] But yet lift not your swords against the
    king.

Lancaster. No ; but we'll lift Gaveston from hence.

Warwick. And war must be the means, or he'll stay
    still.

Queen. Then let him stay, for rather than my lord
    Shall be oppress'd by civil mutinies,
    I will endure a melancholy life,
    And let him frolic with his minion.

[*Canterbury.*] My lords, to ease all this, but hear me
    speak :

We and the rest that are his counsellors,
Will meet, and with a general consent,
Confirm his banishment with our hands and seals.

Lancaster. What we confirm the king will frustrate.

Mortimer jun. Then may we lawfully revolt from him.

Warwick. But say, my lord, where shall this meeting
    be ?

Canterbury.] At the New Temple.

Mortimer jun. Content.

Canterbury.] And, in the meantime, I'll entreat you all
    To cross to Lambeth, and there stay with me.

Lancaster. Come then, let's away.

Mortimer jun. Madam, farewell.

Queen. Farewell, sweet Mortimer ; and for my sake,
    Forbear to levy arms against the king.

Mortimer jun. Ay, if words will serve ; if not, I must.
                          [Exeunt omnes.]

[SCENE III

A Street in London]

Enter GAVESTON *and the* EARL *of* KENT.

Gaveston. Edmund, the mighty prince of Lancaster,
    That hath more earldoms than an ass can bear,
    And both the Mortimers, two goodly men,
    With Guy of Warwick, that redoubted knight,
    Are gone towards Lambeth. There let them remain.
                                Exeunt.

[SCENE IV

The New Temple]

Enter Nobles: [LANCASTER, WARWICK, PEMBROKE,
MORTIMER *senior*, MORTIMER *junior*, BISHOP *of*
CANTERBURY *and* Attendants].

Lancaster. Here is the form of Gaveston's exile :
  May it please your lordship to subscribe your name.
[*Canterbury.*] Give me the paper.   [*He signs it.*]
                    [*They all sign in turn.*]
Lancaster. Quick, quick, my lord ; I long to write my
    name.
Warwick. But I long more to see him banish'd hence.
Mortimer jun. The name of Mortimer shall fright the
    king,
  Unless he be declin'd from that base peasant.

    Enter the KING, GAVESTON, [*and* KENT].

Edward. What ? are you mov'd that Gaveston sits
    here ?
  It is our pleasure : we will have it so.
Lancaster. Your grace doth well to place him by your
    side,
  For nowhere else the new earl is so safe.
    [*The Mortimers, Pembroke, and Warwick draw aside
    and speak to each other.*]

Mortimer sen. What man of noble birth can brook this
    sight ?

    Quam male conveniunt !

    See what a scornful look the peasant casts.

Pembroke. Can kingly lions fawn on creeping ants ?

Warwick. Ignoble vassal, that like Phaeton

  Aspir'st unto the guidance of the sun.

Mortimer jun. Their downfall is at hand, their forces
    down :

  We will not thus be faced and over-peer'd.—

Edward. Lay hands on that traitor Mortimer !

Mortimer sen. Lay hands on that traitor Gaveston !

                                [They seize him.]

Kent. Is this the duty that you owe your king ?

Warwick. We know our duties ; let him know his
    peers.

Edward. Whither will you bear him ? Stay, or ye shall
    die.

Mortimer sen. We are no traitors ; therefore threaten
    not.

Gaveston. No, threaten not, my lord, but pay them
    home !

  Were I a king——

Mortimer jun. Thou villain, wherefore talks thou of a
    king,

  That hardly art a gentleman by birth ?

Edward. Were he a peasant, being my minion,

  I'll make the proudest of you stoop to him.

Lancaster. My lord, you may not thus disparage us.

  Away, I say, with hateful Gaveston !

Mortimer sen. And with the Earl of Kent that favours
      him.   [*Attendants remove Kent and Gaveston.*]
Edward. Nay, then lay violent hands upon your king :
   Here, Mortimer, sit thou in Edward's throne :
   Warwick and Lancaster, wear you my crown :
   Was ever king thus over-rul'd as I ?
Lancaster. Learn then to rule us better, and the realm.
Mortimer jun. What we have done, our heart-blood
      shall maintain.
Warwick. Think you that we can brook this upstart
      pride ?
Edward. Anger and wrathful fury stops my speech.
[*Canterbury.*] Why are you mov'd ? be patient, my
      lord,
   And see what we your counsellors have done.
Mortimer jun. My lords, now let us all be resolute,
   And either have our wills, or lose our lives.
Edward. Meet you for this, proud overdaring peers ?
   Ere my sweet Gaveston shall part from me,
   This Isle shall fleet upon the Ocean,
   And wander to the unfrequented Inde.
[*Canterbury.*] You know that I am a legate to the
      Pope ?
   On your allegiance to the see of Rome,
   Subscribe as we have done to his exile.
Mortimer jun. Curse him, if he refuse, and then may
      we
   Depose him and elect another king.
Edward. Ay, there it goes : but yet I will not yield :
   Curse me, depose me, do the worst you can.

Lancaster. Then linger not, my lord, but do it straight.

[*Canterbury.*] Remember how the bishop was abus'd :
  Either banish him that was the cause thereof,
  Or I will presently discharge these lords
  Of duty and allegiance due to thee.

Edward [*aside*]. It boots me not to threat ; I must speak
    fair :
  The legate of the Pope will be obey'd.—
  My lord, you shall be Chancellor of the realm ;
  Thou, Lancaster, High Admiral of our fleet ;
  Young Mortimer and his uncle shall be earls ;
  And you, Lord Warwick, President of the North ;
  And thou of Wales. If this content you not,
  Make several kingdoms of this monarchy,
  And share it equally amongst you all,
  So I may have some nook or corner left,
  To frolic with my dearest Gaveston.

Canterbury. Nothing shall alter us : we are resolv'd.

Lancaster [*presenting the paper*]. Come, come, subscribe.

Mortimer jun. Why should you love him whom the
    world hates so ?

Edward. Because he loves me more than all the world.
  Ah, none but rude and savage-minded men
  Would seek the ruin of my Gaveston ;
  You that be noble-born should pity him.

Warwick. You that are princely-born should shake him
    off :
  For shame subscribe, and let the lown depart.

Mortimer sen. Urge him, my lord.

[*Canterbury.*] Are you content to banish him the realm ?

Edward. I see I must, and therefore am content :
  Instead of ink I'll write it with my tears.

                              [*He signs the warrant.*]

Mortimer jun. The king is love-sick for his minion.
Edward. 'Tis done, and now, accursed hand, fall off !
Lancaster. Give it me ; I'll have it publish'd in the
      streets.
Mortimer jun. I'll see him presently dispatch'd away.
[*Canterbury.*] Now is my heart at ease.
Warwick.   And so is mine.
Pembroke. This will be good news to the common sort.
Mortimer sen. Be it or no, he shall not linger here.

                              Exeunt Nobles.

Edward. How fast they run to banish him I love.
  They would not stir, were it to do me good.
  Why should a king be subject to a priest ?
  Proud Rome, that hatchest such imperial grooms,
  For these thy superstitious taper-lights,
  Wherewith thy antichristian churches blaze,
  I'll fire thy crazed buildings, and enforce
  The papal towers to kiss the lowly ground.
  With slaughter'd priests may Tiber's channel swell,
  And banks rais'd higher with their sepulchres.
  As for the peers that back the clergy thus,
  If I be king, not one of them shall live.

[*Re-*]*enter* GAVESTON.

Gaveston. My lord, I hear it whispered everywhere,
  That I am banish'd, and must fly the land.
Edward. 'Tis true, sweet Gaveston—O ! were it false !

The legate of the Pope will have it so,
And thou must hence, or I shall be depos'd.
But I will reign to be reveng'd of them,
And therefore, sweet friend, take it patiently.
Live where thou wilt, I'll send thee gold enough;
And long thou shalt not stay, or if thou dost,
I'll come to thee; my love shall ne'er decline.

Gaveston. Is all my hope turn'd to this hell of grief?

Edward. Rend not my heart with thy too-piercing
      words:
Thou from this land, I from myself am banish'd.

Gaveston. To go from hence grieves not poor Gaveston;
   But to forsake you, in whose gracious looks
   The blessedness of Gaveston remains:
   For nowhere else seeks he felicity.

Edward. And only this torments my wretched soul,
   That whether I will or no thou must depart.
   Be governor of Ireland in my stead,
   And there abide till fortune call thee home.
   Here take my picture, and let me wear thine.
                              [*They exchange pictures.*]
   O, might I keep thee here as I do this,
   Happy were I: but now most miserable.

Gaveston. 'Tis something to be pitied of a king.

Edward. Thou shalt not hence; I'll hide thee,
      Gaveston.

Gaveston. I shall be found, and then 'twill grieve me
      more.

Edward. Kind words and mutual talk makes our grief
   greater:

Therefore, with dumb embracement, let us part—
Stay, Gaveston, I cannot leave thee thus.
Gaveston. For every look, my lord, drops down a tear :
    Seeing I must go, do not renew my sorrow.
Edward. The time is little that thou hast to stay,
    And therefore give me leave to look my fill :
    But come, sweet friend, I'll bear thee on thy way.
Gaveston. The peers will frown.
Edward. I pass not for their anger. Come, let's go.
    O that we might as well return as go.

Enter QUEEN ISABEL.

Queen. Whither goes my lord ?
Edward. Fawn not on me, French strumpet ; get thee
        gone.
Queen. On whom but on my husband should I fawn ?
Gaveston. On Mortimer, with whom, ungentle queen—
    I say no more, judge you the rest, my lord.
Queen. In saying this, thou wrongst me, Gaveston ;
    Is't not enough that thou corrupts my lord,
    And art a bawd to his affections,
    But thou must call mine honour thus in question ?
Gaveston. I mean not so ; your grace must pardon
        me.
Edward. Thou art too familiar with that Mortimer,
    And by thy means is Gaveston exil'd ;
    But I would wish thee reconcile the lords,
    Or thou shalt ne'er be reconcil'd to me.
Queen. Your highness knows it lies not in my power.

Edward. Away then ; touch me not. Come, Gaveston.

Queen. Villain ! 'tis thou that robb'st me of my lord.

Gaveston. Madam, 'tis you that rob me of my lord.

Edward. Speak not unto her ; let her droop and pine.

Queen. Wherein, my lord, have I deserv'd these words ?

   Witness the tears that Isabella sheds,

   Witness this heart, that sighing for thee breaks,

   How dear my lord is to poor Isabel.

Edward. And witness heaven how dear thou art to

    me.

   There weep : for till my Gaveston be repeal'd,

   Assure thyself thou com'st not in my sight.

                  [Exeunt Edward and Gaveston.

Queen. O miserable and distressed queen !

   Would, when I left sweet France and was embark'd,

   That charming Circes, walking on the waves,

   Had chang'd my shape, or at the marriage-day

   The cup of Hymen had been full of poison,

   Or with those arms that twin'd about my neck

   I had been stifled, and not lived to see

   The king my lord thus to abandon me.

   Like frantic Juno will I fill the earth

   With ghastly murmur of my sighs and cries ;

   For never doted Jove on Ganymede

   So much as he on cursed Gaveston.—

   But that will more exasperate his wrath ;

   I must entreat him, I must speak him fair,

   And be a means to call home Gaveston :

   And yet he'll ever dote on Gaveston ;

   And so am I for ever miserable.

[*Re-*]*enter the Nobles to the* QUEEN : [LANCASTER,
WARWICK, PEMBROKE, MORTIMER *senior,
and* MORTIMER *junior*].

Lancaster. Look where the sister of the king of France
  Sits wringing of her hands, and beats her breast !
Warwick. The king, I fear, hath ill intreated her.
Pembroke. Hard is the heart that injures such a saint.
Mortimer jun. I know 'tis 'long of Gaveston she weeps.
Mortimer sen. Why ? He is gone.
Mortimer jun.   Madam, how fares your grace ?
Queen. Ah, Mortimer ! now breaks the king's hate
      forth,
  And he confesseth that he loves me not.
Mortimer jun. Cry quittance, madam, then, and love
      not him.
Queen. No, rather will I die a thousand deaths :
  And yet I love in vain ; he'll ne'er love me.
Lancaster. Fear ye not, madam ; now his minion's gone,
  His wanton humour will be quickly left.
Queen. O never, Lancaster ! I am enjoin'd
  To sue unto you all for his repeal ;
  This wills my lord, and this must I perform,
  Or else be banish'd from his highness' presence.
Lancaster. For his repeal, madam ! He comes not
      back,
  Unless the sea cast up his shipwrack'd body.
Warwick. And to behold so sweet a sight as that,
  There's none here but would run his horse to
      death.

Mortimer jun. But, madam, would you have us call him
    home ?

Queen. Ay, Mortimer, for till he be restor'd,
  The angry king hath banish'd me the court ;
  And therefore, as thou lovest and tendrest me,
  Be thou my advocate unto these peers.

Mortimer jun. What, would ye have me plead for
    Gaveston ?

Mortimer sen. Plead for him he that will, I am resolv'd.

Lancaster. And so am I, my lord : dissuade the queen.

Queen. O Lancaster, let him dissuade the king,
  For 'tis against my will he should return.

Warwick. Then speak not for him, let the peasant go.

Queen. 'Tis for myself I speak, and not for him.

Pembroke. No speaking will prevail, and therefore cease.

Mortimer jun. Fair queen, forbear to angle for the fish
  Which, being caught, strikes him that takes it dead ;
  I mean that vile torpedo, Gaveston,
  That now, I hope, floats on the Irish seas.

Queen. Sweet Mortimer, sit down by me awhile,
  And I will tell thee reasons of such weight
  As thou wilt soon subscribe to his repeal.

Mortimer jun. It is impossible ; but speak your mind.

Queen. Then thus, but none shall hear it but ourselves.
    [*She takes Mortimer junior aside. They sit and talk.*]

Lancaster. My lords, albeit the queen win Mortimer,
  Will you be resolute and hold with me ?

Mortimer sen. Not I, against my nephew.

Pembroke. Fear not, the queen's words cannot alter him.

Warwick. No ? Do but mark how earnestly she pleads.

Lancaster. And see how coldly his looks make denial.

Warwick. She smiles ; now for my life his mind is
  chang'd.

Lancaster. I'll rather lose his friendship, I, than grant.

Mortimer jun. [*to the Queen*]. Well, of necessity it must
  be so.   [*He rises and rejoins the others.*]
 My lords, that I abhor base Gaveston,
 I hope your honours make no question,
 And therefore, though I plead for his repeal,
 'Tis not for his sake, but for our avail ;
 Nay for his realm's behoof, and for the king's.

Lancaster. Fie, Mortimer, dishonour not thyself !
 Can this be true, 'twas good to banish him ?
 And is this true, to call him home again ?
 Such reasons make white black, and dark night day.

Mortimer jun. My lord of Lancaster, mark the respect.

Lancaster. In no respect can contraries be true.

Queen. Yet, my good lord, hear what he can allege.

Warwick. All that he speaks is nothing ; we are resolv'd.

Mortimer jun. Do you not wish that Gaveston were
  dead ?

Pembroke. I would he were.

Mortimer jun. Why then, my lord, give me but leave to
  speak.

Mortimer sen. But, nephew, do not play the sophister.

Mortimer jun. This which I urge is of a burning zeal
 To mend the king, and do our country good.
 Know you not Gaveston hath store of gold,
 Which may in Ireland purchase him such friends

As he will front the mightiest of us all ?
And whereas he shall live and be belov'd,
'Tis hard for us to work his overthrow.

Warwick. Mark you but that, my lord of Lancaster.

Mortimer jun. But were he here, detested as he is,
How easily might some base slave be suborn'd
To greet his lordship with a poniard,
And none so much as blame the murderer,
But rather praise him for that brave attempt,
And in the chronicle enrol his name
For purging of the realm of such a plague.

Pembroke. He saith true.

Lancaster. Ay, but how chance was not this done
before ?

Mortimer jun. Because, my lords, it was not thought
upon.
Nay, more, when he shall know it lies in us
To banish him and then to call him home,
'Twill make him vail the top-flag of his pride,
And fear to offend the meanest nobleman.

Mortimer sen. But how if he do not, nephew ?

Mortimer jun. Then may we with some colour rise in
arms ;
For howsoever we have borne it out,
'Tis treason to be up against the king ;
So shall we have the people of our side,
Which for his father's sake lean to the king,
But cannot brook a night-grown mushrump,
Such a one as my Lord of Cornwall is,
Should bear us down of the nobility.

And when the commons and the nobles join,
'Tis not the king can buckler Gaveston ;
We'll pull him from the strongest hold he hath.
My lords, if to perform this I be slack,
Think me as base a groom as Gaveston.

Lancaster. On that condition, Lancaster will grant.

Warwick. And so will Pembroke and I.

Mortimer sen.   And I.

Mortimer jun. In this I count me highly gratified,
And Mortimer will rest at your command.

Queen. And when this favour Isabel forgets,
Then let her live abandon'd and forlorn.
But see, in happy time, my lord the king,
Having brought the Earl of Cornwall on his way,
Is new return'd. This news will glad him much,
Yet not so much as me ; I love him more
Than he can Gaveston ; would he lov'd me
But half so much, then were I treble-bless'd !

[*Re-*]*enter* KING EDWARD, *mourning* [*and speaking
to himself*].

Edward. He's gone, and for his absence thus I mourn.
Did never sorrow go so near my heart
As doth the want of my sweet Gaveston ;
And could my crown's revenue bring him back,
I would freely give it to his enemies,
And think I gain'd, having bought so dear a friend

Queen. Hark, how he harps upon his minion.

Edward. My heart is as an anvil unto sorrow,

Which beats upon it like the Cyclops' hammers,
And with the noise turns up my giddy brain,
And makes me frantic for my Gaveston.
Ah, had some bloodless Fury rose from hell,
And with my kingly sceptre struck me dead,
When I was forc'd to leave my Gaveston.

Lancaster. Diablo ! What passions call you these ?

Queen. My gracious lord, I come to bring you news.

Edward. That you have parled with your Mortimer.

Queen. That Gaveston, my lord, shall be repeal'd.

Edward. Repeal'd ! The news is too sweet to be
    true.

Queen. But will you love me, if you find it so ?

Edward. If it be so, what will not Edward do ?

Queen. For Gaveston, but not for Isabel.

Edward. For thee, fair queen, if thou lovest Gaveston ;
  I'll hang a golden tongue about thy neck,
  Seeing thou hast pleaded with so good success.

Queen. No other jewels hang about my neck
  Than these, my lord [*putting her hands upon his arms*] ;
      nor let me have more wealth
  Than I may fetch from this rich treasury :

                              [*She kisses him.*]

  O how a kiss revives poor Isabel !

Edward. Once more receive my hand, and let this be
  A second marriage 'twixt thyself and me.

Queen. And may it prove more happy than the first.
  My gentle lord, bespeak these nobles fair,
  That wait attendance for a gracious look,
  And on their knees salute your majesty.

Edward. Courageous Lancaster, embrace thy king,
  And, as gross vapours perish by the sun,
  Even so let hatred with thy sovereign's smile.
  Live thou with me as my companion.
Lancaster. This salutation overjoys my heart.
Edward. Warwick shall be my chiefest counsellor :
  These silver hairs will more adorn my court
  Than gaudy silks, or rich imbrotherie.
  Chide me, sweet Warwick, if I go astray.
Warwick. Slay me, my lord, when I offend your grace.
Edward. In solemn triumphs, and in public shows,
  Pembroke shall bear the sword before the king.
Pembroke. And with this sword Pembroke will fight
    for you.
Edward. But wherefore walks young Mortimer aside ?
  Be thou commander of our royal fleet ;
  Or, if that lofty office like thee not,
  I make thee here Lord Marshal of the realm.
Mortimer jun. My lord, I'll marshal so your enemies,
  As England shall be quiet, and you safe.
Edward. And as for you, Lord Mortimer of Chirke,
  Whose great achievements in our foreign war
  Deserves no common place, nor mean reward ;
  Be you the general of the levied troops,
  That now are ready to assail the Scots.
Mortimer sen. In this your grace hath highly honoured
    me,
  For with my nature war doth best agree.
Queen. Now is the king of England rich and strong,
  Having the love of his renowned peers.

Edward. Ay, Isabel, ne'er was my heart so light.
   Clerk of the crown—

               [*Enter* BEAUMONT.]

                  —direct our warrant forth
   For Gaveston to Ireland : Beaumont, fly
   As fast as Iris or Jove's Mercury.
Beaumont. It shall be done, my gracious lord.   [*Exit.*]
Edward. Lord Mortimer, we leave you to your charge.
   Now let us in, and feast it royally.
   Against our friend the Earl of Cornwall comes,
   We'll have a general tilt and tournament ;
   And then his marriage shall be solemnised.
   For wot you not that I have made him sure
   Unto our cousin, the Earl of Gloucester's heir ?
Lancaster. Such news we hear, my lord.
Edward. That day, if not for him, yet for my sake
   Who in the triumph will be challenger,
   Spare for no cost ; we will requite your love.
Warwick. In this or aught your highness shall command
   us.
Edward. Thanks, gentle Warwick. Come, let's in and
   revel.   *Exeunt. Manent Mortimers.*
Mortimer sen. Nephew, I must to Scotland ; thou
   stayest here.
   Leave now to oppose thyself against the king.
   Thou seest by nature he is mild and calm,
   And, seeing his mind so dotes on Gaveston,
   Let him without controulment have his will.

The mightiest kings have had their minions :
Great Alexander lov'd Hephaestion ;
The conquering Hercules for Hylas wept ;
And for Patroclus stern Achilles droop'd.
And not kings only, but the wisest men :
The Roman Tully lov'd Octavius ;
Grave Socrates, wild Alcibiades.
Then let his grace, whose youth is flexible,
And promiseth as much as we can wish,
Freely enjoy that vain, lighted-headed earl ;
For riper years will wean him from such toys.

Mortimer jun. Uncle, his wanton humour grieves not
     me ;
But this I scorn, that one so basely born
Should by his sovereign's favour grow so pert,
And riot it with the treasure of the realm.
While soldiers mutiny for want of pay,
He wears a lord's revenue on his back,
And, Midas-like, he jets it in the court,
With base outlandish cullions at his heels,
Whose proud fantastic liveries make such show,
As if that Proteus, god of shapes, appear'd.
I have not seen a dapper Jack so brisk.
He wears a short Italian hooded cloak,
Larded with pearl, and in his Tuscan cap
A jewel of more value than the crown.
Whiles other walk below, the king and he
From out a window laugh at such as we,
And flout our train, and jest at our attire.
Uncle, 'tis this that makes me impatient.

Mortimer sen. But, nephew, now you see the king is
        chang'd.

Mortimer jun. Then so am I, and live to do him
        service :

But whiles I have a sword, a hand, a heart,

I will not yield to any such upstart.

You know my mind ; come, uncle, let's away.

                           Exeunt.

[ACT II

SCENE I

A hall in Gloucester's house]

Enter SPENCER [*junior*] *and* BALDOCK.

Baldock. Spencer,
  Seeing that our lord th' Earl of Gloucester's dead,
  Which of the nobles dost thou mean to serve ?
Spencer [*jun.*]. Not Mortimer, nor any of his side ;
  Because the king and he are enemies.
  Baldock, learn this of me, a factious lord
  Shall hardly do himself good, much less us ;
  But he that hath the favour of a king,
  May with one word advance us while we live :
  The liberal Earl of Cornwall is the man
  On whose good fortune Spencer's hope depends.
Baldock. What, mean you then to be his follower ?
Spencer [*jun.*]. No, his companion, for he loves me
    well,
  And would have once preferr'd me to the king.
Baldock. But he is banish'd ; there's small hope of
    him.
Spencer [*jun.*]. Ay, for a while ; but, Baldock, mark
    the end.

A friend of mine told me in secrecy
That he's repeal'd, and sent for back again ;
And even now a post came from the court
With letters to our lady from the king ;
And as she read she smil'd, which makes me think
It is about her lover Gaveston.
Baldock. 'Tis like enough, for since he was exil'd
   She neither walks abroad, nor comes in sight.
   But I had thought the match had been broke off,
   And that his banishment had chang'd her mind.
Spencer [*jun.*]. Our lady's first love is not wavering ;
   My life for thine she will have Gaveston.
Baldock. Then hope I by her means to be preferr'd,
   Having read unto her since she was a child.
Spencer [*jun.*]. Then, Baldock, you must cast the
     scholar off,
   And learn to court it like a gentleman.
   'Tis not a black cloak and a little band,
   A velvet-cap'd cloak, fac'd before with serge,
   And smelling to a nosegay all the day,
   Or holding of a napkin in your hand,
   Or saying a long grace at a table's end,
   Or making low legs to a nobleman,
   Or looking downward with your eyelids close,
   And saying, " Truly, an't may please your honour,"
   Can get you any favour with great men ;
   You must be proud, bold, pleasant, resolute,
   And now and then stab, as occasion serves.
Baldock. Spencer, thou knowest I hate such formal toys,
   And use them but of mere hypocrisy.

Mine old lord while he liv'd was so precise,
That he would take exceptions at my buttons,
And being like pin's heads, blame me for the big-
ness ;
Which made me curate-like in mine attire,
Though inwardly licentious enough,
And apt for any kind of villainy.
I am none of these common pedants, I,
That cannot speak without *propterea quod*.

Spencer [jun.]. But one of those that saith, *quando-
quidem,*
And hath a special gift to form a verb.

Baldock. Leave off this jesting, here my lady comes.

[They draw aside.]

Enter the Lady [the KING's Niece].

Niece. The grief for his exile was not so much,
As is the joy of his returning home.
This letter came from my sweet Gaveston :
What needst thou, love, thus to excuse thyself ?
I know thou couldst not come and visit me :
[*Reads.*] " I will not long be from thee, though I
die."
This argues the entire love of my lord ;
[*Reads.*] " When I forsake thee, death seize on my
heart " :
But rest thee here where Gaveston shall sleep.

[She puts the letter into her bosom.]

Now to the letter of my lord the king.
He wills me to repair unto the court,

And meet my Gaveston. Why do I stay,
Seeing that he talks thus of my marriage-day?
[*Calling.*] Who's there? [*They come forward.*] Bal-
    dock!
See that my coach be ready, I must hence.

Baldock. It shall be done, madam.

Niece. And meet me at the park-pale presently.

                            Exit [*Baldock*].

Spencer, stay you and bear me company,
For I have joyful news to tell thee of;
My lord of Cornwall is a-coming over,
And will be at the court as soon as we.

Spencer [*jun.*]. I knew the king would have him home
    again.

Niece. If all things sort out as I hope they will,
Thy service, Spencer, shall be thought upon.

Spencer [*jun.*]. I humbly thank your ladyship.

Niece. Come, lead the way; I long till I am there.

                              [*Exeunt.*]

[SCENE II

Before Tynemouth Castle]

Enter [KING] EDWARD, *the* QUEEN, LANCASTER,
    MORTIMER [*junior*], WARWICK, PEMBROKE,
    KENT, Attendants.

Edward [*aside*]. The wind is good, I wonder why he
    stays;

I fear me he is wrack'd upon the sea.

Queen. Look, Lancaster, how passionate he is,
And still his mind runs on his minion.

Lancaster. My lord,—

Edward. How now ! what news ? is Gaveston arriv'd ?

Mortimer jun. Nothing but Gaveston ! what means
your grace ?
You have matters of more weight to think upon ;
The King of France sets foot in Normandy.

Edward. A trifle ! we'll expel him when we please.
But tell me, Mortimer, what's thy device
Against the stately triumph we decreed ?

Mortimer jun. A homely one, my lord, not worth the
telling.

Edward. Prithee let me know it.

Mortimer jun. But seeing you are so desirous, thus it is :
A lofty cedar-tree, fair flourishing,
On whose top-branches kingly eagles perch,
And by the bark a canker creeps me up,
And gets unto the highest bough of all :
The motto, *Æque tandem.*

Edward. And what is yours, my lord of Lancaster ?

Lancaster. My lord, mine's more obscure than Morti-
mer's.
Pliny reports there is a flying fish
Which all the other fishes deadly hate,
And therefore, being pursued, it takes the air :
No sooner is it up, but there's a fowl
That seizeth it ; this fish, my lord, I bear,
The motto this : *Undique mors est.*

Edward. Proud Mortimer ! ungentle Lancaster !
  Is this the love you bear your sovereign ?
  Is this the fruit your reconcilement bears ?
  Can you in words make show of amity,
  And in your shields display your rancorous minds ?
  What call you this but private libelling
  Against the Earl of Cornwall and my brother ?
Queen. Sweet husband, be content, they all love you.
Edward. They love me not that hate my Gaveston.
  I am that cedar—shake me not too much—
  And you the eagles : soar ye ne'er so high,
  I have the jesses that will pull you down ;
  And *Æque tandem* shall that canker cry
  Unto the proudest peer of Brittany.
  Though thou compar'st him to a flying fish,
  And threatenest death whether he rise or fall,
  'Tis not the hugest monster of the sea,
  Nor foulest harpy that shall swallow him.
Mortimer jun. If in his absence thus he favours him,
  What will he do whenas he shall be present ?
Lancaster. That shall we see ; look where his lordship
      comes.

Enter GAVESTON.

Edward. My Gaveston !
  Welcome to Tynemouth, welcome to thy friend !
  Thy absence made me droop and pine away ;
  For, as the lovers of fair Danae,
  When she was lock'd up in a brazen tower,
  Desir'd her more, and wax'd outrageous,

So did it sure with me : and now thy sight
Is sweeter far than was thy parting hence
Bitter and irksome to my sobbing heart.

Gaveston. Sweet lord and king, your speech preventeth
mine,
Yet have I words left to express my joy :
The shepherd nipt with biting winter's rage
Frolics not more to see the painted spring,
Than I do to behold your majesty.

Edward. Will none of you salute my Gaveston ?

Lancaster. Salute him ? yes ; welcome Lord Chamberlain.

Mortimer jun. Welcome is the good Earl of Cornwall.

Warwick. Welcome, Lord Governor of the Isle of
Man.

Pembroke. Welcome, Master Secretary.

Kent. Brother, do you hear them ?

Edward. Still will these earls and barons use me thus ?

Gaveston. My lord, I cannot brook these injuries.

Queen [*aside*]. Ay me, poor soul, when these begin to jar.

Edward. Return it to their throats, I'll be thy warrant.

Gaveston. Base, leaden earls, that glory in your birth,
Go sit at home and eat your tenants' beef ;
And come not here to scoff at Gaveston,
Whose mounting thoughts did never creep so low
As to bestow a look on such as you.

Lancaster. Yet I disdain not to do this for you.

[*Draws his sword.*]

Edward. Treason, treason ! where's the traitor ?

Pembroke. Here ! here !

[*Edward*]. Convey hence Gaveston ; they'll murder
    him.

Gaveston. The life of thee shall salve this foul dis-
    grace.

Mortimer jun. Villain, thy life, unless I miss mine
    aim.   [*Wounds Gaveston.*]

Queen. Ah ! furious Mortimer, what hast thou done ?

Mortimer jun. No more than I would answer, were he
    slain.   [*Exit Gaveston with Attendants.*]

Edward. Yes, more than thou canst answer, though he
    live ;

    Dear shall you both aby this riotous deed.

    Out of my presence, come not near the court.

Mortimer jun. I'll not be barr'd the court for Gaveston.

Lancaster. We'll hale him by the ears unto the block.

Edward. Look to your own heads ; his is sure enough.

Warwick. Look to your own crown, if you back him
    thus.

Kent. Warwick, these words do ill beseem thy years.

Edward. Nay, all of them conspire to cross me thus ;

    But if I live, I'll tread upon their heads

    That think with high looks thus to tread me down.

    Come, Edmund, let's away and levy men,

    'Tis war that must abate these barons' pride.

        Exit the King [followed by Queen Isabella and Kent.]

Warwick. Let's to our castles, for the king is mov'd.

Mortimer jun. Mov'd may he be, and perish in his
    wrath !

Lancaster. Cousin, it is no dealing with him now,

    He means to make us stoop by force of arms :

And therefore let us jointly here protest,
To prosecute that Gaveston to the death.

Mortimer jun. By heaven, the abject villain shall not
  live.

Warwick. I'll have his blood, or die in seeking it.

Pembroke. The like oath Pembroke takes.

Lancaster.   And so doth Lancaster.
  Now send our heralds to defy the king ;
  And make the people swear to put him down.

Enter a Post.

Mortimer jun. Letters : from whence ?

Messenger.   From Scotland, my lord.

Lancaster. Why, how now, cousin, how fares all our
  friends ?

Mortimer jun. My uncle's taken prisoner by the Scots.

Lancaster. We'll have him ransom'd, man ; be of good
  cheer.

Mortimer jun. They rate his ransom at five thousand
  pound.
  Who should defray the money but the king,
  Seeing he is taken prisoner in his wars ?
  I'll to the king.

Lancaster. Do, cousin, and I'll bear thee company.

Warwick. Meantime, my lord of Pembroke and myself
  Will to Newcastle here, and gather head.

Mortimer jun. About it then, and we will follow you.

Lancaster. Be resolute and full of secrecy.

Warwick. I warrant you.

                    [*Exeunt all but Mortimer and Lancaster.*]

Mortimer jun. Cousin, and if he will not ransom him,
  I'll thunder such a peal into his ears,
    As never subject did unto his king.
Lancaster. Content, I'll bear my part. Holla! who's
    there?

[Enter Guard.]

Mortimer jun. Ay, marry, such a guard as this doth
    well.
Lancaster. Lead on the way.
Guard. Whither will your lordships?
Mortimer jun. Whither else but to the king?
Guard. His highness is dispos'd to be alone.
Lancaster. Why, so he may, but we will speak to him.
Guard. You may not in, my Lord.
Mortimer jun. May we not?

[Enter the KING *and* KENT.*]*

Edward. How now!—What noise is this?
  Who have we there, is't you?   *[Going.]*
Mortimer jun. Nay, stay, my lord, I come to bring
    you news;
  Mine uncle's taken prisoner by the Scots.
Edward. Then ransom him.
Lancaster. 'Twas in your wars; you should ransom
    him.
Mortimer jun. And you shall ransom him, or else——
Kent. What, Mortimer! you will not threaten him?
Edward. Quiet yourself, you shall have the broad seal,

    To gather for him throughout the realm.

Lancaster. Your minion Gaveston hath taught you this.

Mortimer jun. My lord, the family of the Mortimers
    Are not so poor, but, would they sell their land,
    Would levy men enough to anger you.
    We never beg, but use such prayers as these.

                       [*Putting his hand on his sword.*]

Edward. Shall I still be haunted thus ?

Mortimer jun. Nay, now you are here alone, I'll speak
    my mind.

Lancaster. And so will I, and then, my lord, farewell.

Mortimer [*jun.*]. The idle triumphs, masks, lascivious
    shows,
    And prodigal gifts bestow'd on Gaveston,
    Have drawn thy treasure dry, and made thee weak,
    The murmuring commons overstretched hath.

Lancaster. Look for rebellion, look to be depos'd ;
    Thy garrisons are beaten out of France,
    And, lame and poor, lie groaning at the gates.
    The wild Oneyl, with swarms of Irish kerns,
    Lives uncontroll'd within the English pale.
    Unto the walls of York the Scots made road,
    And unresisted drave away rich spoils.

Mortimer jun. The haughty Dane commands the
    narrow seas,
    While in the harbour ride thy ships unrigg'd.

Lancaster. What foreign prince sends thee ambassadors ?

Mortimer jun. Who loves thee, but a sort of flatterers ?

Lancaster. Thy gentle queen, sole sister to Valois,
    Complains that thou hast left her all forlorn.

Mortimer jun. Thy court is naked, being bereft of those
  That makes a king seem glorious to the world ;
  I mean the peers, whom thou shouldst dearly love :
  Libels are cast again thee in the street,
  Ballads and rhymes, made of thy overthrow.
Lancaster. The Northern borderers seeing their houses
        burnt,
  Their wives and children slain, run up and down,
  Cursing the name of thee and Gaveston.
Mortimer jun. When wert thou in the field with
        banner spread ?
  But once, and then thy soldiers march'd like players,
  With garish robes, not armour, and thyself,
  Bedaub'd with gold, rode laughing at the rest,
  Nodding and shaking of thy spangled crest,
  Where women's favours hung like labels down.
Lancaster. And thereof came it that the fleering Scots
  To England's high disgrace, have made this jig ;
    " Maids of England, sore may you mourn,
      For your lemans you have lost at Bannocksbourn,
        With a heave and a ho !
      What weeneth the King of England,
      So soon to have won Scotland ?—
        With a rombelow."
Mortimer jun. Wigmore shall fly to set my uncle free.
Lancaster. And when 'tis gone, our swords shall pur-
        chase more.
    If ye be mov'd, revenge it as you can ;
  Look next to see us with our ensigns spread.
                                Exeunt [*the two*] *Nobles.*

Edward. My swelling heart for very anger breaks.
How oft have I been baited by these peers?
And dare not be reveng'd, for their power is great.
Yet, shall the crowing of these cockerels
Affright a lion? Edward, unfold thy paws,
And let their lives' blood slake thy fury's hunger.
If I be cruel and grow tyrannous,
Now let them thank themselves, and rue too late.

Kent. My lord, I see your love to Gaveston
Will be the ruin of the realm and you,
For now the wrathful nobles threaten wars,
And therefore, brother, banish him for ever.

Edward. Art thou an enemy to my Gaveston?

Kent. Ay, and it grieves me that I favoured him.

Edward. Traitor, begone! whine thou with Mortimer.

Kent. So will I, rather than with Gaveston.

Edward. Out of my sight, and trouble me no more.

Kent. No marvel though thou scorn thy noble peers,
When I thy brother am rejected thus.

Edward. Away!   *Exit.*
Poor Gaveston, that hast no friend but me,
Do what they can, we'll live in Tynemouth here,
And, so I walk with him about the walls,
What care I though the earls begirt us round?
Here comes she that's cause of all these jars.

Enter the QUEEN [*with the* KING'S Niece, *two Ladies,*
GAVESTON,] BALDOCK *and* SPENCER [*junior*].

Queen. My lord, 'tis thought the earls are up in arms.

Edward. Ay, and 'tis likewise thought you favour him.

Queen. Thus do you still suspect me without cause ?

Niece. Sweet uncle, speak more kindly to the queen.

Gaveston. My lord, dissemble with her, speak her fair.

Edward. Pardon me, sweet, I forgot myself.

Queen. Your pardon is quickly got of Isabel.

Edward. The younger Mortimer is grown so brave,
    That to my face he threatens civil wars.

Gaveston. Why do you not commit him to the Tower ?

Edward. I dare not, for the people love him well.

Gaveston. Why, then we'll have him privily made
    away.

Edward. Would Lancaster and he had both carous'd
    A bowl of poison to each other's health.
    But let them go, and tell me what are these.

Niece. Two of my father's servants whilst he liv'd ;
    May't please your grace to entertain them now ?

Edward. Tell me, where wast thou born ? what is thine
    arms ?

Baldock. My name is Baldock, and my gentry
    I fetcht from Oxford, not from heraldry.

Edward. The fitter are thou, Baldock, for my turn.
    Wait on me, and I'll see thou shalt not want.

Baldock. I humbly thank your majesty.

Edward. Knowest thou him, Gaveston ?

Gaveston.   Ay, my lord ;
    His name is Spencer, he is well allied ;
    For my sake, let him wait upon your grace ;
    Scarce shall you find a man of more desert.

Edward. Then, Spencer, wait upon me ; for his sake
    I'll grace thee with a higher style ere long.

Spencer [*jun.*]. No greater titles happen unto me,
  Than to be favoured of your majesty.
Edward. Cousin, this day shall be your marriage-feast.
  And, Gaveston, think that I love thee well,
  To wed thee to our niece, the only heir
  Unto the Earl of Gloucester late deceased.
Gaveston. I know, my lord, many will stomach me,
  But I respect neither their love nor hate.
Edward. The headstrong barons shall not limit me ;
  He that I list to favour shall be great.
  Come, let's away ; and when the marriage ends,
  Have at the rebels, and their complices.

                          Exeunt omnes.

[SCENE III

Near Tynemouth Castle]

Enter LANCASTER, MORTIMER [*junior*], WARWICK,
PEMBROKE, KENT, [*and others*].

Kent. My lords, of love to this our native land
  I come to join with you and leave the king ;
  And in your quarrel and the realm's behoof
  Will be the first that shall adventure life.
Lancaster. I fear me you are sent of policy,
  To undermine us with a show of love.
Warwick. He is your brother, therefore have we cause
  To cast the worst, and doubt of your revolt.
Kent. Mine honour shall be hostage of my truth :

If that will not suffice, farewell, my lords.

Mortimer jun. Stay, Edmund ; never was Plantagenet
    False of his word, and therefore trust we thee.

Pembroke. But what's the reason you should leave him
       now ?

Kent. I have inform'd the Earl of Lancaster.

Lancaster. And it sufficeth. Now, my lords, know this,
    That Gaveston is secretly arriv'd,
    And here in Tynemouth frolics with the king.
    Let us with these our followers scale the walls,
    And suddenly surprise them unawares.

Mortimer jun. I'll give the onset.

Warwick.   And I'll follow thee.

Mortimer jun. This tottered ensign of my ancestors,
    Which swept the desert shore of that dead sea
    Whereof we got the name of Mortimer,
    Will I advance upon this castle's walls.
    Drums, strike alarum, raise them from their sport,
    And ring aloud the knell of Gaveston.

Lancaster. None be so hardy as to touch the king ;
    But neither spare you Gaveston nor his friends.

                              Exeunt.

[SCENE IV

In Tynemouth Castle]

Enter the KING *and* SPENCER *[junior].*

Edward. O tell me, Spencer, where is Gaveston ?

Spencer [jun.] I fear me he is slain, my gracious lord.

Edward. No, here he comes ; now let them spoil and
kill.

[Enter] to them [the QUEEN, *the* KING'S Niece,]
GAVESTON, *etc.*

Fly, fly, my lords, the earls have got the hold ;
Take shipping and away to Scarborough ;
Spencer and I will post away by land.
Gaveston. O stay, my lord, they will not injure you.
Edward. I will not trust them, Gaveston ; away.
Gaveston. Farewell, my lord.
Edward. Lady, farewell.
Niece. Farewell, sweet uncle, till we meet again.
Edward. Farewell, sweet Gaveston, and farewell, niece.
Queen. No farewell to poor Isabel thy queen ?
Edward. Yes, yes, for Mortimer, your lover's sake.
Queen. Heavens can witness I love none but you :

> *Exeunt omnes, manet Isabella.*

From my embracements thus he breaks away.
O that mine arms could close this isle about,
That I might pull him to me where I would ;
Or that these tears, that drizzle from mine eyes,
Had power to mollify his stony heart,
That when I had him we might never part.

Enter the Barons [LANCASTER, WARWICK, MORTI-
MER *junior, and others*]. *Alarums.*

Lancaster. I wonder how he scap'd ?
Mortimer jun.   Who's this ? the queen !

Queen. Ay, Mortimer, the miserable queen,
  Whose pining heart her inward sighs have blasted,
  And body with continual mourning wasted ;
  These hands are tir'd with haling of my lord
  From Gaveston, from wicked Gaveston,
  And all in vain ; for, when I speak him fair,
  He turns away, and smiles upon his minion.

Mortimer jun. Cease to lament, and tell us where's the
    king ?

Queen. What would you with the King ? is't him you
    seek ?

Lancaster. No, madam, but that cursed Gaveston.
  Far be it from the thought of Lancaster
  To offer violence to his sovereign.
  We would but rid the realm of Gaveston :
  Tell us where he remains, and he shall die.

Queen. He's gone by water unto Scarborough ;
  Pursue him quickly, and he cannot scape ;
  The king hath left him, and his train is small.

Warwick. Forslow no time ; sweet Lancaster, let's
    march.

Mortimer jun. How comes it that the king and he is
    parted ?

Queen. That this your army, going several ways,
  Might be of lesser force : and with the power
  That he intendeth presently to raise,
  Be easily suppress'd ; and therefore be gone.

Mortimer jun. Here in the river rides a Flemish
    hoy ;
  Let's all aboard, and follow him amain.

Lancaster. The wind that bears him hence will fill our
    sails :
  Come, come aboard, 'tis but an hour's sailing.
Mortimer jun. Madam, stay you within this castle here.
Queen. No, Mortimer, I'll to my lord the king.
Mortimer jun. Nay, rather sail with us to Scarborough.
Queen. You know the king is so suspicious,
  As if he hear I have but talk'd with you,
  Mine honour will be call'd in question ;
  And therefore, gentle Mortimer, be gone.
Mortimer jun. Madam, I cannot stay to answer you,
  But think of Mortimer as he deserves.
               [Exeunt all but the Queen.]
Queen. So well hast thou deserv'd, sweet Mortimer,
  As Isabel could live with thee for ever.
  In vain I look for love at Edward's hand,
  Whose eyes are fix'd on none but Gaveston,
  Yet once more I'll importune him with prayers :
  If he be strange and not regard my words,
  My son and I will over into France,
  And to the king my brother there complain,
  How Gaveston hath robb'd me of his love :
  But yet I hope my sorrows will have end,
  And Gaveston this blessed day be slain.   *Exit.*

[SCENE V

The Open Country]

Enter GAVESTON, *pursued*.

Gaveston. Yet, lusty lords, I have escap'd your hands,
  Your threats, your larums, and your hot pursuits ;
  And though divorced from king Edward's eyes,
  Yet liveth Pierce of Gaveston unsurpris'd,
  Breathing, in hope (*malgrado* all your beards,
  That muster rebels thus against your king),
  To see his royal sovereign once again.

> *Enter the Nobles* [WARWICK, LANCASTER, PEM-
> BROKE, MORTIMER *junior*, Soldiers, JAMES,
> *and other* Attendants of Pembroke].

Warwick. Upon him, soldiers, take away his weapons.
Mortimer jun. Thou proud disturber of thy country's
      peace,
  Corrupter of thy king, cause of these broils,
  Base flatterer, yield ! and were it not for shame,
  Shame and dishonour to a soldier's name,
  Upon my weapon's point here shouldst thou fall,
  And welter in thy gore.
Lancaster.   Monster of men !
  That, like the Greekish strumpet, train'd to arms

And bloody wars so many valiant knights ;
Look for no other fortune, wretch, than death.
Kind Edward is not here to buckler thee.
Warwick. Lancaster, why talkst thou to the slave ?
Go, soldiers, take him hence, for, by my sword,
His head shall off : Gaveston, short warning
Shall serve thy turn : it is our country's cause,
That here severely we will execute
Upon thy person. Hang him at a bough.
Gaveston. My lord !—
Warwick. Soldiers, have him away ;
But for thou wert the favourite of a king,
Thou shalt have so much honour at our hands.
Gaveston. I thank you all, my lords : then I perceive,
That heading is one, and hanging is the other,
And death is all.

Enter EARL *of* ARUNDEL.

Lancaster. How now, my lord of Arundel ?
Arundel. My lords, King Edward greets you all by me.
Warwick. Arundel, say your message.
Arundel.   His majesty,
Hearing that you had taken Gaveston,
Entreateth you by me, yet but he may
See him before he dies ; for why, he says,
And sends you word, he knows that die he shall ;
And if you gratify his grace so far,
He will be mindful of the courtesy.
Warwick. How now ?

Gaveston.   Renowmed Edward, how thy name
   Revives poor Gaveston.

Warwick.   No, it needeth not ;
   Arundel, we will gratify the king
   In other matters ; he must pardon us in this.
   Soldiers, away with him.

Gaveston. Why, my lord of Warwick,
   Will not these delays beget my hopes ?
   I know it, lords, it is this life you aim at ;
   Yet grant King Edward this.

Mortimer jun.   Shalt thou appoint
   What we shall grant ? Soldiers, away with him :
   Thus we'll gratify the king,
   We'll send his head by thee ; let him bestow
   His tears on that, for that is all he gets
   Of Gaveston, or else his senseless trunk.

Lancaster. Not so, my lord, lest he bestow more cost
   In burying him than he hath ever earned.

Arundel. My lords, it is his majesty's request,
   And in the honour of a king he swears,
   He will but talk with him, and send him back.

Warwick. When, can you tell ? Arundel, no ; we wot,
   He that the care of realm remits,
   And drives his nobles to these exigents
   For Gaveston, will, if he sees him once,
   Violate any promise to possess him.

Arundel. Then if you will not trust his grace in keep,
   My lords, I will be pledge for his return.

Mortimer jun. It is honourable in thee to offer this ;
   But for we know thou art a noble gentleman,

We will not wrong thee so, to make away
A true man for a thief.

Gaveston. How mean'st thou, Mortimer? that is over-
base.

Mortimer jun. Away, base groom, robber of king's
renowm.

Question with thy companions and thy mates.

Pembroke. My lord Mortimer, and you, my lords, each
one,

To gratify the king's request therein,
Touching the sending of this Gaveston,
Because his majesty so earnestly
Desires to see the man before his death,
I will upon mine honour undertake
To carry him, and bring him back again ;
Provided this, that you my lord of Arundel
Will join with me.

Warwick.   Pembroke, what wilt thou do ?
Cause yet more bloodshed : is it not enough
That we have taken him, but must we now
Leave him on " had I wist," and let him go ?

Pembroke. My lords, I will not over-woo your honours,
But if you dare trust Pembroke with the prisoner,
Upon mine oath, I will return him back.

Arundel. My lord of Lancaster, what say you in this ?

Lancaster. Why, I say, let him go on Pembroke's word.

Pembroke. And you, lord Mortimer ?

Mortimer jun. How say you, my lord of Warwick ?

Warwick. Nay, do your pleasures, I know how 'twill
prove.

Pembroke. Then give him me.

Gaveston.   Sweet sovereign, yet I come
 To see thee ere I die.

Warwick [aside].   Yet not perhaps,
 If Warwick's wit and policy prevail.

Mortimer jun. My lord of Pembroke, we deliver him
   you ;
 Return him on your honour. Sound, away !
  Exeunt manent Pembroke, Arundel, Gaveston, and
  Pembroke's men, four Soldiers.

Pembroke. My lord, you shall go with me.
 My house is not far hence, out of the way
 A little, but our men shall go along.
 We that have pretty wenches to our wives,
 Sir, must not come so near and baulk their lips.

Arundel. 'Tis very kindly spoke, my lord of Pembroke ;
 Your honour hath an adamant of power
 To draw a prince.

Pembroke.   So, my lord. Come hither, James :
 I do commit this Gaveston to thee,
 Be thou this night his keeper ; in the morning
 We will discharge thee of thy charge : be gone.

Gaveston. Unhappy Gaveston, whither goest thou now ?
        Exit cum servis Pembroke.

Horse-boy. My lord, we'll quickly be at Cobham.
         Exeunt ambo.

[ACT III

SCENE I

The Open Country]

Enter GAVESTON *mourning,* [JAMES, *and others of*]
the Earl of Pembroke's men.

Gaveston. O treacherous Warwick, thus to wrong thy
  friend.
James. I see it is your life these arms pursue.
Gaveston. Weaponless must I fall, and die in bands ?
 O, must this day be period of my life ?
 Centre of all my bliss ! An ye be men,
 Speed to the king.

Enter WARWICK *and his company.*

Warwick.   My lord of Pembroke's men,
 Strive you no longer ; I will have that Gaveston.
James. Your lordship doth dishonour to yourself,
 And wrong our lord, your honourable friend.
Warwick. No, James, it is my country's cause I follow.
 Go, take the villain ; soldiers, come away.
 We'll make quick work. Commend me to your
  master,

My friend, and tell him that I watch'd it well.
Come, let thy shadow parley with King Edward.
Gaveston. Treacherous earl, shall I not see the King ?
Warwick. The king of heaven perhaps, no other king.
    Away !
    [*Exeunt Warwick and his men with Gaveston.*
        Manet James cum cœteris.]
[*James*]. Come, fellows, it booted not for us to strive,
We will in haste go certify our lord.   *Exeunt.*

[SCENE II

Near Boroughbridge, in Yorkshire]

Enter KING EDWARD *and* SPENCER [*junior,* BALDOCK,
   and Nobles *of the* King's side, *and* Soldiers] *with
   drums and fifes.*

Edward. I long to hear an answer from the barons
Touching my friend, my dearest Gaveston.
Ah ! Spencer, not the riches of my realm
Can ransom him ; ah, he is mark'd to die.
I know the malice of the younger Mortimer,
Warwick I know is rough, and Lancaster
Inexorable, and I shall never see
My lovely Pierce, my Gaveston again !
The barons overbear me with their pride.
Spencer [*jun.*]. Were I King Edward, England's sover-
    eign,

Son to the lovely Eleanor of Spain,
Great Edward Longshanks' issue, would I bear
These braves, this rage, and suffer uncontroll'd
These barons thus to beard me in my land,
In mine own realm? My lord, pardon my speech:
Did you retain your father's magnanimity,
Did you regard the honour of your name,
You would not suffer thus your majesty
Be counterbuft of your nobility.
Strike off their heads, and let them preach on poles.
No doubt, such lessons they will teach the rest,
As by their preachments they will profit much,
And learn obedience to their lawful king.

Edward. Yea, gentle Spencer, we have been too mild,
Too kind to them ; but now have drawn our sword,
And if they send me not my Gaveston,
We'll steel it on their crest, and poll their tops.

Baldock. This haught resolve becomes your majesty,
Not to be tied to their affection,
As though your highness were a schoolboy still,
And must be aw'd and govern'd like a child.

Enter HUGH SPENCER, *an old man, father to the*
young SPENCER, *with his truncheon and* Soldiers.

Spencer sen. Long live my sovereign, the noble
Edward,
In peace triumphant, fortunate in wars !

Edward. Welcome, old man, com'st thou in Edward's
aid ?
Then tell thy prince of whence, and what thou art.

Spencer sen. Lo, with a band of bowmen and of pikes,
  Brown bills and targeteers, four hundred strong,
  Sworn to defend King Edward's royal right,
  I come in person to your majesty,
  Spencer, the father of Hugh Spencer there,
  Bound to your highness everlastingly,
  For favours done, in him, unto us all.

Edward. Thy father, Spencer?

Spencer jun.   True, an it like your grace,
  That pours, in lieu of all your goodness shown,
  His life, my lord, before your princely feet.

Edward. Welcome ten thousand times, old man, again.
  Spencer, this love, this kindness to thy king,
  Argues thy noble mind and disposition.
  Spencer, I here create thee Earl of Wiltshire,
  And daily will enrich thee with our favour,
  That, as the sunshine, shall reflect o'er thee.
  Beside, the more to manifest our love,
  Because we hear Lord Bruce doth sell his land,
  And that the Mortimers are in hand withal,
  Thou shalt have crowns of us t' outbid the barons:
  And, Spencer, spare them not, but lay it on.
  Soldiers, a largess, and thrice welcome all.

Spencer [jun.]. My lord, here comes the queen.

    Enter the QUEEN *and her son* [PRINCE EDWARD],
        and LEVUNE, *a Frenchman.*

Edward.   Madam, what news?

Queen. News of dishonour, lord, and discontent.
  Our friend Levune, faithful and full of trust,

Informeth us, by letters and by words,
That lord Valois our brother, King of France,
Because your highness hath been slack in homage,
Hath seized Normandy into his hands.
These be the letters, this the messenger.

Edward. Welcome, Levune. [*To the* QUEEN.] Tush,
    Sib, if this be all,
Valois and I will soon be friends again.
But to my Gaveston ; shall I never see,
Never behold thee now ? Madam, in this matter,
We will employ you and your little son ;
You shall go parley with the king of France.
Boy, see you bear you bravely to the king,
And do your message with a majesty.

Prince. Commit not to my youth things of more weight
Than fits a prince so young as I to bear,
And fear not, lord and father, heaven's great beams
On Atlas' shoulder shall not lie more safe,
Than shall your charge committed to my trust.

Queen. Ah, boy ! this towardness makes thy mother
    fear
Thou art not mark'd to many days on earth.

Edward. Madam, we will that you with speed be
    shipp'd,
And this our son ; Levune shall follow you
With all the haste we can despatch him hence.
Choose of our lords to bear you company ;
And go in peace, leave us in wars at home.

Queen. Unnatural wars, where subjects brave their
    king ;

    God end them once !   My lord, I take my leave,
To make my preparation for France.
                                [Exit with Prince Edward.]

                  Enter [ARUNDEL].

Edward. What, lord [Arundel,] dost thou come alone ?
[*Arundel.*] Yea, my good lord, for Gaveston is dead.
Edward. Ah, traitors ! have they put my friend to
      death ?
  Tell me, [Arundel,] died he ere thou cam'st,
  Or didst thou see my friend to take his death ?
[*Arundel.*] Neither, my lord ; for as he was surpris'd,
  Begirt with weapons, and with enemies round,
  I did your highness' message to them all ;
  Demanding him of them, entreating rather,
  And said, upon the honour of my name,
  That I would undertake to carry him
  Unto your highness, and to bring him back.
Edward. And tell me, would the rebels deny me that ?
Spencer [*jun.*]. Proud recreants.
Edward.   Yea, Spencer, traitors all.
[*Arundel.*] I found them at the first inexorable ;
  The Earl of Warwick would not bide the hearing,
  Mortimer hardly ; Pembroke and Lancaster
  Spake least : and when they flatly had denied,
  Refusing to receive me pledge for him,
  The Earl of Pembroke mildly thus bespake ;
  " My lords, because our sovereign sends for him,
  And promiseth he shall be safe return'd,

I will this undertake, to have him hence,
And see him re-delivered to your hands."

Edward. Well, and how fortunes that he came not ?

Spencer [*jun.*]. Some treason, or some villainy, was
cause.

[*Arundel.*] The Earl of Warwick seiz'd him on his
way ;
For being delivered unto Pembroke's men,
Their lord rode home thinking his prisoner safe ;
But ere he came, Warwick in ambush lay,
And bare him to his death ; and in a trench
Strake off his head, and march'd unto the camp.

Spencer [*jun.*]. A bloody part, flatly against law of arms.

Edward. O shall I speak, or shall I sigh and die !

Spencer [*jun.*]. My lord, refer your vengeance to the
sword
Upon these barons ; hearten up your men ;
Let them not unreveng'd murther your friends !
Advance your standard, Edward, in the field,
And march to fire them from their starting holes.

Edward kneels and saith

Edward. By earth, the common mother of us all,
By heaven, and all the moving orbs thereof,
By this right hand, and by my father's sword,
And all the honours longing to my crown,
I will have heads, and lives for him, as many
As I have manors, castles, towns, and towers.

[*Rises.*]

Treacherous Warwick ! traitorous Mortimer !
If I be England's king, in lakes of gore

Your headless trunks, your bodies will I trail,
That you may drink your fill, and quaff in blood,
And stain my royal standard with the same,
That so my bloody colours may suggest
Remembrance of revenge immortally
On your accursed traitorous progeny,
You villains, that have slain my Gaveston.
And in this place of honour and of trust,
Spencer, sweet Spencer, I adopt thee here :
And merely of our love we do create thee
Earl of Gloucester, and Lord Chamberlain,
Despite of times, despite of enemies.

Spencer [*jun.*]. My lord, here's a messenger from the
         barons
Desires access unto your majesty.

Edward. Admit him near.

Enter the [Messenger, *a*] Herald *from the* Barons,
with his coat of arms.

Messenger. Long live King Edward, England's lawful
         lord.
Edward. So wish not they, I wis, that sent thee hither.
Thou comst from Mortimer and his complices,
A ranker rout of rebels never was.
Well, say thy message.
Messenger. The barons up in arms by me salute
Your highness with long life and happiness ;
And bid me say, as plainer to your grace,
That if without effusion of blood

You will this grief have ease and remedy,
That from your princely person you remove
This Spencer, as a putrifying branch,
That deads the royal vine, whose golden leaves
Empale your princely head, your diadem,
Whose brightness such pernicious upstarts dim,
Say they ; and lovingly advise your grace,
To cherish virtue and nobility,
And have old servitors in high esteem,
And shake off smooth dissembling flatterers :
This granted, they, their honours, and their lives,
Are to your highness vow'd and consecrate.

Spencer [*jun.*]. Ah, traitors ! will they still display their
    pride ?

Edward. Away, tarry no answer, but be gone.
Rebels, will they appoint their sovereign
His sports, his pleasures, and his company ?
Yet, ere thou go, see how I do divorce

                            Embrace Spencer

Spencer from me. Now get thee to thy lords,
And tell them I will come to chastise them
For murthering Gaveston ; hie thee, get thee gone.
Edward with fire and sword follows at thy heels.

                             [*Exit Herald.*]

My lord, perceive you how these rebels swell ?
Soldiers, good hearts, defend your sovereign's right,
For now, even now, we march to make them stoop.
Away !

    *Exeunt. Alarums, excursions, a great fight, and a
      retreat* [*sounded, within*].

[SCENE III

The battle-field, Boroughbridge]

Enter the KING, SPENCER *the Father* [*senior*], SPENCER
the son [*junior*], *and the* Noblemen *of the King's
side.*

Edward. Why do we sound retreat? upon them, lords!
This day I shall pour vengeance with my sword
On those proud rebels that are up in arms,
And do confront and countermand their king.

Spencer [*jun.*]. I doubt it not, my lord, right will prevail.

Spencer [*sen.*]. 'Tis not amiss, my liege, for either part
To breathe awhile; our men, with sweat and dust
All chok'd well near, begin to faint for heat;
And this retire refresheth horse and man.

Spencer [*jun.*]. Here come the rebels.

Enter the Barons: MORTIMER [*junior*], LANCASTER,
WARWICK, PEMBROKE, *cum cæteris.*

Mortimer [*jun.*]. Look, Lancaster, yonder is Edward
Among his flatterers.

Lancaster.   And there let him be
Till he pay dearly for their company.

Warwick. And shall, or Warwick's sword shall smite
in vain.

Edward. What, rebels, do you shrink and sound
    retreat ?

Mortimer [jun.]. No, Edward, no, thy flatterers faint
    and fly.

Lancaster. They'd best betimes forsake thee, and their
    trains,
For they'll betray thee, traitors as they are.

Spencer [jun.]. Traitor on thy face, rebellious Lancaster

Pembroke. Away, base upstart, brav'st thou nobles thus

Spencer [sen.]. A noble attempt, and honourable deed,
  Is it not, trow ye, to assemble aid,
  And levy arms against your lawful king ?

Edward. For which ere long their heads shall satisfy,
  T' appease the wrath of their offended king.

Mortimer jun. Then, Edward, thou wilt fight it to the
    last,
  And rather bathe thy sword in subjects' blood,
  Than banish that pernicious company.

Edward. Ay, traitors all, rather than thus be brav'd,
  Make England's civil towns huge heaps of stones,
  And ploughs to go about our palace-gates.

Warwick. A desperate and unnatural resolution.
  Alarum ! to the fight ! St. George for England,
  And the barons' right.

Edward. Saint George for England, and King Edward'
    right. [*Alarums. Exeunt the two parties severally.*

   Enter [KING] EDWARD [*and his followers,*] *with the*
           Barons, *captives.*

Edward. Now, lusty lords, now, not by chance of war

But justice of the quarrel and the cause,
Vail'd is your pride ; methinks you hang the heads,
But we'll advance them, traitors ; now 'tis time
To be aveng'd on you for all your braves,
And for the murther of my dearest friend,
To whom right well you knew our soul was knit,
Good Pierce of Gaveston, my sweet favourite.
Ah, rebels, recreants, you made him away !

Kent. Brother, in regard of thee, and of thy land,
Did they remove that flatterer from thy throne.

Edward. So, sir, you have spoke ; away, avoid our
    presence.   [_Exit Kent._]
Accursed wretches, was't in regard of us,
When we had sent out messenger to request
He might be spared to come to speak with us,
And Pembroke undertook for his return,
That thou, proud Warwick, watch'd the prisoner,
Poor Pierce, and headed him against law of arms ?
For which thy head shall overlook the rest,
As much as thou in rage outwentst the rest.

Warwick. Tyrant, I scorn thy threats and menaces ;
'Tis but temporal that thou canst inflict.

Lancaster. The worst is death, and better die to live
Than live in infamy under such a king.

Edward. Away with them, my lord of Winchester.
These lusty leaders, Warwick and Lancaster,
I charge you roundly—off with both their heads.
Away !

Warwick. Farewell, vain world.

Lancaster.   Sweet Mortimer, farewell.

Mortimer jun. England, unkind to thy nobility,
 Groan for this grief, behold how thou art maimed.

Edward. Go, take that haughty Mortimer to tl
   Tower,
 There see him safe bestow'd ; and for the rest,
 Do speedy execution on them all.
 Begone !

Mortimer jun. What, Mortimer ! can ragged ston
   walls
 Immure thy virtue that aspires to heaven ?
 No, Edward, England's scourge, it may not be ;
 Mortimer's hope surmounts his fortune far.

                          [*The captive Barons are led off*

Edward. Sound drums and trumpets ! March wit
   me, my friends,
 Edward this day hath crown'd him king anew.

     Exeunt ; manent Spencer [*junior*], *Levune, and Baldoc*

Spencer [*jun.*]. Levune, the trust that we repose in thee
 Begets the quiet of King Edward's land.
 Therefore begone in haste, and with advice
 Bestow that treasure on the lords of France,
 That therewith all enchanted, like the guard
 That suffered Jove to pass in showers of gold
 To Danae, all aid may be denied
 To Isabel, the queen, that now in France
 Makes friends, to cross the seas with her young son
 And step into his father's regiment.

Levune. That's it these barons and the subtle queen
 Long levell'd at.

Baldock.   Yea, but, Levune, thou seest

These barons lay their heads on blocks together ;
What they intend, the hangman frustrates clean.
Levune. Have you no doubts, my lords, I'll clap so close
Among the lords of France with England's gold,
That Isabel shall make her plaints in vain,
And France shall be obdurate with her tears.
Spencer [jun.]. Then make for France amain ; Levune,
    away.
Proclaim King Edward's wars and victories.

Exeunt omnes.

[ACT IV

SCENE I

Near the Tower of London]

Enter EDMUND [Earl of Kent].

Kent. Fair blows the wind for France ; blow, gentle
    gale,
  Till Edmund be arriv'd for England's good.
  Nature, yield to my country's cause in this.
  A brother, no, a butcher of thy friends,
  Proud Edward, dost thou banish me thy presence ?
  But I'll to France, and cheer the wronged queen,
  And certify what Edward's looseness is.
  Unnatural king, to slaughter noble men
  And cherish flatterers.   Mortimer, I stay
  Thy sweet escape : stand gracious, gloomy night,
  To his device.

      Enter MORTIMER [*junior*], *disguised*.

Mortimer [*jun.*].   Holla ! who walketh there ?
  Is't you, my lord ?
Kent.   Mortimer, 'tis I ;
  But hath thy potion wrought so happily ?

Mortimer [*jun.*]. It hath, my lord ;   the warders all
        asleep,
    I thank them, gave me leave to pass in peace.
    But hath your grace got shipping unto France ?
Kent. Fear it not.   *Exeunt.*

[SCENE II

Paris]

Enter the QUEEN *and her son* [PRINCE EDWARD].

Queen. Ah, boy, our friends do fail us all in France :
    The lords are cruel, and the king unkind ;
    What shall we do ?
Prince.   Madam, return to England,
    And please my father well, and then a fig
    For all my uncle's friendship here in France.
    I warrant you, I'll win his highness quickly ;
    'A loves me better than a thousand Spencers.
Queen. Ah, boy, thou art deceiv'd, at least in this,
    To think that we can yet be tun'd together ;
    No, no, we jar too far.   Unkind Valois,
    Unhappy Isabel, when France rejects,
    Whither, oh, whither dost thou bend thy steps ?

Enter *Sir* JOHN *of* HAINAULT.

Sir John. Madam, what cheer ?
Queen.   Ah, good Sir John of Hainault,

361

Never so cheerless, nor so far distrest.

Sir John. I hear, sweet lady, of the king's unkindness
 But droop not, madam ; noble minds contemn
 Despair : will your grace with me to Hainault,
 And there stay time's advantage with your son ?
 How say you, my lord, will go with your friends
 And shake off all our fortunes equally ?

Prince. So pleaseth the queen, my mother, me it likes
 The King of England, nor the court of France,
 Shall have me from my gracious mother's side,
 Till I be strong enough to break a staff ;
 And then have at the proudest Spencer's head.

Sir John. Well said, my lord.

Queen. O, my sweet heart, how do I moan thy wrongs
 Yet triumph in the hope of thee, my joy.
 Ah, sweet Sir John, even to the utmost verge
 Of Europe, or the shore of Tanais,
 Will we with thee to Hainault, so we will ;
 The marquis is a noble gentleman ;
 His grace, I dare presume, will welcome me.
 But who are these ?

Enter EDMUND [Earl of Kent] *and* MORTIMER [junior].

Kent.   Madam, long may you live,
 Much happier than your friends in England do.

Queen. Lord Edmund and lord Mortimer alive !
 Welcome to France ; the news was here, my lord,
 That you were dead, or very near your death.

Mortimer jun. Lady, the last was truest of the twain :

But Mortimer, reserv'd for better hap,
Hath shaken off the thraldom of the Tower,
And lives t' advance your standard, good my lord.

Prince. How mean you ? and the king, my father,
    lives !
No, my Lord Mortimer, not I, I trow.

Queen. Not, son ! why not ? I would it were no
    worse.
But, gentle lords, friendless we are in France.

Mortimer jun. Monsieur le Grand, a noble friend of
    yours,
Told us, at our arrival, all the news—
How hard the nobles, how unkind the king
Hath showed himself ; but, madam, right makes
    room
Where weapons want ; and, though a many friends
Are made away, as Warwick, Lancaster,
And others of our party and faction ;
Yet have we friends, assure your grace, in England
Would cast up caps, and clap their hands for joy,
To see us there appointed for our foes.

Kent. Would all were well, and Edward well reclaim'd,
For England's honour, peace, and quietness.

Mortimer jun. But by the sword, my lord, it must be
    deserv'd ;
The king will ne'er forsake his flatterers.

Sir John. My lords of England, sith the ungentle king
Of France refuseth to give aid of arms
To this distressed queen his sister here,
Go you with her to Hainault ; doubt ye not,

We will find comfort, money, men and friends
    Ere long, to bid the English king a base.
    How say, young prince, what think you of the
        match ?

Prince. I think King Edward will outrun us all.

Queen. Nay, son, not so ; and you must not discourage
    Your friends, that are so forward in your aid.

Kent. Sir John of Hainault, pardon us, I pray ;
    These comforts that you give our woful queen
    Bind us in kindness all at your command.

Queen. Yea, gentle brother ; and the God of heaven
    Prosper your happy motion, good Sir John.

Mortimer jun. This noble gentleman, forward in arms,
    Was born, I see, to be our anchor-hold.
    Sir John of Hainault, be it thy renown,
    That England's Queen, and nobles in distress,
    Have been by thee restor'd and comforted.

Sir John. Madam, along, and you, my lord, with me,
    That England's peers may Hainault's welcome see.

                                     [Exeunt.

[SCENE III

The Royal Palace, London]

Enter the KING, [ARUNDEL], *the two* SPENCERS,
with others.

Edward. Thus after many threats of wrathful war,
    Triumpheth England's Edward with his friends ;

And triumph, Edward, with his friends uncon-
    troll'd.
My lord of Gloucester, do you hear the news ?
Spencer jun. What news, my lord ?
Edward. Why, man, they say there is great execution
    Done through the realm ; my lord of Arundel,
    You have the note, have you not ?
[*Arundel.*] From the lieutenant of the Tower, my lord.
Edward. I pray let us see it. [*Takes the note.*]   What
    have we there ?
    Read it, Spencer.
      [*Hands it to*] *Spencer* [*junior, who*] *reads their names.*
    Why, so ; they bark'd apace a month ago :
    Now, on my life, they'll neither bark nor bite.
    Now, sirs, the news from France ?   Gloucester, I
      trow
    The lords of France love England's gold so well
    As Isabella gets no aid from thence.
    What now remains ? have you proclaim'd, my lord,
    Reward for them can bring in Mortimer ?
Spencer jun. My lord, we have ; and if he be in
      England,
    'A will be had ere long, I doubt it not.
Edward. If, dost thou say ? Spencer, as true as death,
    He is in England's ground ; our portmasters
    Are not so careless of their king's command.

             Enter a Post.

    How now, what news with thee ? from whence
      come these ?

Post. Letters, my lord, and tidings forth of France ;
  To you, my lord of Gloucester, from Levune.
                    [*Gives letters to Spencer junior.*]
Edward. Read.
Spencer [*junior*] *reads the letter :*
       " My duty to your honour premised, &c. I
    have, according to instructions in that behalf,
    dealt with the king of France his lords, and
    effected, that the Queen, all discontented and
    discomforted, is gone : whither, if you ask, with
    Sir John of Hainault, brother to the marquis, into
    Flanders. With them are gone lord Edmund, and
    the lord Mortimer, having in their company
    divers of your nation, and others ; and, as
    constant report goeth, they intend to give King
    Edward battle in England, sooner than he can
    look for them. This is all the news of import.
                    Your honour's in all service, LEVUNE."

Edward. Ah, villains, hath that Mortimer escap'd ?
    With him is Edmund gone associate ?
    And will Sir John of Hainault lead the round ?
    Welcome, a God's name, madam, and your son.
    England shall welcome you and all your rout.
    Gallop apace, bright Phœbus, through the sky,
    And dusky night, in rusty iron car,
    Between you both shorten the time, I pray,
    That I may see that most desired day
    When we may meet these traitors in the field.
    Ah, nothing grieves me, but my little boy

Is thus misled to countenance their ills.
Come, friends, to Bristow, there to make us strong ;
And, winds, as equal be to bring them in,
As you injurious were to bear them forth.

[Exeunt.]

[SCENE IV

Near Harwich]

Enter the QUEEN, *her son* [PRINCE EDWARD], EDMUND
    [Earl of Kent], MORTIMER [*junior*], *and Sir* JOHN
    [*of* HAINAULT].

Queen. Now, lords, our loving friends and countrymen,
    Welcome to England all, with prosperous winds.
    Our kindest friends in Belgia have we left,
    To cope with friends at home ; a heavy case
    When force to force is knit, and sword and glaive
    In civil broils makes kin and countrymen
    Slaughter themselves in others, and their sides
    With their own weapons gor'd. But what's the
        help ?
    Misgoverned kings are cause of all this wrack ;
    And, Edward, thou art one among them all,
    Whose looseness hath betrayed thy land to spoil,
    And made the channels overflow with blood
    Of thine own people ; patron shouldst thou be,
    But thou——

367

Mortimer jun. Nay, madam, if you be a warrior,
    You must not grow so passionate in speeches.
    Lords, sith that we are by sufferance of heaven
    Arriv'd, and armed in this prince's right,
    Here for our country's cause swear we to him
    All homage, fealty, and forwardness ;
    And for the open wrongs and injuries
    Edward hath done to us, his queen and land,
    We come in arms to wreck it with the swords,
    That England's queen in peace may repossess
    Her dignities and honours : and withal
    We may remove these flatterers from the king,
    That havocks England's wealth and treasury.
Sir John. Sound trumpets, my lord, and forward let us
    march.
    Edward will think we come to flatter him.
Kent. I would he never had been flattered more.

                             [Exeunt.]

[SCENE V

Near Bristol]

Enter the KING, BALDOCK, *and* SPENCER *[junior],*
    flying about the stage.

Spencer [jun.]. Fly, fly, my lord, the queen is over-
    strong ;
    Her friends do multiply, and yours do fail.

Shape we our course to Ireland, there to breathe.
Edward. What, was I born to fly and run away,
  And leave the Mortimers conquerors behind?
  Give me my horse, and let's r'enforce our troops:
  And in this bed of honour die with fame.
Baldock. O no, my lord, this princely resolution
  Fits not the time; away, we are pursued.

                                        [*Exeunt.*]

[*Enter*] EDMUND [Earl of Kent] *alone, with a sword
                    and target.*

Kent. This way he fled, but I am come too late.
  Edward, alas, my heart relents for thee.
  Proud traitor, Mortimer, why dost thou chase
  Thy lawful king, thy sovereign, with thy sword?
  Vile wretch, and why hast thou, of all unkind,
  Borne arms against thy brother and thy king?
  Rain showers of vengeance on my cursed head,
  Thou God, to whom in justice it belongs
  To punish this unnatural revolt.
  Edward, this Mortimer aims at thy life.
  O fly him, then! But, Edmund, calm this rage,
  Dissemble, or thou diest; for Mortimer
  And Isabel do kiss, while they conspire:
  And yet she bears a face of love forsooth.
  Fie on that love that hatcheth death and hate.
  Edmund, away. Bristow to Longshanks' blood
  Is false; be not found single for suspect:
  Proud Mortimer pries near into thy walks.

Enter the QUEEN, MORTIMER [*junior*], *the young*
PRINCE [EDWARD], *and Sir* JOHN *of* HAINAULT.

Queen. Successful battles gives the God of kings
  To them that fight in right and fear his wrath.
  Since then successfully we have prevailed,
  Thanks be heaven's great architect, and you.
  Ere farther we proceed, my noble lords,
  We here create our well-beloved son,
  Of love and care unto his royal person,
  Lord Warden of the realm, and sith the fates
  Have made his father so infortunate,
  Deal you, my lords, in this, my loving lords,
  As to your wisdoms fittest seems in all.
Kent. Madam, without offence, if I may ask,
  How will you deal with Edward in his fall ?
Prince. Tell me, good uncle, what Edward do you mean?
Kent. Nephew, your father : I dare not call him king.
Mortimer [*jun.*]. My lord of Kent, what needs these
    questions ?
  'Tis not in her controlment, nor in ours,
  But as the realm and parliament shall please,
  So shall your brother be disposed of.
  [*Aside to the Queen.*] I like not this relenting mood in
    Edmund.
  Madam, 'tis good to look to him betimes.
Queen. My lord, the Mayor of Bristow knows our
    mind.
Mortimer [*jun.*]. Yea, madam, and they scape not easily
  That fled the field.

370

Queen.   Baldock is with the King.
  A goodly chancellor, is he not my lord ?
Sir John. So are the Spencers, the father and the son.
Kent. This, Edward, is the ruin of the realm.

Enter RICE AP HOWELL, *and the* Mayor of Bristow, *with*
  SPENCER [*senior, prisoner, and* Attendants].

Rice. God save Queen Isabel, and her princely son.
  Madam, the mayor and citizens of Bristow,
  In sign of love and duty to this presence,
  Present by me this traitor to the state,
  Spencer, the father to that wanton Spencer,
  That, like the lawless Catiline of Rome,
  Revell'd in England's wealth and treasury.
Queen. We thank you all.
Mortimer jun.   Your loving care in this
  Deserveth princely favours and rewards.
  But where's the king and the other Spencer fled ?
Rice. Spencer the son, created Earl of Gloucester,
  Is with that smooth-tongu'd scholar Baldock gone,
  And shipp'd but late for Ireland with the King.
Mortimer jun. Some whirlwind fetch them back or sink them
      all :
  They shall be started thence, I doubt it not.
Prince. Shall I not see the king my father yet ?
Kent [*aside*]. Unhappy is Edward, chas'd from Eng-
      land's bounds.
Sir John. Madam, what resteth, why stand you in a
      muse ?

Queen. I rue my lord's ill-fortune ; but alas,
    Care of my country call'd me to this war.
Mortimer [*jun.*]. Madam, have done with care and sad
       complaint ;
    Your king hath wrong'd your country and himself,
    And we must seek to right it as we may.
    Meanwhile, have hence this rebel to the block.
    Your lordship cannot privilege your head.
Spencer [*sen.*]. Rebel is he that fights against his prince ;
    So fought not they that fought in Edward's right.
Mortimer [*jun.*]. Takes him away, he prates ;
              [*Exeunt Attendants with Spencer senior.*]
                  You, Rice ap Howell,
    Shall do good service to her majesty,
    Being of countenance in your country here,
    To follow these rebellious runagates.
    We in meanwhile, madam, must take advice,
    How Baldock, Spencer, and their complices,
    May in their fall be followed to their end.
                          Exeunt omnes.

[SCENE VI

The Abbey of Neath, Glamorganshire]

Enter the Abbot, Monks, [KING] EDWARD, SPENCER
[*junior*], *and* BALDOCK [*the three latter disguised*].

Abbot. Have you no doubt, my lord ; have you no fear ;
    As silent and as careful will we be,

To keep your royal person safe with us,
Free from suspect, and fell invasion
Of such as have your majesty in chase,
Yourself, and those your chosen company,
As danger of this stormy time requires.

Edward. Father, thy face should harbour no deceit.
O, hadst thou ever been a king, thy heart,
Pierced deeply with sense of my distress,
Could not but take compassion of my state.
Stately and proud, in riches and in train,
Whilom I was, powerful and full of pomp :
But what is he whom rule and empery
Have not in life or death made miserable ?
Come, Spencer ; come, Baldock, come, sit down by
    me ;
Make trial now of that philosophy,
That in our famous nurseries of arts
Thou suckedst from Plato and from Aristotle.
Father, this life contemplative is heaven.
O that I might this life in quiet lead.
But we, alas, are chas'd ; and you, my friends,
Your lives and my dishonour they pursue.
Yet, gentle monks, for treasure, gold nor fee,
Do you betray us and our company.

Monks. Your grace may sit secure, if none but we
Do wot of your abode.

Spencer [*jun.*]. Not one alive ; but shrewdly I suspect
A gloomy fellow in a mead below.
'A gave a long look after us, my lord ;
And all the land I know is up in arms,

Arms that pursue our lives with deadly hate.

Baldock. We were embark'd for Ireland, wretched we,
  With awkward winds and sore tempests driven
  To fall on shore, and here to pine in fear
  Of Mortimer and his confederates.

Edward. Mortimer, who talks of Mortimer?
  Who wounds me with the name of Mortimer,
  That bloody man? Good father, on thy lap
  Lay I this head, laden with mickle care.
  O might I never open these eyes again,
  Never again lift up this drooping head,
  O never more lift up this dying heart!

Spencer [jun.]. Look up, my lord. Baldock, this drow-
    siness
  Betides no good; here even we are betray'd.

Enter, with Welsh hooks, RICE AP HOWELL, *a* Mower,
    and the EARL *of* LEICESTER.

Mower. Upon my life, those be the men ye seek.

Rice. Fellow, enough. My lord, I pray be short,
  A fair commission warrants what we do.

Leicester. The Queen's commission, urged by Mortimer.
  What cannot gallant Mortimer with the queen?
  Alas, see where he sits, and hopes unseen
  T' escape their hands that seek to reave his life.
  Too true it is, *Quem dies vidit veniens superbum,*
  Hunc dies vidit fugiens jacentem.
  But, Leicester, leave to grow so passionate.
  Spencer and Baldock, by no other names,
  I arrest you of high treason here.

Stand not on titles, but obey th' arrest ;
'Tis in the name of Isabel the Queen.
My lord, why droop you thus ?

Edward. O day ! the last of all my bliss on earth,
Centre of all misfortune ! O my stars !
Why do you lour unkindly on a king ?
Comes Leicester, then, in Isabella's name
To take my life, my company from me ?
Here, man, rip up this panting breast of mine,
And take my heart in rescue of my friends !

Rice. Away with them.

Spencer jun.   It may become thee yet
To let us take our farewell of his grace.

Abbot. My heart with pity earns to see this sight,
A king to bear these words and proud commands.

Edward. Spencer, ah, sweet Spencer, thus then must
        we part.

Spencer jun. We must, my lord ; so will the angry
        heavens.

Edward. Nay, so will hell and cruel Mortimer ;
The gentle heavens have not to do in this.

Baldock. My lord, it is in vain to grieve or storm.
Here humbly of your grace we take our leaves ;
Our lots are cast ; I fear me, so is thine.

Edward. In heaven we may, in earth never shall we
        meet :
And, Leicester, say, what shall become of us ?

Leicester. Your majesty must go to Killingworth.

Edward. Must ! 'tis somewhat hard, when kings must
        go.

Leicester. Here is a litter ready for your grace,
  That waits your pleasure, and the day grows old.
Rice. As good be gone, as stay and be benighted.
Edward. A litter hast thou ? lay me in a hearse,
  And to the gates of hell convey me hence ;
  Let Pluto's bells ring out my fatal knell,
  And hags howl for my death at Charon's shore,
  For friends hath Edward none but these and these,
  And these must die under a tyrant's sword.
Rice. My lord, be going ; care not for these,
  For we shall see them shorter by the heads.
Edward. Well, that shall be, shall be : part we must.
  Sweet Spencer, gentle Baldock, part we must.
  Hence feigned weeds ! unfeigned are my woes ;
                       [*Throws off his disguise.*]
  Father, farewell. Leicester, thou stay'st for me,
  And go I must. Life, farewell, with my friends.
                [*Exeunt [King] Edward and Leicester.*
Spencer jun. O, is he gone ? is noble Edward gone ?
  Parted from hence ? never to see us more ?
  Rent, sphere of heaven, and, fire, forsake thy orb,
  Earth, melt to air ! gone is my sovereign,
  Gone, gone, alas, never to make return.
Baldock. Spencer, I see our souls are fleeted hence ;
  We are depriv'd the sunshine of our life :
  Make for a new life, man ; throw up thy eyes
  And heart and hand to heaven's immortal throne,
  Pay nature's debt with cheerful countenance ;
  Reduce we all our lessons unto this,
  To die, sweet Spencer, therefore live we all ;

Spencer, all live to die, and rise to fall.

Rice. Come, come, keep these preachments till you
come to the place appointed. You, and such
as you are, have made wise work in England.
Will your lordships away ?

Mower. Your worship, I trust, will remember me ?

Rice. Remember thee, fellow ! what else ? Follow me
to the town. [*Exeunt.*]

[ACT V

SCENE I

Kenilworth Castle]

Enter the KING, LEICESTER, *with the* BISHOP [OF WINCHESTER] *for the crown,* [*and* TRUSSEL].

Leicester. Be patient, good my lord, cease to lament,
   Imagine Killingworth Castle were your court,
   And that you lay for pleasure here a space,
   Not of compulsion or necessity.
Edward. Leicester, if gentle words might comfort me,
   Thy speeches long ago had eas'd my sorrows ;
   For kind and loving hast thou always been.
   The griefs of private men are soon allay'd,
   But not of kings. The forest deer, being struck,
   Runs to an herb that closeth up the wounds ;
   But when the imperial lion's flesh is gor'd,
   He rends and tears it with his wrathful paw,
   [And] highly scorning that the lowly earth
   Should drink his blood, mounts up into the air.
   And so it fares with me, whose dauntless mind
   The ambitious Mortimer would seek to curb,

And that unnatural queen, false Isabel,
That thus hath pent and mew'd me in a prison;
For such outrageous passions cloy my soul,
As with the wings of rancour and disdain
Full often am I soaring up to heaven,
To plain me to the gods against them both.
But when I call to mind I am a king,
Methinks I should revenge me of the wrongs
That Mortimer and Isabel have done.
But what are kings, when regiment is gone,
But perfect shadows in a sunshine day?
My nobles rule, I bear the name of king;
I wear the crown, but am controll'd by them,
By Mortimer, and my unconstant queen,
Who spots my nuptial bed with infamy;
Whilst I am lodg'd within this cave of care,
Where sorrow at my elbow still attends,
To company my heart with sad laments,
That bleeds within me for this strange exchange.
But tell me, must I now resign my crown,
To make usurping Mortimer a king?
Bishop. Your grace mistakes; it is for England's good,
And princely Edward's right we crave the crown.
Edward. No, 'tis for Mortimer, not Edward's head;
For he's a lamb, encompassed by wolves,
Which in a moment will abridge his life.
But if proud Mortimer do wear this crown,
Heavens turn it to a blaze of quenchless fire;
Or, like the snaky wreath of Tisiphon,
Engirt the temples of his hateful head;

So shall not England's vine be perished,
But Edward's name survives, though Edward dies.
Leicester. My lord, why waste you thus the time away ?
They stay your answer ; will you yield your crown ?
Edward. Ah, Leicester, weigh how hardly I can brook
To lose my crown and kingdom without cause ;
To give ambitious Mortimer my right,
That like a mountain overwhelms my bliss,
In which extreme my mind here murthered is.
But what the heavens appoint, I must obey !
Here, take my crown ; the life of Edward too ;
                          [*Taking off the crown.*]
Two kings in England cannot reign at once.
But stay awhile, let me be king till night,
That I may gaze upon this glittering crown ;
So shall my eyes receive their last content,
My head, the latest honour due to it,
And jointly both yield up their wished right.
Continue ever thou celestial sun ;
Let never silent night possess this clime :
Stand still you watches of the element ;
All times and seasons, rest you at a stay,
That Edward may be still fair England's king.
But day's bright beams doth vanish fast away,
And needs I must resign my wished crown.
Inhuman creatures, nurs'd with tiger's milk,
Why gape you for your sovereign's overthrow ?
My diadem I mean, and guiltless life.
See, monsters, see, I'll wear my crown again !
                          [*He puts on the crown.*]

What, fear you not the fury of your king?
But, hapless Edward, thou art fondly led;
They pass not for thy frowns as late they did,
But seek to make a new-elected king;
Which fills my mind with strange despairing
    thoughts,
Which thoughts are martyred with endless torments,
And in this torment comfort find I none,
But that I feel the crown upon my head,
And therefore let me wear it yet awhile.

Trussel. My lord, the parliament must have present
    news,
  And therefore say, will you resign or no?

                      The King rageth.

Edward. I'll not resign; but whilst I live [be King].
  Traitors, be gone! and join you with Mortimer!
  Elect, conspire, install, do what you will,
  Their blood and yours shall seal these treacheries!

Bishop. This answer we'll return, and so farewell.

Leicester. Call them again, my lord, and speak them
    fair;
  For if they go, the prince shall lose his right.

Edward. Call thou them back, I have no power to
    speak.

Leicester. My lord, the king is willing to resign.

Bishop. If he be not, let him choose.

Edward. O would I might! but heavens and earth
    conspire
  To make me miserable. Here receive my crown;
  Receive it? no, these innocent hands of mine

Shall not be guilty of so foul a crime.
He of you all that most desires my blood,
And will be called the murtherer of a king,
Take it. What, are you mov'd? pity you me?
Then send for unrelenting Mortimer,
And Isabel, whose eyes, being turn'd to steel,
Will sooner sparkle fire than shed a tear.
Yet stay, for rather than I will look on them,
Here, here!   [*Gives the crown.*]
          Now, sweet God of heaven,
Make me despise this transitory pomp,
And sit for aye enthronized in heaven.
Come, death, and with thy fingers close my eyes,
Of if I live, let me forget myself.

Enter BERKELEY.

Berkeley. My lord—
Edward. Call me not lord; away—out of my sight:
   Ah, pardon me: grief makes me lunatic.
   Let not that Mortimer protect my son;
   More safety is there in a tiger's jaws,
   Than his embracements. Bear this to the queen,
   Wet with my tears, and dried again with sighs;
                         [*Gives a handkerchief.*]
   If with the sight thereof she be not moved,
   Return it back and dip it in my blood.
   Commend me to my son, and bid him rule
   Better than I. Yet how have I transgress'd,
   Unless it be with too much clemency?

Trussel. And thus most humbly do we take our leave.
      [*Exeunt the Bishop of Winchester and Trussel.*]
Edward. Farewell; I know the next news that they
    bring
  Will be my death; and welcome shall it be;
  To wretched men death is felicity.

[BERKELEY *gives a paper to* LEICESTER.]

Leicester. Another post. What news brings he?
Edward. Such news as I expect: come, Berkeley, come,
  And tell thy message to my naked breast.
Berkeley. My lord, think not a thought so villainous
  Can harbour in a man of noble birth.
  To do your highness service and devoir,
  And save you from your foes, Berkeley would die.
Leicester. My lord, the council of the Queen commands
  That I resign my charge.
Edward. And who must keep me now? Must you,
    my lord?
Berkeley. Ay, my most gracious lord, so 'tis decreed.
Edward [*taking the paper*]. By Mortimer, whose name is
    written here.
  Well may I rent his name that rends my heart!
                    [*Tears the paper.*]
  This poor revenge hath something eas'd my mind.
  So may his limbs be torn, as is this paper.
  Hear me, immortal Jove, and grant it too.
Berkeley. Your grace must hence with me to Berkeley
    straight.

Edward. Whither you will ; all places are alike,
  And every earth is fit for burial.
Leicester. Favour him, my lord, as much as lieth in you.
Berkeley. Even so betide my soul as I use him.
Edward. Mine enemy hath pitied my estate,
  And that's the cause that I am now remov'd.
Berkeley. And thinks your grace that Berkeley will be
      cruel ?
Edward. I know not ; but of this am I assured,
  That death ends all, and I can die but once.
  Leicester, farewell.
Leicester. Not yet, my lord ; I'll bear you on your way.
                                          Exeunt omnes.

[SCENE II

The Royal Palace, London]

Enter MORTIMER [*junior*] *and* QUEEN ISABEL.

Mortimer [*jun.*]. Fair Isabel, now have we our desire ;
  The proud corrupters of the light-brain'd king
  Have done their homage to the lofty gallows,
  And he himself lies in captivity.
  Be rul'd by me, and we will rule the realm.
  In any case take heed of childish fear,
  For now we hold an old wolf by the ears,
  That, if he slip, will seize upon us both,
  And gripe the sorer, being grip'd himself.

Think therefore, madam, that imports us much
To erect your son with all the speed we may,
And that I be protector over him ;
For our behoof will bear the greater sway
Whenas a king's name shall be under writ.
Queen. Sweet Mortimer, the life of Isabel,
  Be thou persuaded that I love thee well,
  And therefore, so the prince my son be safe,
  Whom I esteem as dear as these mine eyes,
  Conclude against his father what thou wilt,
  And I myself will willingly subscribe.
Mortimer jun. First would I hear news that he were
      depos'd,
  And then let me alone to handle him.

Enter Messenger.

Mortimer jun. Letters ! from whence ?
Messenger.   From Killingworth, my lord.
Queen. How fares my lord the king ?
Messenger. In health, madam, but full of pensiveness.
Queen. Alas, poor soul, would I could ease his grief.

[*Enter the* BISHOP OF WINCHESTER *with the crown.*]

Thanks, gentle Winchester.
  [*To the Messenger.*] Sirrah, be gone.   [*Exit Messenger.*]
Bishop. The king hath willingly resign'd his crown.
Queen. O happy news ! send for the prince, my son.
Bishop. Further, ere this letter was seal'd, Lord
      Berkeley came,

So that he now is gone from Killingworth ;
And we have heard that Edmund laid a plot
To set his brother free ; no more but so.
The lord of Berkeley is so pitiful
As Leicester that had charge of him before.
Queen. Then let some other be his guardian.
Mortimer jun. Let me alone, here is the Privy Seal.
                    [*Exit the Bishop of Winchester.*]
[*Mortimer junior, calling.*] Who's there ?—Call hither
        Gurney and Matrevis.
    To dash the heavy-headed Edmund's drift,
    Berkeley shall be discharg'd, the king remov'd,
    And none but we shall know where he lieth.
Queen. But, Mortimer, as long as he survives,
    What safety rests for us, or for my son ?
Mortimer jun. Speak, shall he presently be dispatch'd
        and die ?
Queen. I would he were, so it were not by my means.

        Enter MATREVIS *and* GURNEY.

Mortimer jun. Enough.
    Matrevis, write a letter presently
    Unto the lord of Berkeley from ourself
    That he resign the king to thee and Gurney ;
    And when 'tis done, we will subscribe our name.
Matrevis. It shall be done, my lord.   [*Writes.*]
Mortimer jun.   Gurney !
Gurney.   My lord.
Mortimer jun. As thou intendest to rise by Mortimer,
    Who now makes Fortune's wheel turn as he please,

Seek all the means thou canst to make him droop,
And neither give him kind word nor good look.

Gurney. I warrant you, my lord.

Mortimer jun. And this above the rest : because we
    hear
That Edmund casts to work his liberty,
Remove him still from place to place by night,
[Till] at the last he come to Killingworth,
And then from thence to Berkeley back again ;
And by the way, to make him fret the more,
Speak curstly to him ; and in any case
Let no man comfort him if he chance to weep,
But amplify his grief with bitter words.

Matrevis. Fear not, my lord, we'll do as you command.
                [*He presents the letter, which Mortimer signs.*]

Mortimer jun. So now away ; post thitherwards amain.

Queen. Whither goes this letter ? to my lord the king ?
Commend me humbly to his majesty,
And tell him that I labour all in vain
To ease his grief, and work his liberty ;
And bear him this as witness of my love.
                         [*Gives a ring.*]

Matrevis. I will, madam.
    Exeunt Matrevis and Gurney. Manent Isabella and
    Mortimer.

Enter the young PRINCE [EDWARD] *and the* EARL OF
    KENT *talking with him.*

Mortimer jun. Finely dissembled. Do so still, sweet
    queen.

Here comes the young prince with the Earl of Kent.

Queen. Something he whispers in his childish ears.

Mortimer jun. If he have such access unto the prince,
  Our plots and stratagems will soon be dash'd.

Queen. Use Edmund friendly as if all were well.

Mortimer jun. How fares my honourable lord of Kent ?

Kent. In health, sweet Mortimer : how fares your
      grace ?

Queen. Well, if my lord your brother were enlarg'd.

Kent. I hear of late he hath depos'd himself.

Queen. The more my grief.

Mortimer jun. And mine.

Kent [*aside*]. Ah, they do dissemble.

Queen. Sweet son, come hither, I must talk with thee.

Mortimer jun. Thou being his uncle, and the next of
      blood,
  Do look to be protector over the prince.

Kent. Not I, my lord ; who should protect the son,
  But she that gave him life ? I mean the queen.

Prince. Mother, persuade me not to wear the crown :
  Let him be king. I am too young to reign.

Queen. But he content, seeing it his highness' pleasure.

Prince. Let me but see him first, and then I will.

Kent. Ay, do, sweet nephew.

Queen. Brother, you know it is impossible.

Prince. Why, is he dead ?

Queen. No, God forbid.

Kent. I would those words proceeded from your heart.

Mortimer jun. Inconstant Edmund, dost thou favour
      him,

That wast a cause of his imprisonment ?

Kent. The more cause have I now to make amends.

Mortimer jun. I tell thee, 'tis not meet that one so false

    Should come about the person of a prince.

    My lord, he hath betray'd the king his brother,

    And therefore trust him not.

Prince. But he repents, and sorrows for it now.

Queen. Come, son, and go with this gentle lord and me.

Prince. With you I will, but not with Mortimer.

Mortimer jun. Why, youngling, 'sdain'st thou so of Mortimer ?

    Then I will carry thee by force away [*seizing him*].

Prince. Help, Uncle Kent, Mortimer will wrong me.

Queen. Brother Edmund, strive not ; we are his friends ;

    Isabel is nearer than the Earl of Kent.

Kent. Sister, Edward is my charge, redeem him.

Queen. Edward is my son, and I will keep him.

Kent. Mortimer shall know that he hath wronged me.

    Hence will I haste to Killingworth Castle,

    And rescue aged Edward from his foes,

    To be reveng'd on Mortimer and thee.

    Exeunt omnes : [*on one side the Queen, Prince*
        Edward, and Mortimer junior ; on the other,
        Kent.]

[SCENE III

Near Kenilworth Castle]

Enter MATREVIS *and* GURNEY [*and* Soldiers], *with the* KING.

Matrevis. My lord, be not pensive, we are your friends ;
    Men are ordain'd to live in misery,
    Therefore come : dalliance dangereth our lives.
Edward. Friends, whither must unhappy Edward go ?
    Will hateful Mortimer appoint no rest ?
    Must I be vexed like the nightly bird,
    Whose sight is loathsome to all winged fowls ?
    When will the fury of his mind assuage ?
    When will his heart be satisfied with blood ?
    If mine will serve, unbowel straight this breast,
    And give my heart to Isabel and him ;
    It is the chiefest mark they level at.
Gurney. Not so, my liege, the queen hath given this
       charge
    To keep your grace in safety ;
    Your passions make your dolours to increase.
Edward. This usage makes my misery increase.
    But can my air of life continue long
    When all my senses are annoy'd with stench ?
    Within a dungeon England's king is kept,
    Where I am starv'd for want of sustenance.

My daily diet is heart-breaking sobs,
That almost rents the closet of my heart ;
Thus lives old Edward not reliev'd by any,
And so must die, though pitied by many.
O, water, gentle friends, to cool my thirst,
And clear my body from foul excrements.
Matrevis. Here's channel water, as our charge is given ;
    Sit down, for we'll be barbers to your grace.
Edward. Traitors, away ! what, will you murther me,
    Or choke your sovereign with puddle water ?
Gurney. No ; but wash your face, and shave away your
            beard,
Lest you be known and so be rescued.
Matrevis. Why strive you thus ? your labour is in vain.
Edward. The wren may strive against the lion's
            strength,
But all in vain : so vainly do I strive
To seek for mercy at a tyrant's hand.
    *They wash him with puddle water, and shave his beard
        away.*
Immortal powers ! that knows the painful cares
That waits upon my poor distressed soul,
O level all your looks upon these daring men,
That wrongs their liege and sovereign, England's
            king.
O Gaveston, it is for thee that I am wrong'd,
For me, both thou and both the Spencers died !
And for your sakes a thousand wrongs I'll take.
The Spencers' ghosts, wherever they remain,
Wish well to mine ; then tush, for them I'll die.

Matrevis. 'Twixt theirs and yours shall be no enmity.
  Come, come away ; now put the torches out,
  We'll enter in by darkness to Killingworth.

Enter KENT.

Gurney. How now, who comes there ?
Matrevis. Guard the king sure : it is the Earl of Kent.
Edward. O gentle brother, help to rescue me.
Matrevis. Keep them asunder ; thrust in the king.
Kent. Soldiers, let me but talk to him one word.
Gurney. Lay hands upon the earl for this assault.
Kent. Lay down your weapons, traitors ; yield the king.
Matrevis. Edmund, yield thou thyself, or thou shalt
      die.
Kent. Base villains, wherefore do you gripe me thus ?
Gurney. Bind him and so convey him to the court.
Kent. Where is the court but here ? he is the king ;
  And I will visit him ; why stay you me ?
Matrevis. The court is where lord Mortimer remains ;
  Thither shall your honour go ; and so farewell.
    [*Exeunt Matrevis and Gurney, with the King. Manent
      Edmund [Earl of Kent] and the Soldiers.*
Kent. O miserable is that commonweal,
  Where lords keep courts, and kings are lock'd in
      prison !
Soldier. Wherefore stay we ? On, sirs, to the court.
Kent. Ay, lead me whither you will, even to my death,
  Seeing that my brother cannot be releas'd.
                                  Exeunt omnes.

[SCENE IV

The Royal Palace, London]

Enter MORTIMER [*junior*] *alone.*

Mortimer jun. The king must die, or Mortimer goes
    down :
  The commons now begin to pity him :
  Yet he that is the cause of Edward's death,
  Is sure to pay for it when his son is of age ;
  And therefore will I do it cunningly.
  This letter, written by a friend of ours,
  Contains his death, yet binds them save his life.
                                   [*Reads.*

  "Edwardum occidere nolite timere bonum est :
  Fear not to kill the king, 'tis good he die."
  But read it thus, and that's another sense :
  " Edwardum occidere nolite timere bonum est ;
  Kill not the king, 'tis good to fear the worst."
  Unpointed as it is, thus shall it go,
  That, being dead, if it chance to be found,
  Matrevis and the rest may bear the blame,
  And we be quit that caus'd it to be done.
  Within this room is lock'd the messenger
  That shall convey it, and perform the rest :
  And by a secret token that he bears,
  Shall he be murdered when the deed is done.
  Lightborn, come forth !

[*Enter* LIGHTBORN.]

Art thou as resolute as thou wast ?

Lightborn. What else, my lord ? and far more resolute.

Mortimer jun. And hast thou cast how to accomplish it ?

Lightborn. Ay, ay, and none shall know which way he died.

Mortimer jun. But at his looks, Lightborn, thou wilt relent.

Lightborn. Relent ! ha, ha ! I use much to relent.

Mortimer jun. Well, do it bravely, and be secret.

Lightborn. You shall not need to give instructions ;
'Tis not the first time I have killed a man.
I learn'd in Naples how to poison flowers ;
To strangle with a lawn thrust through the throat ;
To pierce the windpipe with a needle's point ;
Or whilst one is asleep, to take a quill
And blow a little powder in his ears :
Or open his mouth and pour quicksilver down.
But yet I have a braver way than these.

Mortimer jun. What's that ?

Lightborn. Nay, you shall pardon me ; none shall know my tricks.

Mortimer jun. I care not how it is, so it be not spied.
Deliver this to Gurney and Matrevis. [*Giving a letter.*]
At every ten miles' end thou hast a horse.
Take this ; [*Gives money*] away, and never see me more.

Lightborn. No.

Mortimer jun. No.
  Unless thou bring me news of Edward's death.
Lightborn. That will I quickly do.   Farewell, my lord.
                                                    [*Exit.*]
Mortimer [*jun.*]. The prince I rule, the queen do I
      command,
  And with a lowly congé to the ground,
  The proudest lords salute me as I pass ;
  I seal, I cancel, I do what I will.
  Fear'd am I more than lov'd ;—let me be fear'd,
  And when I frown, make all the court look pale.
  I view the prince with Aristarchus' eyes,
  Whose looks were as a breeching to a boy.
  They thrust upon me the protectorship,
  And sue to me for that that I desire.
  While at the council-table, grave enough,
  And not unlike a bashful puritan,
  First I complain of imbecility,
  Saying it is *onus quam gravissimum* ;
  Till, being interrupted by my friends,
  Suscepi that *provinciam* as they term it ;
  And to conclude, I am Protector now.
  Now is all sure : the queen and Mortimer
  Shall rule the realm, the king ; and none rule us.
  Mine enemies will I plague, my friends advance ;
  And what I list command who dare control ?
  Major sum quam cui possit fortuna nocere.
  And that this be the coronation-day,
  It pleaseth me, and Isabel the queen.
                                          [*Trumpets within.*]

The trumpets sound, I must go take my place.

Enter the young KING [EDWARD III.], BISHOP [OF
CANTERBURY], Champion, Nobles, QUEEN.

Bishop [*of Canterbury*]. Long live King Edward, by the
    grace of God,
King of England and lord of Ireland.
Champion. If any Christian, Heathen, Turk, or Jew,
    Dares but affirm that Edward's not true king,
    And will avouch his saying with the sword,
    I am the champion that will combat him.
Mortimer [*jun.*]. None comes, sound trumpets.
                           [*Trumpets sound.*]
King [*Edward III.*].   Champion, here's to thee.
                              [*Gives a purse.*]
Queen. Lord Mortimer, now take him to your charge.

Enter Soldiers, *with the* EARL OF KENT *prisoner.*

Mortimer jun. What traitor have we there with blades
    and bills?
Soldier. Edmund, the Earl of Kent.
King [*Edward III.*].   What hath he done?
Soldier. 'A would have taken the king away perforce,
    As we were bringing him to Killingworth.
Mortimer jun. Did you attempt his rescue, Edmund?
    Speak.
Kent. Mortimer, I did; he is our king,
    And thou compellst this prince to wear the crown.

Mortimer jun. Strike off his head ! he shall have martial law.

Kent. Strike off my head ! base traitor, I defy thee.

King [*Edward III.*]. My lord, he is my uncle, and shall live.

Mortimer jun. My lord, he is your enemy, and shall die.

Kent. Stay, villains !

King [*Edward III.*]. Sweet mother, if I cannot pardon him,

Entreat my lord Protector for his life.

Queen. Son, be content ; I dare not speak a word.

King [*Edward III.*]. Nor I, and yet methinks I should command ;

But, seeing I cannot, I'll entreat for him.

My lord, if you will let my uncle live,

I will requite it when I come to age.

Mortimer jun. 'Tis for your highness' good, and for the realm's.

How often shall I bid you bear him hence ?

Kent. Art thou king ? must I die at thy command ?

Mortimer jun. At our command. Once more away with him.

Kent. Let me but stay and speak ; I will not go.

Either my brother or his son is king,

And none of both them thirst for Edmund's blood :

And therefore, soldiers, whither will you hale me ?

They hale Edmund away and carry him to be beheaded.

King [*Edward III.*]. What safety may I look for at his hands,

If that my uncle shall be murthered thus ?

Queen. Fear not, sweet boy, I'll guard thee from thy
   foes ;
   Had Edmund liv'd, he would have sought thy
      death.
   Come, son, we'll ride a-hunting in the park.

King [Edward III.]. And shall my uncle Edmund ride
   with us ?

Queen. He is a traitor ; think not on him ; come.

                                        Exeunt omnes.

[SCENE V

Berkeley Castle]

Enter MATREVIS *and* GURNEY.

Matrevis. Gurney, I wonder the king dies not,
   Being in a vault up to the knees in water,
   To which the channels of the castle run,
   From whence a damp continually ariseth,
   That were enough to poison any man,
   Much more a king brought up so tenderly.

Gurney. And so do I, Matrevis : yesternight
   I opened but the door to throw him meat,
   And I was almost stifled with the savour.

Matrevis. He hath a body able to endure
   More than we can inflict : and therefore now
   Let us assail his mind another while.

Gurney. Send for him out thence, and I will anger him.
Matrevis. But stay, who's this?

Enter LIGHTBORN.

Lightborn.   My lord Protector greets you. [*Gives letter.*]
Gurney. What's here? I know not how to conster it.
Matrevis. Gurney, it was left unpointed for the nonce;
  " *Edwardum occidere nolite timere,*"
  That's his meaning.
Lightborn. Know you this token? [*Gives token.*] I must
    have the king.
Matrevis. Ay, stay awhile, thou shalt have answer
    straight.
  [*Aside*]. This villain's sent to make away the king.
Gurney [*aside*]. I thought as much.
Matrevis [*aside*].   And when the murder's done,
  See how he must be handled for his labour.
  Pereat iste! Let him have the king.
  What else? here is the keys, this is the lake,
  Do as you are commanded by my lord.
Lightborn. I know what I must do. Get you away.
  Yet be not far off, I shall need your help;
  See that in the next room I have a fire,
  And get me a spit, and let it be red-hot.
Matrevis. Very well.
Gurney.   Need you anything besides?
Lightborn. What else? A table and a feather-bed.
Gurney. That's all?
Lightborn. Ay, ay; so, when I call you, bring it in.

Matrevis. Fear not you that.

Gurney [*giving him a torch*]. Here's a light, to go into
       the dungeon.   [*Exeunt Gurney and Matrevis.*]

Lightborn. So now
  Must I about this gear ; ne'er was there any
  So finely handled as this king shall be
              [*Opening the dungeon door.*
  Foh, here's a place indeed, with all my heart.

Edward. Who's there ? What light is that ? Where-
    fore comes thou ?

Lightborn. To comfort you, and bring you joyful news.

Edward. Small comfort finds poor Edward in thy looks.
  Villain, I know thou comst to murther me.

Lightborn. To murther you, my most gracious lord,
  Far is it from my heart to do you harm.
  The queen sent me to see how you were used,
  For she relents at this your misery :
  And what eyes can refrain from shedding tears,
  To see a king in this most piteous state ?

Edward. Weepst thou already ? list awhile to me
  And then thy heart, were it as Gurney's is,
  Or as Matrevis', hewn from the Caucasus,
  Yet will it melt, ere I have done my tale.
  This dungeon where they keep me is the sink
  Wherein the filth of all the castle falls.

Lightborn. O villains !

Edward. And there in mire and puddle have I stood
  This ten days' space ; and, lest that I should sleep,
  One plays continually upon a drum.
  They give me bread and water, being a king ;

So that, for want of sleep and sustenance,
My mind's distempered, and my body's numb'd,
And whether I have limbs or no I know not.
O, would my blood dropp'd out from every vein,
As doth this water from my tattered robes.
Tell Isabel, the queen, I look'd not thus,
When for her sake I ran at tilt in France,
And there unhors'd the Duke of Cleremont.

Lightborn. O speak no more, my lord ; this breaks my
 heart.
Lie on this bed, and rest yourself awhile.

Edward. These looks of thine can harbour nought but
 death :
I see my tragedy written in thy brows.
Yet stay awhile ; forbear thy bloody hand,
And let me see the stroke before it comes,
That even then when I shall lose my life,
My mind may be more steadfast on my God.

Lightborn. What means your highness to mistrust me
 thus ?

Edward. What means thou to dissemble with me
 thus ?

Lightborn. These hands were never stain'd with innocent
 blood,
Nor shall they now be tainted with a king's.

Edward. Forgive my thought for having such a thought.
One jewel have I left ; receive thou this.

        [Giving jewel.]

Still fear I, and I know not what's the cause,
But every joint shakes as I give it thee.

O, if thou harbourst murther in thy heart,
Let this gift change thy mind, and save thy soul.
Know that I am a king : O, at that name
I feel a hell of grief ! Where is my crown ?
Gone, gone, and do I remain alive ?

Lightborn. You're overwatch'd, my lord ; lie down and
     rest.

Edward. But that grief keeps me waking, I should
     sleep ;
For not these ten days have these eyes' lids clos'd.
Now as I speak they fall, and yet with fear
Open again. O wherefore sits thou here ?

Lightborn. If you mistrust me, I'll begone, my lord.

Edward. No, no, for if thou meanst to murther me,
     Thou wilt return again, and therefore stay. [*Sleeps.*]

Lightborn. He sleeps.

Edward [*waking*]. O let me not die yet : stay, O stay a
     while !

Lightborn. How now, my lord ?

Edward. Something still buzzeth in mine ears,
     And tells me if I sleep I never wake ;
This fear is that which makes me tremble thus ;
And therefore tell me, wherefore art thou come ?

Lightborn. To rid thee of thy life. Matrevis, come !

[*Enter* MATREVIS *and* GURNEY.]

Edward. I am too weak and feeble to resist :
     Assist me, sweet God, and receive my soul !

Lightborn. Run for the table.

Edward. O spare me, or despatch me in a trice.
                [Matrevis brings in a table.]

Lightborn. So, lay the table down, and stamp on it,
  But not too hard, lest that you bruise his body.
                [King Edward is murdered.]

Matrevis. I fear me that this cry will raise the town,
  And therefore let us take horse and away.

Lightborn. Tell me, sirs, was it not bravely done ?

Gurney. Excellent well : take this for thy reward.
             Then Gurney stabs Lightborn.

  Come, let us cast the body in the moat,
  And bear the king's to Mortimer our lord :
  Away !   *Exeunt omnes.*

[SCENE VI

The Royal Palace, London]

Enter MORTIMER *[junior] and* MATREVIS.

Mortimer jun. Is't done, Matrevis, and the murtherer
    dead ?

Matrevis. Ay, my good lord ; I would it were undone.

Mortimer jun. Matrevis, if thou now growest penitent
  I'll be thy ghostly father ; therefore choose,
  Whether thou wilt be secret in this,
  Or else die by the hand of Mortimer.

Matrevis. Gurney, my lord, is fled, and will, I fear,
  Betray us both, therefore let me fly.

Mortimer jun. Fly to the savages.

Matrevis. I humbly thank your honour.   [*Exit.*]
Mortimer jun. As for myself, I stand as Jove's huge
        tree,
And others are but shrubs compar'd to me.
All tremble at my name, and I fear none ;
Let's see who dare impeach me for his death.

Enter the QUEEN.

Queen. Ah, Mortimer, the king my son hath news
His father's dead, and we have murdered him !
Mortimer jun. What if he have ? the king is yet a
        child.
Queen. Ay, ay, but he tears his hair, and wrings his
        hands,
And vows to be reveng'd upon us both.
Into the council-chamber he is gone,
To crave the aid and succour of his peers.
Ay me, see where he comes, and they with him ;
Now, Mortimer, begins our tragedy.

Enter the KING [EDWARD THE THIRD], *with the* Lords, [*and Attendants*].

[*1st*] *Lord.* Fear not, my lord, know that you are a king.
King [*Edward III.*]. Villain !—
Mortimer jun. How now, my lord ?
King [*Edward III.*]. Think not that I am frighted with
        thy words.
My father's murdered through thy treachery ;
And thou shalt die, and on his mournful hearse
Thy hateful and accursed head shall lie,

To witness to the world that by thy means

His kingly body was too soon interr'd.

Queen. Weep not, sweet son.

King [Edward III.]. Forbid not me to weep; he was
    my father;

And had you lov'd him half so well as I,

You could not bear his death thus patiently.

But you, I fear, conspir'd with Mortimer.

[1st] Lord. Why speak you not unto my lord the king?

Mortimer jun. Because I think scorn to be accus'd.

Who is the man dare say I murdered him?

King [Edward III.]. Traitor, in me my loving father
    speaks,

And plainly saith, 'twas thou that murdredst him.

Mortimer jun. But hath your grace no other proof than
    this?

King [Edward III.] [showing letter]. Yes, if this be the
    hand of Mortimer.

Mortimer jun. [aside]. False Gurney hath betray'd me
    and himself.

Queen [aside]. I fear'd as much; murther cannot be
    hid.

Mortimer jun. 'Tis my hand; what gather you by
    this?

King [Edward III.]. That thither thou didst send a
    murtherer.

Mortimer jun. What murtherer? Bring forth the man
    I sent.

King [Edward III.]. Ah, Mortimer, thou knowest that
    he is slain;

And so shalt thou be too. Why stays he here,
Bring him unto a hurdle, drag him forth ;
Hang him, I say, and set his quarters up ;
But bring his head back presently to me.

Queen. For my sake, sweet son, pity Mortimer.

Mortimer jun. Madam, entreat not, I will rather die,
Than sue for life unto a paltry boy.

King [Edward III.]. Hence with the traitor, with the
    murderer !

Mortimer jun. Base Fortune, now I see, that in thy
    wheel
There is a point, to which when men aspire,
They tumble headlong down : that point I touch'd,
And, seeing there was no place to mount up higher,
Why should I grieve at my declining fall ?
Farewell, fair queen. Weep not for Mortimer,
That scorns the world, and, as a traveller,
Goes to discover countries yet unknown.

King [Edward III.]. What ! suffer you the traitor to
    delay ?

    [*Mortimer junior is taken away by 1st Lord and
        Attendants.*]

Queen. As thou receivedst thy life from me,
Spill not the blood of gentle Mortimer !

King [Edward III.]. This argues that you spilt my
    father's blood,
Else would you not entreat for Mortimer.

Queen. I spill his blood ? no.

King [Edward III.]. Ay, madam, you ; for so the
    rumour runs.

Queen. That rumour is untrue ; for loving thee,
  Is this report rais'd on poor Isabel.
King [*Edward III.*]. I do not think her so unnatural.
[*2nd*] *Lord.* My lord, I fear me it will prove too true.
King [*Edward III.*]. Mother, you are suspected for his
    death,
  And therefore we commit you to the Tower
  Till further trial may be made thereof ;
  If you be guilty, though I be your son,
  Think not to find me slack or pitiful.
Queen. Nay, to my death, for too long have I lived,
  Whenas my son thinks to abridge my days.
King [*Edward III.*]. Away with her, her words enforce
    these tears,
  And I shall pity her if she speak again.
Queen. Shall I not mourn for my beloved lord,
  And with the rest accompany him to his grave ?
[*2nd*] *Lord.* Thus, madam, 'tis the king's will you shall
    hence.
Queen. He hath forgotten me ; stay, I am his mother.
[*2nd*] *Lord.* That boots not ; therefore, gentle madam,
    go.
Queen. Then come, sweet death, and rid me of this
    grief.   [*Exit.*]

[*Re-enter* 1st Lord, *with the head of* MORTIMER *junior*].

[*1st*] *Lord.* My lord, here is the head of Mortimer.
King [*Edward III.*]. Go fetch my father's hearse, where
    it shall lie ;

407

And bring my funeral robes.   [*Exeunt Attendants.*]
                                            Accursed head,
Could I have rul'd thee then, as I do now,
Thou hadst not hatch'd this monstrous treachery !
Here comes the hearse ; help me to mourn, my
    lords.

[*Re-enter Attendants with the hearse and funeral robes.*]

Sweet father, here unto thy murdered ghost
I offer up this wicked traitor's head ;
And let these tears, distilling from mine eyes,
Be witness of my grief and innocency.

FINIS

IMPRINTED AT LONDON FOR WILLIAM
JONES, AND ARE TO BE SOLD AT HIS
SHOP, NEAR UNTO HOLBORN CONDUIT,
                    1594

GLOSSARY

GLOSSARY

A

abject : abase.
abjection : degradation.
aby : pay the penalty for.
accidental (heat) : excessive.
adamant : loadstone.
adjunct : star.
affection, their : whatever they affect or wish.
affections : fancies, feelings in general.
age : old man.
air of life : breath.
Almain rutters : German horsemen.
annoyeth : molests.
answerable : corresponding, proportionate.
Argier : Algeria.
argin : glacis ; banks sloping down from a fortress, on which attackers would be exposed to the defenders' fire.
argosies : large merchant ships.
armadoes : large warships, or fleets.
arms : coat-of-arms.
artier : artery.
artisan : student of the arts.
Asant : Zante (¿).
aspire : aspire to.
asseized : taken possession of (legal phrase).
Auster and *Aquilon :* south-west and north-west winds.

B

bands : bonds.

bandy : exchange blows.

banned : repressed.

Barbarian steeds : Barbary horses, " barbs."

base, bid the English king a : make him risk a run—referring to the boys' game of Prisoner's Base or Jack Catch All.

basilisks : cannon.

bastones : cudgels, staves.

bevers : refreshments between meals.

bewrays : betrays.

bickering : skirmish, battle.

bills, brown : halberds bronzed to prevent rust.

bird that spreads her wings upon the city walls : ibis.

bootless : unavailing.

boots : avails.

boss : gross, fat woman.

brave : fine, gallant, presumptuous.

braved : challenged, treated with bravado.

braves : insults.

brent : burnt.

brigandines : brigantines—small vessels which could be sailed or rowed.

Britainy : England.

buckler : shield.

bugs (will make the hair stand) : bugbears, horrors.

C

carbonadoes : strips of meat.

Cario : Cairo (?).

casemate : chamber in the ramparts with embrasures for cannon, etc.

cast : anticipate.

cavalieros : mounds for cannon, raised above the rest of the works of a fortress.

certify : inform.

champion plains : open, level country.

chance how : how chances it.

channel : collar-bone.

channel : gutter, sewer.

charming (Circes) : casting spells.

check (the ground) : stamp.

Chorus : speaker of prologue.

Cimmerian : black.

claps : pats.

clout : centre of the archery target.

colour : pretext, excuse.

competitor (with me) : partner, comrade.

conceit : fancy, idea, imagination.

congé : bow, usually at leaving.

consort of music : company of musicians.

conster : construe, translate.

continent to : bordering upon.

countenance : importance, influence.

counterbuft : thrown back by, forcibly rebuffed.

counterfort : buttress, supporting a wall or terrace.

countermand : command, control.

counterscarps : the walls of the ditch which face in towards the fortress.

countervail : equal in number.

cousin : any collateral relative except brother and sister ; used frequently to mean nephew or niece.

crazed : ruined.

crownets : coronets, bracelets.

curse : excommunicate.

curstly : harshly.

curtain : wall joining the towers of a fortress.

curtle-axe : cutlass, heavy sword for slashing.

D

dapper Jack : smart fellow (derogatory).
dated (*health*) : having its end preordained.
declined : turned away.
defy (*the King*) : renounce allegiance to.
device : painting on a shield.
die : swoon with joy.
dispensive faith : faith subject to special dispensations.
dominion (or *intelligentia*) : controlling spirit.
doubtlessly : free from doubt.
drift : plot, intention.

E

earns : grieves deeply.
ecstasies : profound emotions, either joyous or tragic.
egregious : distinguished, noble.
empery : empire.
engines : instruments.
enlarge : set free.
estates : states, positions.
events (*of mercy*) : effects, results (?).
expressless : inexpressible.

F

faced : out-faced, bullied.
facts (*of war*) : feats, deeds.
false (*his service*) : betray.
fancy (*one that*) : fall in love with.
fear (*not Orcanes*) : frighten.
fearing (*his love*) : fearing for.
females' miss : loss of the females.
fire them from : smoke them out of.
fleering : gibing.

414

fleet : float.
foil : disgrace.
foil : sword.
forest : wilderness.
for me : as far as I am concerned.
forslow : waste.
for why, forwhy : because.
furniture (Tamburlaine's) : dress, weapons, etc., and possibly tent also.
fustian : nonsense.

G

gabions : baskets filled with earth and used for protection as sandbags are used now.
gather head : collect soldiers.
gear : business.
glaive : lance.
glorious (tyrants) : boastful.
glozing : flattering.
gravelled : puzzled.
groom : slave, servant.

H

hand : handwriting.
haunted : followed persistently.
hay : kind of country dance.
hest : command.
hey-pass : juggler.
high-minded : arrogant.
horse-courser : horse-dealer.
hoy : small vessel, rigged as a sloop.
hugy : huge.
humidum and calor : moisture and warmth.
hurdle : framework on which criminals were dragged to execution.
hypostasis : excess of blood in the organs of the body.

I

illustrate : beautify.
imbrotherie : embroidery.
imprecations : prayers.
intreated : asked earnestly.
investion . investiture.
ippocras : a spiced wine.

J

Jacob's staff : instrument for measuring distances and heights.
jesses : short straps fastened to the legs of a (trained) hawk, by
    which it was held.
jets : struts.
jig : a kind of dance, a tune for the dance, a mocking song.
Jubalter : Gibraltar.

K

kern : lightly armed Irish foot-soldier.
knave's acre : a mean street—with special reference to Poultney
    Street, Soho, a haunt of rag and bottle dealers.

L

labels : strips of parchment or paper by which seals were fastened
    to documents.
lachryma Christi : " tears of Christ," a sweet South Italian wine.
lanch : cut.
larded : decorated.
leaguer : camp, especially the camp of a besieging army.
legs, making low : bowing low.
lemans : lovers.
let : hinder.

levelled at : aimed at.
licentiate : graduate licensed to enter for a doctor's or master's
    degree.
like thee not : please thee not.
lusty (grove) : pleasant.

M

made him sure : betrothed him.
mails : baggage.
main : sea.
malgrado : in spite of.
manage arms : make war.
march beer : a choice ale usually made in March.
mate : assist.
mated : made helpless.
metaphysical science : magic.
mettle : temperament.
mickle : much.
minion : favourite, darling.
monstrous : abnormal.
mushrump : mushroom.

O

observations, martial : martial rites, customs.
Oneyl : Irish rebel leader.
ordinance : cannon.
organons : instruments, means.
orifex : orifice.
ostry : hostelry.
outlandish : foreign.
outrageous : committing outrages.
over-peered : looked down upon.

P

pale, the English : the part of Ireland in which English jurisdiction
    was established.

parcel of (his fame) : essential part of.

parled : parleyed.

pash : smash.

pass (not for their anger) : care.

passionate : possessed by any strong emotion—love, anger, etc.

pathetical : moving, persuasive.

peevish : silly.

perpendicular (at Damascus) : i.e. zero meridian, longitude o°, of the world which Tamburlaine is making.

pickadevaunts : beards cut to a sharp point.

pin (that thousands seek to cleave) : nail in the very centre of an archery target.

pioners : pioneers.

pitch (of Atlas) : shoulders.

plage : region, coast.

plainer : complainant.

policy : trickery, stratagem.

porpintine : porcupine.

Portingale : Portugal.

portly : stately.

ports : gates.

preachments : sermons.

precisian : puritan.

preferred : recommended.

presently : now, at once.

prest : ready.

prevail : avail.

preventeth : anticipates.

proof, armour of : armour which has been proved, tested.

proof, to the : irrefutably.

proper : own.

protest : vow.

public schools : university classrooms.

purchase : acquire—not necessarily by buying.

purchase : undertaking, a fine acquisition.

Q

quiddity : subtlety.
quinque-angle form : fortress in the form of a five-pointed star.
quite : requite, reward.

R

racking (clouds) : moving before the wind.
rampiers : ramparts.
rape : seizure, carrying off.
raze : graze.
rebated : blunted.
record : call to mind, set down in writing.
Rector (of university) : Principal.
redoubted : feared.
regiment : rule, authority.
remits : gives up.
renied : renegade.
renowmed : renowned.
rent : rend.
respect : consideration of special circumstances.
resteth : remains to be done.
retorqued : twisted in upon themselves.
Rhamnusia : Nemesis.
road : raid.
rombelow, rumbelow : meaningless refrain of a song.
round : dance.
rude : barbarous, unlearned, brutal.
runagates : deserters, renegades.
rutters : horsemen.

S

Saba : Sheba.
sarell : seraglio, women's quarters.

scald : mean, contemptible.

Scalonian : Ascalon.

seen : well seen, well versed.

sennet : set of notes played on a trumpet as a signal for the approach or departure of processions.

shadow : ghost, spirit.

sib : wife, kinswoman.

silly : helpless, harmless, simple, lowly, inexpert, untrained.

sled : sledge.

slop, round : loose breeches, trunk hose.

sophister, play the : use fallacious arguments.

spials : spies.

state, offer present dukedoms to our : offer to make us dukes at once.

state : position, rank.

stature : statue.

stavesacre : (?) stauracia ; a silk figured with small crosses.

stay : stay for, await.

still : distil.

stomach him : resent him.

stuffed with (treasure) : supported by.

success : result, consequence, whether good or bad.

suspect, Be not single for : Do not be found alone, since you are suspected.

sway To some direction in : give me some control of.

swowns, zounds : God's wounds—an oath.

T

tainted : touched, struck.

tall : valiant, bold.

taratantaras : trumpet calls.

target : shield.

targeteers : foot soldiers with shields.

tartar : dregs of wine.

tendrest : carest for.

theoria : contemplation, survey (?).

timeless : untimely, premature.
tires (*on my life*) : seizes upon and tears. A term used in falconry.
tongues : languages.
torpedo : electric ray fish.
tottered : tattered.
toward (*brother*) : promising.
trained : enticed, decoyed.
triumph : tournament.
turtle : turtle-dove.

U

unkind : unnatural.

V

vailing : doffing (headgear), lowering, dipping (a flag, a sail).
valurous : valuable.
vild : vile.
villany : discourtesy, dishonour.
villeiness : female servant.
virtue (*is the fount*) : ability.

W

wanton : flighty, amorous, licentious.
weeds : garments.
Welsh hooks : bill-books, with a cross-piece under the blade.
while : until.
whilom : formerly.
wis : know.
witty : wise, intelligent.

Printed in Great Britain by
Thomas Nelson and Sons Ltd, Edinburgh